WAITING
FOR
WAR

WAITING
FOR
WAR

BRITAIN 1939–1940

BARRY TURNER

ICON

Praise for *The Berlin Airlift* (Icon Books, 2017)

'In this fine piece of popular history, Barry Turner provides an engaging and vivid account of this first major episode of the Cold War.'   *BBC History*

'A crisply written, suitably dramatic and ultimately heartening book.'   *Daily Mail*

'This new history of "Operation Vittles" based on hitherto unexplored archives and interviews with veterans paints a fresh, vivid picture of the Berlin airlift, whose repercussions – the role of the USA as a global leader, German ascendancy, Russian threat – are still being felt today.'   *The Bookseller*

Praise for *Karl Doenitz and the Last Days of the Third Reich* (Icon Books, 2015)

'A page-turning narrative'   *Daily Mail*

First published in the UK in 2019
by Icon Books Ltd, Omnibus Business Centre,
39–41 North Road, London N7 9DP
email: info@iconbooks.com
www.iconbooks.com

Sold in the UK, Europe and Asia
by Faber & Faber Ltd, Bloomsbury House,
74–77 Great Russell Street,
London WC1B 3DA or their agents

Distributed in the UK, Europe and Asia
by Grantham Book Services,
Trent Road, Grantham NG31 7XQ

Distributed in Australia and New Zealand
by Allen & Unwin Pty Ltd, PO Box 8500,
83 Alexander Street, Crows Nest, NSW 2065

Distributed in South Africa
by Jonathan Ball, Office B4,
The District, 41 Sir Lowry Road,
Woodstock 7925

Distributed in India
by Penguin Books India,
7th Floor, Infinity Tower – C, DLF Cyber City,
Gurgaon 122002, Haryana

ISBN: 978-178578-548-1

Typeset in Dante by Marie Doherty

Printed and bound in Great Britain
by Clays Ltd, Elcograf S.p.A.

CONTENTS

ABOUT THE AUTHOR

Barry Turner is a celebrated historian, the author most recently of *The Berlin Airlift* (Icon, 2017), described by *BBC History* magazine as a 'fine piece of popular history'. He is also the author of *Karl Doenitz and the Last Days of the Third Reich* (Icon, 2015), and of *Suez 1956* (Hodder, 2006) and, with Tony Rennell, of *When Daddy Came Home* (Arrow, 2014). He lives in London and south-west France.

LIST OF ILLUSTRATIONS

Plate section

A butcher painting a meat registration
notice on the window of his shop.

Soldiers helping with the harvest where
farmhands have been called up.

David Low, the *Evening Standard*'s political cartoonist.

A British wartime poster appearing in the streets of London.

Neville Chamberlain inspects a field gun in northern France.

The sandbagged structure used to protect
the statue of Eros in Piccadilly Circus.

Signposts removed from their positions in
Kent, to confound the enemy.

ARP workers digging trenches for air-raid
shelters in St James's Park, London.

An Austin Therm balloon car with a bag full of coal gas.

A farmer has his herd of cows painted with
white stripes during the blackout.

A poster recruiting women into the war effort.

A female member of the Auxiliary Fire Service.

A poster providing guidance on good practice during an air raid.

A heap of scrap iron collected from householders
to help in the salvage scheme.

A propaganda poster encouraging mothers
to leave their children in the countryside.

Villagers saying goodbye to the evacuee
children they adopted for the war.

INTRODUCTION

The stand-off between Britain and Germany from September 1939 to May 1940 has entered the history books as the 'Phoney War'. But this is not to say that it was without drama. The story of this critical period in the nation's history is of political infighting, missed opportunities and of military and civil incompetence on a monumental scale. Defeatism was deeply ingrained in a people dreading, above all, a return to the carnage of the Great War.

Revisionist interpretations of events have attempted to excuse Neville Chamberlain and his foreign secretary Lord Halifax for doing no more than bowing to the dictate of public opinion. The voters wanted peace and the government tried its best to give it to them. But this is to ignore the prime function of a political leader which is to lead.

Portrayed as a victim of circumstances or as a misguided idealist, Chamberlain can be forgiven many things but not for his failure to recognise Hitler's ruthless villainy. While Chamberlain fondly imagined that he was shaping events, in fact he allowed the events, with Hitler as their driving force, to shape him.

The hindsight justification for the Phoney War, that it gave Britain time to build up its strength for the struggle ahead, is hard if not impossible to sustain. Britain was in better military shape by May 1940 but so too was Germany. The big difference was that while Britain put its energy into building up its defence, Germany focused on attack. In September 1938 the RAF had five squadrons of Hurricanes and one of Spitfires. A year later it had 26 squadrons equipped with one or the other. But these were light monoplane fighter aircraft built for defence. The strength of Bomber Command actually fell in the same period. The RAF had barely a single aircraft that could reach Germany with even a modest bomb load.

Moreover, by holding back when Germany was occupied with crushing Czechoslovakia and Poland, the Anglo-French Allies sacrificed the support of Eastern Europe with its highly committed fighting forces at a time when Germany had only thirteen divisions on the western front. No amount of rearmament could make up for the lost opportunity of stopping Hitler when he was at his most vulnerable.

With Britain adrift with a government that had neither the will nor the appetite for conducting a war, policy was dictated by the false hope that economic pressure would bring Germany to its senses or, failing that, an internal upheaval would lead to Hitler's downfall.

A catalogue of errors that almost cost Britain the war started with the failure of military and diplomatic intelligence to penetrate the Nazi regime or to understand that Hitler and the other dictators, Mussolini and Franco, held in contempt the conventions of international diplomacy.

On the home front, an ambitious programme of civil defence was dictated by the entirely erroneous assumption that Germany had the capacity and the immediate aim to bomb London and other cities to near total destruction. Public morale suffered an unnecessary mass evacuation and an over-officious administration, along with ham-fisted efforts to mould public opinion to suit the prejudices of the political elite. Arrogance and ignorance combined to undermine morale.

Seen from this distance, the commanding features of everyday life in 1939 – the blackout, gas-masks, air-raid shelters, evacuees, rationing and the profusion of often contradictory rules and regulations – seem bizarre almost to the point of farce. But they were real enough to those who had to live the experience. So too was the action at sea and in the air where combat brought occasional triumphs to balance against the more frequent tragedies of a misguided and poorly implemented strategy. A compensating factor was the ability of the country to laugh at the absurdities of life under the shadow of the swastika.

But there can be no escaping the conclusion that the Chamberlain government took the country to the brink of defeat. As Churchill remarked to his personal bodyguard, Inspector Walter Thompson: 'I hope it is not too late. I am very much afraid it is.'

It was a close-run thing.

CHAPTER 1

We Are At War

The ultimatum to Germany was delivered on the morning of September 3rd, 1939. Shortly before 9.00am, in the role of reluctant messenger, Sir Nevile Henderson, British ambassador in Berlin, arrived at the German Foreign Office. He was expecting to meet Hitler's foreign minister but Joachim von Ribbentrop was disinclined to receive him. Instead, he sent Paul Schmidt, interpreter for the Nazi top brass in their dealings with foreign dignitaries, as his understudy.

Schmidt almost did not make it. After several days of round-the-clock duties and September 3rd being a Sunday, he overslept.

> I had to take a taxi to the Foreign Office. I could just see Henderson entering the building as I drove across Wilhelmsplatz. I used a side entrance and stood in Ribbentrop's office ready to receive Henderson punctually at 9 a.m. Henderson was announced as the hour struck. He came in looking very serious, shook hands but declined my invitation to be seated, remaining standing solemnly in the middle of the room.[1]

An arch-appeaser who saw his world dissolving, Henderson found it hard to get out his words. But he felt bound to read aloud the document in his hand. It was short and to the point.

'More than twenty-four hours have elapsed since an immediate reply was requested to the warning of 1 September [that Britain would take action when German forces were withdrawn from Polish territory], and since then the attacks on Poland have intensified. If His Majesty's Government has not received satisfactory assurances of the cessation of all aggressive action against Poland and the withdrawal of German troops from that country by eleven o'clock British Summer Time, from that time a state of war will exist between Great Britain and Germany.'

The deadline was set for just two hours ahead. Schmidt made his way to the Reich Chancellery.

Hitler was seated at his desk, Ribbentrop to his right near the window ... I stopped at some distance from the desk and then slowly translated the British ultimatum. When I finished there was complete silence.

Hitler sat immobile, gazing before him ... He sat completely still and unmoving.

After an interval that seemed an age, he turned to Ribbentrop, who had remained standing by the window. 'What now?' he asked. ...

Ribbentrop answered: 'I assume that the French will hand in a similar ultimatum within the hour.'[2]

As Schmidt was leaving, Hermann Goering, commander-in-chief of the Luftwaffe and economics supremo, was heard to mutter, 'If we lose this war, then God have mercy on us'.

In London, with no expectation of Hitler backing down, Prime Minister Neville Chamberlain was standing by in 10 Downing Street, preparing himself for a nationwide broadcast. BBC engineers were putting the finishing touches to a makeshift studio when Big Ben struck eleven o'clock.

Chamberlain was set to follow the morning service broadcast from Croydon parish church, where the congregation sang 'Oh, For a Faith Which Will Not Shrink' and 'God is Working His Purpose Out'. Later in the day, with exquisite sensitivity, the BBC followed up with a talk by Dom Bernard Clements, vicar of All Saints, Margaret Street, on the theme of 'What happens when I die'.

At 11.10, with no news from Berlin, the prime minister gave orders for the armed forces to be put on a war footing. With telephone confirmation from the British embassy in Berlin that the ultimatum had indeed failed to elicit a response, Chamberlain took his place before the microphone.

> Meanwhile, on the steps of the Royal Exchange there gathered a group of incongruously dressed officials, two in cocked hats, short gold-fringed capes and long coats with brass buttons down to the floor, one in a morning suit with a tall top hat with a gold band around it, and two City policemen wearing tin helmets and carrying gas-masks slung on khaki-web shoulder straps; a crowd of City maintenance workers watched a gowned official in a short barrister's wig read the official proclamation of war.[3]

At 11.15 Chamberlain spoke. His thin, metallic voice was not suited to a rallying call. In contrast to Hitler's lengthy tub-thumping epistles, he gave himself just a few minutes to summarise a catalogue of failure.

Every effort had been made to achieve a 'peaceful and honourable settlement between Germany and Poland, but Hitler would not have it. He had evidently made up his mind to attack Poland whatever happened.' Chamberlain made no effort to hide his remorse.

> 'You can imagine what a bitter blow it is to me that my long struggle to win peace has failed … Yet I cannot believe that there is anything more, or anything different I could have done that would have been more successful.'

In those few words, Chamberlain revealed his inadequacy in a time of crisis. Unable to accept, or even understand, any judgement but his own, he was a victim of myopia and arrogance. But there it was. There could be no going back. For the second time in little more than a quarter of a century, Britain was at war with Germany.

Chamberlain ended his broadcast to the nation on what, for him, was a high note.

> 'It is the evil things that we shall be fighting against – brute force, bad faith, injustice, oppression and persecution – and against them I am certain that right will prevail.'

After a short pause, a BBC announcer took over the microphone: 'And now, an announcement about food.'

This was followed by a long silence broken only by the shuffling of paper and a low whisper. Then the national anthem was played. Mid-way came the wail of air-raid sirens. Chamberlain was standing back from the microphone chatting with staff and colleagues. They fell silent. So this was it. The anticipated Luftwaffe onslaught was about to begin. As the prime minister and his entourage made their way to the cellar, the national anthem was still playing on the radio.

Anticipating hours of nervous waiting, Mrs Chamberlain took along a selection of books.

In the event, it was a false alarm triggered by who knows what? A French aircraft carrying the French assistant military attaché back to Paris was one possibility; another was an RAF plane on a reconnaissance trip over Heligoland in the North Sea. In some quarters, English tourists in a hurry to get back from France were blamed. Later, the Air Ministry made its excuses.

> An aircraft was observed approaching the South Coast of England. As its identity could not be readily determined, an air raid warning was given. It was shortly afterwards identified as a friendly aircraft and the All Clear was given.

As war minister, Leslie Hore-Belisha blamed an over-sensitive radar station, one of twenty recently installed with a range, imperfect as it turned out, of between 50 and 120 miles.

> Radar had given us a backhander and warned us of two of our own civil machines that were flying over the Channel.[4]

A few minutes earlier, Berlin had responded formally to the British ultimatum with a refusal 'to receive, accept, let alone to fulfil [the demands] made upon the German government'. The tame justification for action against Poland, including the supposed 'ill treatment' of Germans within the Polish borders, was familiar stuff. The following evening German diplomats, consuls and other officials left, under police escort, for Berlin via Gravesend and Rotterdam. As foreign secretary, Lord Halifax pledged to find a new home for the embassy dog. All defences were on the alert for an imminent attack from German bombers.

On September 3rd [writes L.S. Bailey], I was a Warrant
Officer pilot with No. 1 Meteorological Flight, stationed at
Mildenhall, Suffolk. Immediately following the speech by
Neville Chamberlain, I was summoned to Headquarters
No. 3 Group, Bomber Command, then located on the same
station. The area officer commanding handed me three top
secret packages, and I was given instructions to deliver these
personally, with all possible speed, by air to the R.A.F. Station
Commanders at Wyton, Grantham and Linton on Ouse.

I flew a Gauntlet aircraft to carry out this mission,
and thanks to the prior briefing by 3 Group, the Station
Commander of each Station met the aircraft on arrival and
signed for their package without my having to leave the cock-
pit. Within 1 hr. 10 mins. all the packages, the first operational
instructions for Bomber Stations, had been delivered.

Another flight, mission unknown, ended catastrophically. Doris
MacDonald lived nearby in west London.

After lunch we took the dog for a walk from here to Hendon
where we had heard there had been some trouble. For the first
time we carried our gas-masks. On arriving near St Mary's
Church, we found a number of houses had been extensively
damaged – not by a bomb as it might have appeared – but by
a falling British aircraft. I do not know if the pilot was killed;
no doubt he had hoped to land on the adjacent airfield. He
was probably the first casualty of the war.

The fallibility of the new defence technology was corroborated by
the experience of those in the front line of plane spotting. A.P. Perry
was part of a Territorial Army coastal battery.

Suddenly the Spotter yelled 'Plane!' and pointed to the sky over London. Three little dots were sliding out from behind a cloud.

We jumped to our posts and swung the long telescopic tube onto the target. 'On!' shouted No. 2 as he got them in his wide-view finder. I turned the fine-adjustment wheel of my narrow-angle range lens to catch the planes in its view. It was up to me to feed the correct height into the Predictor. If I failed to pick up the fleeting target or made a bad 'cut', so that the wrong height was set, all our efforts would be in vain.

Slowly the dots came into the middle of my viewer. 'On Target!', I shouted as I twisted the knob which would bring the upper and lower images of the leading plane together. The planes were light bombers. But the Brasshats had never provided us with any system of aircraft recognition training. We had to pick up what we could, mostly from the newspapers. So we could not be sure whether the dots were friend or foe. We waited for them to fire the Colours of the Day for recognition. Nothing happened except that the planes disappeared behind a cloud.

Half a minute later we heard 'Boom! Boom!' from the next gunsite on the defence perimeter and saw little puffs of white smoke around the dots, now far out of our range. We had muffed our first chance of action! But we had the last laugh. The 'enemy' were our own Bristol Blenheims.

WHOEVER IT WAS who ordered the alarm on September 3rd could be forgiven for being over-cautious. For years the received wisdom among military pundits was of enemy bombers delivering death and destruction on an unprecedented scale. Winston Churchill, huddled in his shelter, was not alone in imagining 'ruin and carnage and vast explosions shaking the ground; [...] buildings clattering down in dirt and rubble, [...] fire-brigades and ambulances scurrying through the smoke beneath the drone of hostile aeroplanes'.

Another confident prediction soon to prove unfounded was of panic in the streets. For the most part, calm and good humour prevailed. All traffic came to a halt while police and steel-helmeted wardens acted as guides to the nearest public shelter. Their job was made easier by the Sunday closing of most shops and businesses. Even so, for those caught up in the open or at home preparing lunch, the sense of impending disaster was intense. Valerie Ranzetta, a mother of three who lived on the south coast, was called to her garden gate.

I was alarmed by the extraordinary sight of my next-door-neighbour's husband running down the road, arms waving, umbrella flailing the air, mouth wide open, shouting something, which, as he drew nearer, proved to be, 'I've got to *go* – *now!*' He belonged to the Territorial Army, and had been ordered to report for immediate duty. That morning, his wife and children had gone to Suffolk, for their annual holiday, there to await Father. They would have to wait a long time, I remember thinking. Well, he panicked, I panicked. He needed a flask of coffee, sandwiches, night-clothes, a change of linen, and as most of his best things were in his wife's two suitcases, this wasn't as easy as it sounded. Somehow, between us, we managed it, and the taxi carried him off, waving from the window, face pale with tense bewilderment, like most of us at that time. Just then, my husband came hurrying down the street, astonished by the sight of Harry leaning from the cab, and shouting at the top of his lungs! When my husband reached

me, all he could say was: *'He's in full uniform!'* and I knew what
he meant. It brought the war home to us.

In Aldershot, 'the home of the British Army', Tom Childerhouse
was expected to collect his two younger sisters from their holiday in
Norfolk. He had decided on an overnight drive. 'Leaving home soon
after work at 6.30 p.m. on September 2nd, I anticipated being back
by dawn in time for the next day's work.'

Getting to Norfolk was no problem. Getting back was another
matter.

We arrived in that rather deserted stretch of the A11 between
Newmarket and Thetford at around midnight on the 3rd. ...
Suddenly a red light was seen swinging back and forth and a
party of R.A.F. personnel stood firm, blocking my way. I was
questioned, 'Where had I come from, where was I going',
but most important of all, why had I been driving with full
headlights? I was told pilots from the nearby aerodromes had
reported my illuminated car. ... I was told to drive the rest of
my journey, over unfamiliar roads, without headlights. ... In
the end, I fixed one of those celluloid fog-light covers to one
headlight and removed the bulb of the other. I completed the
journey both ways in almost total darkness, arriving home at
dawn as expected.

Mrs Calver, of Petts Wood, lived near a railway cutting that held
morning mist. Responding to violent banging on her door, she
found an old lady in hysterics saying the Germans were coming,
she could see the gas along the railway line. It took some explaining to prove to her that she was threatened by nothing worse than
shifting fog.

Mrs Cottrell's husband was an ARP (Air Raid Precautions) warden. When the first siren went, he decided that his training must be put into full operation at once. The kitchen was to be the refuge. His elderly mother and her friend were hurried in. All blankets were taken off the beds. Some were nailed to tops of doors and windows in case of gas attacks. The oven cloth was stuffed up the boiler chimney and sticky tape stuck over cracks in the windows and back door. The sink was filled with water in case of fire. Her mother sat in the kitchen with a canary on one knee, a bottle of whisky on the other. The 'All Clear' sounded. The only ill-effects came the next day when the family was nearly choked by smoke when the boiler was lit. They had forgotten the cloth stuffed up the chimney.

A correspondent's landlady, having attended ARP classes, set up a shelter in her basement. But where was the wet blanket to protect against a gas attack?

> As soon as the warning went, I raced up to my room, snatched a blanket from my bed, tumbled it into the bath and waited a few anxious moments whilst it became soaking wet. Then galloping down the stairs two at a time, trailing water all the way, the landlady and I fitted it over the door, getting our clothes almost as wet as the blanket doing so. Our discomfort was quickly relieved by the All Clear. As we went up to tidy ourselves we were met by a cascade of water splashing down the stairs. I had forgotten to turn off the bath taps.

Maurice Brandon, on holiday in Brighton, was walking on the front when the first sirens sounded. A woman fainted. He laid her out on a bench, thinking as he did so, 'I must take a course in First Aid'.

While Neville Chamberlain was on air, 23-year-old Kate Quennell, who lived with her mother in Coventry, had domestic work on hand.

I was busy nailing up black-out material over the frosted glass above the front door, and the window by the side of the door. I wondered how long it would be before I would be able to take the material down again.

For the third time, WAR had interfered with my life. My father had succumbed to the influenza epidemic following the Great War; my twin sister had died as a result of bronchitis contracted during an air raid in the Great War, when we were living at Upper Tooting in London.

I never took the black-out material down; during the blitz on Coventry on 14th November, 1940, a bomb fell in the corner of the back garden and the blast sucked out the back of the house. The front door was blown in against the foot of the staircase behind which my mother and I were sheltering.

EMERGING FROM THE Downing Street shelter, Chamberlain made his way to the House of Commons where the benches were packed with members waiting to be uplifted with a call to arms. Instead, they were treated to an effusion of self-pity.

> This is a sad day for all of us, but to none is it sadder than to me. Everything that I have worked for, everything that I have hoped for, everything that I have believed in during my public life, has crashed into ruins.

It was left to Churchill to strike a suitably belligerent note. Agreeing with the prime minister that it was indeed a 'solemn hour', he went on to praise the 'strength and energy' of national unity in the face of tyranny.

Outside, the storms of war may blow and the lands may be lashed with the fury of its gales, but in our own hearts this Sunday morning there is peace. Our hands may be active, but our consciences are at rest.

It was no longer simply a question of fighting to save Poland.

We are fighting to save the whole world from the pestilence of Nazi tyranny and in defence of all that is most sacred to man. This is no war for domination or imperial aggrandisement or material gain; no war to shut any country out of its sunlight and means of progress. It is a war, viewed in its inherent quality, to establish, on impregnable rocks, the rights of the individual, and it is a war to establish and revive the stature of man.[5]

The contrast with the dejected Chamberlain could not have been greater. As a leader in the making, Churchill had made his pitch. Nearly eight months were to pass before he was able to take up the challenge.

For many people, the immediate problem was getting accustomed to new patterns of daily life. Frank Turner was a journalist with the Press Association. On September 3rd he was expecting to be in the PA building in Fleet Street by 4.00pm to start his shift as night editor. But the call came for him to be in earlier to sub-edit the speeches from Parliament before they were sent by teleprinter to the daily and Sunday papers and to the foreign news agencies.

Living out in south London, Turner was one of the first to come up against the complexities of travel in wartime.

Living half a mile from Penge East railway station, I went to the nearby main road hoping for a bus. The only transport in sight was a motorcyclist with a sidecar. I cadged a lift to the station and caught a train to Victoria, but as usual had to change at Herne Hill for a train to Blackfriars.

Herne Hill platforms were almost deserted and very quiet during the few minutes' wait, but suddenly the Sunday morning air was split by the wailing sound of air raid sirens ... as the sirens died away we few passengers heard a man somewhere on the station say loudly, 'Well, I'm buggered!'

I reached Blackfriars only to find myself locked in behind the collapsible gates of the District station with many other passengers. An Air Raid Warden yielded to my entreaties and let me out. 'At your own risk,' said he.

Through deserted New Bridge Street and Fleet Street I made my way only to find frustration at the doors of the Press Association building. They were locked! Knowing the building, I found a back door open and was met by a procession of people of all departments trudging from the air raid shelter in the basement up to the fourth, fifth and sixth floors to resume the jobs they had left. The 'All Clear' siren had been sounded.

We slogged away all the rest of that afternoon and then at 4 p.m. I took over my real job as night editor. I remember the mass of official Proclamations, including Conscription and regulations, also 13 or 14 Bills to be rushed through Parliament the next day.

About 1 a.m. I said 'I'm going home; we've broken the back of it for tonight' and caught the 1.15 a.m. train from Blackfriars. About 2 a.m., as I was sitting on my bed taking off my socks, the air raid siren sounded again, with the 'All Clear' ten minutes or so later.

WHILE THE WAITING for something – anything – to happen continued into the first week of the war, Britain looked to her friends in the wider world. A French ultimatum was presented in Berlin, not as Ribbentrop had predicted, an hour after that from Britain but at 12 noon. The delay was explained by the dithering on the part of foreign minister Georges Bonnet who held out to the last moment for a negotiated settlement of the Polish question.

The countries of the British empire and Commonwealth declared war in the next few days, though the commitment was hedged. A body of isolationist opinion in Canada ('We live in a fireproof house, far from inflammable materials')[6] was led by prime minister Mackenzie King. The decision was taken out of his hands by parliament voting to back the mother country. Canada declared war on September 10th.

Isolationism was also evident in Australia where painful memories from the Great War of the disastrous Gallipoli campaign cast doubts on a successful outcome of the latest conflict. However, along with New Zealand, where there was unqualified backing for Britain, war with Germany was declared on the day the British ultimatum ran out.

The trickiest alliance was with South Africa where, trading on the anti-British sentiment among the Boer population, prime minister James Hertzog favoured neutrality. The interventionist argument was put by his deputy, the soldier and statesman Jan Smuts, who was able to win a majority of the cabinet to his side. Subsequently, a two-day debate in the House of Assembly ended with the defeat of Hertzog's motion of neutrality. A new government led by Smuts declared war on Germany on September 6th.

The British colonies had no choice but to take their orders from London, though in remote parts of the empire it took some time for the news to get through. Employed by United Africa, a trading company dealing in hides and skins, gum and ground nuts, G.E. Higham was stationed at Geidam in north-east Nigeria, some 100 miles from Lake Chad.

My nearest neighbours were five days travel away, walking or by horse or camel, in Maiduguri or in N'Guru (to the east and west). There was no other means of communication. In those days, for better or for worse, we did not fraternise with the local Africans though we were on the best of terms. Like all others in similar circumstances I had become a little 'eccentric' being so long on my own.

My one means of contact with the world outside Geidam was a Philips battery radio set on which I got wonderful reception. For months I listened to the war developing with the speeches of Hitler, Mussolini and the others coming over perfectly.

But on September 3rd, just as Mr Chamberlain said 'We shall be fighting evil things' the batteries ran out. I could only guess that we were at war, but to make sure I sent off two runners – one to N'Guru and one to Maiduguri to make sure. I promised each man extra pay if he could get there and back in seven days – no mean feat.

They did it in six with the news that we were, most certainly, at war.

Though Italy was not to declare war on the Allies until June 1940, Mr Higham reckoned that the nearest likely enemy airbase was in Italian-held Libya, more than a thousand miles away. Nonetheless, he felt it wise to take precautions, particularly when a plane passed overhead.

I could only just see it glinting in the sun but it convinced me that Mussolini or Hitler was after my blood. So, believe it or not, I had an air raid shelter dug for myself and my boys – 8ft × 8ft × 8ft with places to keep food and drink, particularly the latter.

Looking back on this, I have often wondered just how 'eccentric' I had become. Geidam was just about as far away from anywhere that one could get in those parts. It wasn't far from French territory and the desert – in fact during the dry season one might just as well have been in the desert. But I had become convinced that I was a very important person.

Finally, the local Paramount Chief, the Kaigama, a wonderful old man came and asked me what we should do about the prospect of air raids. I told him that the only thing he could do to get warning was to send out his tribesmen in three lines – about 15 miles to the north west, north east and dead north – and when they saw or heard the Italian planes coming to bomb us they were to start beating their drums in the style of the bush telegraph and when we heard them we would all dive for cover and grab our rifles – such as they were.

BRITAIN WAS BACK on air alert on September 6th when the sirens disrupted the early morning. Ursula Bloom, in north London, was in bed reading when she heard the alarm.

I shot up and grabbed the gas-mask. I dashed into my clothes, had a last furtive look through the mullioned window beyond which absolutely nothing was happening, then went downstairs.

The residents [of her boarding house] had collected in the lounge, the idea being with the reminder of the 1914–18 hostilities that if one stood with one's back to the main wall of the house nothing could possibly happen to the person – I suppose it is very satisfactory to be so sure. Nothing happened to any of us.

One gets a little tired of standing with one's back to the main wall so I sat down and did some of my knitting. The milkman, making the most of an exciting occasion, came round and said that Romford had been raided, and that Chatham was already in ruins! All sorts of things were going on on the east coast, and I, who had lived there in the previous war, thought this quite likely. An hour later when the all clear sounded, I felt pretty silly as I took my gas-mask back upstairs and then started a belated breakfast away from the main wall of the house.[7]

Better prepared was Hilde Hoile who lived in Burgess Hill, West Sussex, in the days before it was urbanised: 'Whenever the siren sounded we got under our beds which we had brought down to the dining room.' Hilde took comfort from the wall built by the council to protect the glass doors against blast but reflected later that the wall itself was hardly strong enough to withstand more than a gentle push.

As recorded by her friend, an elderly resident of Bedford demanded protection for herself and a neighbour that went beyond the official guidelines.

She asked for an oilskin cape for mustard gas protection, and a tin hat, for herself and her neighbour, also an old lady over seventy.

They were determined to survive at all costs, and their applications not being successful, the indomitable pair decided on their own outfit, so they purchased cyclist's oilskin capes. When the sirens sounded they donned their gas-masks, capes and with saucepans on their grey heads solemnly marched down to their Anderson shelters.

It was an image, said their friend, worthy of Bruce Bairnsfather, creator of the 'Old Bill' cartoons from the Great War.

As bizarre but more tragically came a lesson to those in the civilian front line not to exaggerate their duties. After climbing a drainpipe in an attempt to put out a light in an upstairs room, police constable George Southworth was killed falling from a third floor in Harley Street. He had been unable to get a reply when he knocked on the door.

Of war news there was little that was encouraging. Poland fought nobly and hopelessly. Eager to get their unfair share of the country, Soviet forces invaded from the east on September 17th. Warsaw surrendered eleven days later after suffering bombing and fire storms, intensifying fears in London and Paris that they would be next. But there were compensations, as Marian Rees noted in her diary.

Now the weather is so glorious – the morning haze, the hot mellow September sun, the heavy dew, the yellow sunflowers and the myriad blackberries in the garden, the peaceful river that I walk alongside on my way to work. Perhaps it is as well to live in these things, and not to live in the future. Only the sky is filled with barrage balloons, but even these are beautiful in the twilight, and in the field at the bottom of the garden there is a company of Territorials, with a camp, a gun and a searchlight. Even they seem to be peacefully enjoying themselves, digging in the sun, getting browner and browner skinned, smoking and talking.

A junior diplomat at Canada House on Trafalgar Square, Charles Ritchie set down his impressions of a city with a delayed sentence of blitzkrieg.

> While the general London scene is the same, there are oddities of detail – brown paper pasted over fan-lights and walled-in windows on the ground floors of the buildings, the sand-bags around hospitals and museums, the coffin-like enclosures around the statues in the central court of the Foreign Office. And there are odd tableaux too – glimpses of people in shirt-sleeves digging air-raid shelters in their back gardens, or offices debouching typewriters and desks for removal to country premises. Then there is the outcropping of uniforms, raw-looking young soldiers in very new uniforms unload themselves from Army trucks and stand about awkwardly in front of public buildings. Women in uniform looking dowdy as old photographs of the last war, full-bosomed, big-bottomed matrons who carry their uniforms with a swagger, and young girls copying their brothers – a spectacle to make their lovers quail.[8]

There was still time to think and to wonder, how did it come to this?

CHAPTER 2

Butter Before Guns

For more than a decade after the Great War with its terrible cost in lives lost and damaged, the hope was of a peaceful settlement of differences between nations bonded by a system of interlocking treaties. With the League of Nations to see fair play (a wretched illusion), there would be no further need to waste resources on military prowess. In Britain the budget for the armed forces was cut in almost every year up to 1932 while the armaments industry was allowed to wind down.

But the dread of another conflict was never far from the public imagination. Terrifying images were created by the power of the unknown with a consensus building up of a future war being fought, not on land or at sea, but in the air by machines of huge if yet untested destructive power. The bombs that fell from German airships and aircraft in 1917–18 were an intimation of what was possible. Asked to peer into the future, South African statesman Jan Smuts declared that there was 'absolutely no limit' to the use to which planes could be put.

As the high point of aerial warfare, Giulio Douhet, Italian career soldier and an early champion of Mussolini, promoted the idea of pre-emptive bombing to destroy civilian morale and bring a speedy end to conflict. In *Il Dominio dell'Aria* (Command of the Air), Douhet presented as fact that 'Within a few minutes [of an attack] some twenty tons of high explosive, incendiary and gas bombs will rain down ... As the hours pass and night advances, the fires will spread while the poison gas will paralyse all life.' In Britain, the theme was taken up by J.F.C. (Boney) Fuller, another professional soldier and fascist sympathiser. In *The Reformation of War*, he described how 'great cities, such as London, will be attacked from the air':

> Picture, if you will, what the result will be: London for several days will be one vast raving Bedlam, the hospitals will be stormed, traffic will cease, the homeless will shriek for help, the city will be in pandemonium. What of the government at Westminster? It will be swept away by an avalanche of terror. Then will the enemy dictate his terms ... Thus may a war be won in forty-eight hours and the losses of the winning side may actually be nil!

There was some evidence to support the soothsayers. The air raids on London towards the end of the Great War caused 4,820 deaths and injuries, a casualty rate of sixteen for every ton of bombs. In 1919, the newly formed Royal Air Force, the first of its kind, made short measure of an uprising in Somaliland led by the 'Mad Mullah'. The RAF then saw action in Iraq, Aden, Sudan and on the North West Frontier of India. Up against lightly armed natives who had never before encountered sky machines with destructive power, this was fighting made easy for the imperial forces. But the science of war was not static. It was by no means fanciful that forthcoming advances in air technology would allow for a more damaging delivery of high explosives and, probably, of poison gas.

In 1922, in his role as chairman of the Committee of Imperial Defence, Lord Balfour, recalling German raids of the Great War, predicted that in a reprise of a European conflict, a continental enemy could 'drop on London a continuous torrent of high explosives at the rate of seventy-five tons a day for an indefinite period'.

A harder look at the evidence by a sub-committee of the Committee of Imperial Defence, set up in 1924 under Sir John Anderson, soon to be the administrative and political driving force for civil defence, concluded that on the first day of war 200 tons of bombs would be dropped on London with a smaller tonnage thereafter, causing 50,000 casualties within the month.

For a war-weary Britain and France, doom-laden predictions strengthened the movement for peace at almost any price. Even the rise of fascism with its militaristic slant, first in Italy and then in Germany, did little to dent the widespread conviction that passive resistance or no resistance at all was the only antidote to aggression. The famous debate of 1933 at the Oxford University Union, the elite finishing school for the next generation of political leaders, when students voted 225 to 153 that 'in no circumstances' would they fight for King and Country, was enthusiastically endorsed on both sides of the Channel, with other universities urged to follow Oxford's example.

The groundswell of anti-war sentiment in Britain found expression in the Peace Pledge Union led by Dick Sheppard, a former padre and crowd-pulling preacher who had been traumatised by what he had experienced on the Western Front. In 1934, having launched his Peace Ballot, over 100,000 sent postcards renouncing war and promising to 'never again, directly or indirectly, support or sanction another'. Sheppard was only 57 when he died of a heart attack. Such was his popularity, not least as a broadcaster who made his listeners feel they were part of a friendly, informal conversation, his funeral had thousands lining the route of his cortege.

There were other big names attached to pacifism. Aldous Huxley was among those who rejected the 'collective security' promised by the League of Nations as a contradiction in terms. Peace could not be secured by threatening to punish an aggressor. The only way forward was unilateral disarmament with Britain setting an example for the world to follow. Labour leader George Lansbury was a Christian socialist pacifist. At a by-election speech at Fulham in 1933, he pledged to 'close every recruiting station, disband the army and dismiss the air force'. A 32 per cent swing of votes gave this supposedly safe Tory seat to Labour with a majority of nearly five thousand. As Lansbury's successor as Labour leader, Clement Attlee, though no pacifist, declared his party 'unalterably opposed to anything in the nature of rearmament'.

In the fortnight leading up to the Oxford Union debate, a rather more significant historical landmark was observed in Germany, where Adolf Hitler was proclaimed chancellor. As the soon-to-be dictator began moving his people into senior positions, Neville Chamberlain, chancellor of the exchequer in the national but largely Conservative government led by Stanley Baldwin, had his mind elsewhere, as he disclosed in a letter to *The Times*:

> Sir. It may be of interest to record that, in walking through St James's Park today, I noticed a grey wagtail running about on the now temporarily dry bed of the lake, near the dam below the bridge, and occasionally picking small insects out of the cracks in the dam.
>
> Probably the occurrence of this bird in the heart of London has been recorded before, but I have not myself previously noted it in the Park.

I am your obedient servant,
Neville Chamberlain

P.S. For the purpose of removing doubts, as we say in the House of Commons, I should perhaps add that I mean a grey wagtail and not a pied.[1]

Clearly, and despite vitriolic speeches and the evidence of a diseased mind contained in his memoir *Mein Kampf*, the government was not fazed by Hitler's rise. Indeed, there was consolation to be found in a resurgent Germany. It was a common belief in Britain, if not in France, that Germany had been given a rough deal in the Versailles peace treaty that ended the Great War. In addition to losing one eighth of its territory, all its colonies had been redistributed among the victors. To shore up the defence of France, German troops were barred from territory west of the Rhine and from 50 kilometres to the east of the river. Though Allied occupation forces withdrew from the Rhineland in 1930, it remained a demilitarised buffer zone against a German attack on France.

As an added precaution, the German military, limited to 100,000 men, was forbidden tanks, heavy artillery, aircraft, gas, submarines and a general staff. Massive reparations, though subsequently modified, contributed to a giddy spirit of inflation and the collapse of the deutschmark.

Among those who argued that Germany deserved better were fascist sympathisers who found much to praise in the new Germany. While the world was struggling with failing economies and social disruption, here was a leader who, like Mussolini in Italy, got things done. Fascist methods were crude but who could deny the benefits? When Hitler came to power, well over a third of Germany's working population was unemployed, and the national income was down by

40 per cent on the previous three years. Helped by a recovery in the world economy, he launched his version of America's New Deal by pouring money into construction and, later, into rearmament. This in contrast to Britain and France where recession had been made worse by politicians adhering to the book-keeping school of economics with cutbacks in national expenditure in a vain effort to balance the accounts. German unemployment fell from 4 million in 1933 to 1.7 million in 1935 to close to zero by 1937.

The 1936 Olympic Games, held in Berlin, was a masterclass in public relations. Trailing a giant Olympic banner, the airship *Hindenburg* floated majestically over an athletics stadium designed to accommodate 100,000 spectators. The right-leaning politician and playboy, Chips Channon, heaped praise on his German hosts as the 'masters of the art of party-giving'[2] (propaganda minister Joseph Goebbels entertained 2,000 guests at his Sommerfest), while the more serious-minded Randolph Hughes found 'health, character and order', a contrast to Britain with its 'louts and hooligans and wastrels'.[3] 'We plod behind', declared Virginia Woolf. The German team came out top of the Olympic medal table with 33 gold, 26 silver and 30 bronze. Britain lagged far behind with just four gold, seven silver and three bronze.

The image of Germany as a fresh, disciplined and inventive nation was further endorsed at the 1937 Paris Exposition Universelle where the German-built 54-metre tower, topped by an eagle embraced by a swastika, dwarfed the British pavilion with its emphasis on traditional crafts and hobbies illustrated by a giant photograph of Chamberlain in wading boots wielding his fishing rod.

The Nazi regime made certain that the signs of progress were highly visible. Ambitious public works included over seven thousand kilometres of autobahns by 1936 (Britain had to wait until 1958 for its first stretch of motorway). Consumers, used only to shortages, rushed to buy the Volksempfaenger, a household radio made afford-able for almost everyone. As the first of the Volkswagens rolled off the production line, the promise was held out for the debut of a 'peo-ple's car'. Factory workers, often subject to long hours in primitive conditions, were mollified by state-subsidised holidays.

Playing down the injustices and brutalities of Nazism, British right-wingers saw in Germany a reflection of their yearning for regeneration. Retired army officers were among Hitler's most ardent supporters. Oswald Mosley made headlines with his Blackshirt demonstrations but his influence was superficial compared to the Anglo-German Group. Set up in 1933, it had among its members leading editors and journal-ists and other opinion leaders able to put pressure on the government to build good relations with Nazi Germany.

Foremost among those who cosied up to Hitler was the 7th Marquess of Londonderry, 'a scion of one of Britain's grandest and wealthiest aristocratic families',[4] a cousin of Winston Churchill, who by virtue of his gold-plated connection was secretary of state for air from 1931 to 1935. Courted by the Nazi elite with flattering atten-tion to his opinions and with lavish entertainment including weekend shoots with Hermann Goering, Londonderry was seen in Berlin as a useful adjunct to a campaign to present Germany in a favourable light. Ill-equipped to be a politician, his arrogance and superior man-ner caused him to be sacked as air minister in 1935. Henceforth, he put his energy into promoting a peaceful understanding with Britain's continental rival.

It was not just Londonderry who spoke up for fascism. Paeans of praise for Hitler littered the media in the 1930s. *The Times*, the *Daily Express* and the *Daily Mail* argued that Nazi rule was bring-ing great benefits to Germany and that Hitler was a force for good. Journalists who showed willing such as George Ward Price, foreign correspondent for the *Daily Mail*, were favoured with privileged access to Hitler's inner circle. As owner of the *Mail*, Lord Rothermere was gushingly eager to please the dictators. A regular visitor to Germany since 1930, his first praise of Hitler appeared under the headline, 'A Nation Reborn'. In 1930 he told *Mail* readers that any 'minor misdeeds of individual Nazis will be submerged by the immense benefits the new regime is already bestowing on Germany'. Hitler was delighted to welcome Rothermere to Nazi functions and there were many exchanges of mutual goodwill.

Bookshops sold soft propaganda on behalf of the new Germany. In *Germany Speaks*, leading members of the regime wrote persuasively of their role in restoring Germany to its rightful place in the international community. Joachim von Ribbentrop, German ambassador in London and from 1938 Reich foreign minister, expounded his duty 'to assist in every way possible any movement genuinely desirous of promoting understanding between two great nations'. As minister of justice, Dr Franz Guertner assured his readers that in his country 'law and justice are at the root of every activity'.[5]

Incredibly, as it must now seem, the excesses of Nazi power – with political opponents falling under the state-wielded cosh – were excused or minimised by writers who held to the end justifying the means. *These Germans* had the travel writer Eric Taverner quoting his Hamburg friend, a 'broad minded man of the world ... with a deep appreciation of what we Englishmen mean by fair play', on how international Jewry was intent on communist domination of Europe and how, in Germany, the 'secret grip' of the Jews had stifled medicine, law and the creative industries', and the Jews were linked to the liberal press activity for 'anonymous interests'. The spread of concentration camps was praised for clearing the 'do-nothings', 'parasites' and 'foreign elements' off the streets. Similarly, the well publicised sterilisation campaign against 'recidivists and degenerates' was justified as a contribution to the greater good.

To capture the young, Britain's private schools were provided with free textbooks for first-stage German with conversation exercises that lauded Hitler and Nazi ideology. The writer Peter Vansittart was at Haileybury in the mid-1930s.

We had a German Club: sweet cakes, *lieder* and guitars, solemn Teutonic visitors glad of our parrot denunciations of Versailles. One of them announced that modern psychology was invented by Goering's brother. A lively film, *Marching through Germany with Hitler's Armies*, was shown in Big School. Processions, uniforms, cheap but stirring tunes, had narcotic powers which I have found easier to condemn than to expurgate ...

One master, a Christian Union leader, encouraged us to spend summer holidays at a German Labour Camp, where, he guaranteed, most interesting things were occurring. These camps, apparently, had the happy results of completing the breakdown of snobbery and class-distinction. The disadvantages are equally clear. While fitting the individuals to take their place without question in a highly organised national life, the system gives them no time to think for themselves, and actually discourages any such desire ... If the ideal is co-operation and peace, perhaps the price is justified; if it is not, the outcome can only be disaster in an unparalleled scale.[6]

REGISTERING THE PUBLIC mood (as home secretary Sir Samuel Hoare observed, 'There is a strong pro-German feeling in this country'), the government looked upon Hitler not so much as a threat but as a strong leader with whom they could settle European relations. The first priority was to resolve German grievances. Hitler had his own way of doing this. Given that neither Britain nor France was prepared to deny him, he felt free to abandon the disarmament conference in Geneva and, in October 1933, to stalk out of the League of Nations. These moves were universally regretted but not roundly condemned. Was not Germany justified in its resentment at being treated as a second-rate power in thrall to its former enemies?

Hitler was not alone in reneging on international agreements and abusing diplomatic conventions. The myopia of the democracies in the 1930s extended to the Italian rape of Ethiopia (then known as Abyssinia), the Japanese assault on Manchuria, and to the overthrow of the legitimate government in Spain. So it was that criticism was muted when, in blatant defiance of the Treaty of Versailles, Hitler reintroduced conscription in 1935 and announced the creation of an air force and a five-fold increase in the size of the German army to 600,000. In the first two years of Nazi rule, military expenditure as a proportion of national income jumped from 1 per cent to 10 per cent.

Noting the ambitious scale of German rearmament, the thinking in London held to a European pact guaranteeing mutual defence against an aggressor. An Anglo-French accord for 'a general settlement freely negotiated between Germany and the other powers' was taken forward, with foreign secretary Sir John Simon visiting Berlin for 'a full exchange of views with Herr Hitler'. Apart from vague and soon to be broken German promises to limit military spending, the only development of any note was an agreement in principle for Germany's naval strength to be allowed to increase to 35 per cent of Royal Navy tonnage. Simon took credit for the subsequent Anglo-German Naval Treaty, 'the only agreement for arms limitation which has ever been secured out of all the welter of discussion'. In reality, it was an extraordinary climbdown by Britain. In quick order, Germany was given the go-ahead to build up its navy to 21 cruisers and 64 destroyers. Such was the sense of urgency – or panic – that no one thought to consult France or Italy, the other two European naval powers. Nor was any account taken of the views of Sweden and Denmark, where there was an understandable fear of German dominance in the Baltic.

On March 7th, 1936, German troops crossed into demilitarised Rhineland. If Britain and France wanted to stop Hitler in his tracks, this was the time. There was every legitimate reason to resist the weakening of the defence of France by allowing Germany to cross the Rhine. Instead, there was merely a shrugging of shoulders. After all, Hitler was simply 'moving into his own back yard'.[7] The Fuehrer put it more grandly when he addressed the Reichstag. 'Germany has regained its honour, found belief again, overcome its greatest economic distress and finally, ushered in a new cultural ascent', he claimed, adding: 'We have no territorial claims to make in Europe.' In the German elections that followed on March 29th, Hitler and the National Socialist party (the only party allowed to stand) secured 98.9 per cent of the vote.

Thus, by May 1937 when Neville Chamberlain succeeded Stanley Baldwin as prime minister, the scene was set for the finale in Europe's power play with Hitler in the leading role. His gamble on reoccupying the Rhineland without incurring repercussions (he later called it the most nerve-wracking 48 hours of his life) strengthened his belief that he was walking with destiny. Unfolding events seemed to confirm his good opinion of himself. The outbreak of the Spanish Civil War was an opportunity to proclaim the German model of fascism as the European bulwark against Bolshevism; the news from Italy was of Mussolini's desire to strengthen the Rome–Berlin Axis, while in France, the political gulf between left and right mitigated efforts to maintain the alliances built up to contain Germany. The new centre of power was in Berlin.

Chamberlain's up-front involvement with appeasement started in late 1937 when Lord Halifax, in his grand-sounding but non-departmental role of Lord President of the Council, was in Berlin for the International Sporting Exhibition. Though himself a hunting and shooting enthusiast, it would not have occurred to Halifax to make the trip had not an official invitation arrived on his desk and had not Chamberlain seized on the chance for a senior colleague to meet the Nazi hierarchy. Informal conversation in convivial surroundings must surely help to clear away mutual suspicion. That, at least, was Chamberlain's reckoning.

As foreign secretary, Anthony Eden was not so sure. His senior adviser, Robert Vansittart, was opposed to a visit that could be interpreted as kowtowing to an insalubrious dictatorship. But Eden, as a young (he was only 40) and ambitious politician was hardly in a position to defy the prime minister over what few would regard as a vital issue.

More controversially, Eden made no objection to the appointment of the egocentric, emotional and susceptible Nevile Henderson to be ambassador in Berlin. Pro-German and a faithful ally to Chamberlain, it was disturbing that Henderson felt 'specially selected by Providence for the definite mission of … helping to preserve the peace of the world'. He made no promise of objective judgement.

The red carpet was rolled out for Halifax when he flew to Germany on November 17th. A round of semi-official functions gave him the opportunity to be polite and attentive, while nodding approval at the catalogue of German achievements and acquiescing at vaguely formulated ambitions for the greater glory of the Reich. When faced with contentious issues, such as a closer attachment to Austria, the re-absorption of Danzig, Poland's access to the Baltic, and an adjustment of the boundaries of Czechoslovakia to satisfy that country's German minority, Halifax showed himself willing to consider 'possible alternatives in the European order which might be destined to come about with the passage of time'. His patience held even when he had to listen to Joseph Goebbels complain of the rare occasions when anti-German sentiment appeared in the British press.

Halifax went away well pleased that he had made a favourable impression. His hosts were equally pleased to have pulled off a triumph of play-acting. It was less than a fortnight earlier that Hitler had called together his service chiefs to give one of his rambling diatribes on his plans for extending the boundaries of the Reich. On that occasion, there had been no kind words for Britain and France, pilloried as 'hate-inspired antagonists' in decadent decline. The old stale European order had to give way to the new, invigorated Germany. To prove the point, and here his audience was shocked into close attention, the Nazi flag would soon fly over Austria and Czechoslovakia.

When, full of optimism, Halifax returned from his mission of reconciliation, Chamberlain was delighted. Presumably he did not see or chose to ignore the David Low cartoon in the *Evening Standard* showing Hitler proudly displaying his sporting trophies to a trembling Halifax. Up on the wall were two empty places reserved for Austria and Czechoslovakia.

Anthony Eden's first tenure at the Foreign Office came to an end with his resignation in February 1938. Though by no means an opponent of Chamberlain's foreign policy, which he accurately defined as 'peace at almost any price', he had become increasingly irritated by the prime minister's readiness to negotiate without preconditions, thereby sidelining the Foreign Office. In particular, he was incensed by Chamberlain's enthusiasm for talks with Mussolini before there was a guarantee that Italian troops would be withdrawn from Spain where they were supporting the fascist insurrection. Eden was replaced by Halifax, a 'feudal anachronism'[8] and a like mind for

Chamberlain who had the added virtue of being a peer and thus restricted to the House of Lords. This left Chamberlain effectively in charge of foreign affairs.

The annexation of Austria in March 1938 was another spectacular gamble that paid off for Hitler. Forcing the pace with demands that threatened the sovereignty of Czechoslovakia and Poland, he had all the evidence he needed to be convinced that Britain and France would not act to save their friends. In July, Chamberlain spoke of the absurdity of war on account of 'a quarrel in a far away country between people of whom we know nothing'.

His words were echoed by the hard core of Nazi sympathisers who cared little for the threatened states of central and eastern Europe. In his book *Why Britain Prospers* (1938), William Teeling put the rhetorical question, 'How far are we interested in the future of these small countries?' Since they were no threat to the British empire, the answer was 'that the people, as a whole, would never go to war to defend them'.[9] He had a point. Whatever now is thought of Chamberlain and Halifax, their inadequate response to momentous events matched the mood of the time.

On May 14th, 1938, at the start of a friendly football match at the Olympic Stadium in Berlin and with Chamberlain's encouragement, the English captain, Eddie Hapgood, led his team in giving the Nazi salute while the German national anthem was played.

CHAMBERLAIN IS STUCK with his image as a dry old stick. With his dark suit and starched wing collar which emphasised his scrawny neck, he was the epitome of a superannuated bank manager. That he was intelligent and well-read there could be no doubt, but he had an inflated view of his talent as a political operator well able to take the measure of his opponents. His fatal error in assessing Hitler was his assumption that he was dealing with a rational being who was open to reasoned argument.

As for Halifax, rich and sophisticated, holding to the correct manners of old-world diplomacy, he could not bring himself to believe that two great countries – Germany and Italy – had fallen to those for whom lies and duplicity were second nature. There was, he believed, 'a rational solution to all problems and all that was needed was to find a *modus vivendi* comfortable to all parties'.[10] Oozing sanctity, (someone said of him that he would have been happier as Archbishop of Canterbury), Halifax was the perfect complement to Chamberlain's self-belief and arrogance.

As J.B. Priestley, dramatist and popular broadcaster pointed out, 'When Chamberlain and Halifax talk about appeasement, they are referring to a Germany and Italy that do not exist. They are trying to settle the world of 1909.'[11]

Destined to be Chief of the Imperial General Staff on the outbreak of war, General Edmund Ironside met Hitler and Goering in Berlin towards the end of 1937. On the evening of his departure,

I was sitting in the hall of the Adlon Hotel by myself after dinner, and had told my British Gunner servant to signal to me when I had to leave for the midnight train. I was thinking over what I had seen, including Marshal Badoglio (Italian Chief of Staff). I found him a great man. We had to talk in French which he spoke none too well and I could not speak Italian though I understood it. I had gained the impression that Badoglio did not wish to fight against us and he did not take kindly to Hitler's policies. As I was ruminating I found that Reichenau (one of Hitler's favourite generals), with his jackal Koch, and Goering had come up to me and were bowing deeply. They told me that I could not be enjoying myself as I was not drinking. They ordered three bottles of whisky and the four of us started taking our drams neat with a very little water afterwards. They gradually became more and more intoxicated. When they were well away I saw my servant signalling to me. I said that I must go and at last Goering said that before I went he wished to make a toast. 'I drink to the peace which ought to be between our two great nations.' Then in a drunken whisper he said to Reichenau, 'but only for two years'. I then said goodbye and cleared off.[12]

Thinking this over, Ironside concluded that a German offensive could be expected around September 1939: 'I told Mr Chamberlain of this instance of German ideas, but he rather pooh-poohed its value.'

Not everyone subscribed to the meek and mild route to everlasting peace. In Britain, the lobby for rearmament was led by the chiefs of staff of the three services. In 1933 and early 1934, they got together with senior civil servants in a Defence Requirements Committee, the better to feed the government with the fruits of their expertise. Quicker than the politicians to identify a resurgent Germany as a likely threat, they pointed out the risk of being caught in a pincer with an aggressively inclined Japan challenging Britain's imperial reach in the Far East. The country simply did not have the military backup to meet its responsibilities. An ambitious programme of rearmament was called for.

As chancellor of the exchequer from 1931 to 1937, Chamberlain was ambivalent on defence. He made no complaint at the dropping of the ten-year rule whereby military planning was based on the assumption that the next conflict was at least a decade away, and he recognised the virtue of negotiating from a position of strength but his first concern was for the health of the economy as it emerged from years of recession. He was sensitive, as he wrote, to the 'further sacrifice of our commerce to the manufacture of arms'. That rearmament and economic growth were not mutually exclusive, the former helping to stimulate industry and commerce across a broad front, seems never to have occurred to him.

In any case, the very idea of building prosperity on the back of rearmament was anathema to Chamberlain who, above all, wanted to be recorded in history as a man of peace. In his vision of the future it was only by general disarmament that the security of mankind could be assured. When that prospect faded as the world order began to crumble, Chamberlain reluctantly went along with the majority view that there was no alternative 'but to provide the necessary means both of safeguarding ourselves against aggression and to play our part in the enforcement of common action of international obligations'.[13]

In December 1937, the Cabinet agreed to an upper limit of £1,500 million, to be spent on rearmament for the period up to 1941. This was a substantial increase on previous estimates but was still way short of what the service chiefs regarded as the essential minimum. To go further, argued Chamberlain, would be to undermine attempts to satisfy Germany's grievances by rational discussion leading to mutually agreed solutions.

Once installed as prime minister in May 1937, Chamberlain put himself at the forefront of pacifying the bullies while, to his credit, putting in place as war minister an energiser and innovator. As minister of transport from 1934, Leslie Hore-Belisha had introduced a new highway code and pedestrian crossings. The winking of Belisha beacons to warn motorists to slow down was a permanent reminder of his talents, not least for self-publicity. Welcoming the challenge of a move to the War Office, he started on a series of reforms to modernise the army and improve service conditions to attract more recruits.

With direct commissioning from the ranks, by-passing Woolwich and Sandhurst, a new breed of officer began to emerge, much to the consternation of the old guard. Even Chamberlain was moved to observe 'the obstinacy of some of the Army heads in sticking to obsolete methods is incredible'. It was not until Hore-Belisha came on the scene that the army could boast a single armoured division.

By late 1938 the regular army consisted of no more than five divisions of which only two were fully equipped. Moreover, the brief for the army was to focus on protecting the empire by keeping up to strength its overseas garrisons. There were no plans to fight on the European mainland.

The German military structure was tighter and psychologically in better shape to fight a war closer to home. The mass intake and training of the young was an opportunity to impose Nazi ideology on impressionable minds and to instil unquestioning obedience to higher authority. But it was the strategy of dynamic mobility that gave the German army its unique edge. The break with tradition of relying on the slow mass movement of troops and cavalry started with a young infantry captain. Joining the motor transport staff in 1922, Heinz Guderian became the chief proponent of armoured warfare.

An experimental armoured division took part in Germany's summer exercises of 1935, and that autumn the first three armoured divisions were formed. Next year they were regrouped into an armoured corps. Massed armour appeared in the manoeuvres of 1937 and again in 1938. In March 1937, under Guderian, the Panzers enjoyed their first triumph when one armoured and one SS motorised division entered Vienna, having driven 420 miles in 48 hours. They went on to prove their worth in the attacks on Czechoslovakia and Poland. By September 1939, Guderian, at age 51, was commander of XIX Panzer Corps, one of the new generation of commanders to give the German army its head start.

The naval balance was thought to be more favourable to Britain. The Royal Navy, though clamouring for more resources, was confident of holding its own against all-comers. Britain had more battleships than any country except America and new aircraft carriers were planned. But British battleships were mostly older than those of America and Japan, the other two leading maritime nations, and by 1939 the carrier *Ark Royal* was the only serious newcomer in the fleet. The poor performance of carrier-borne aircraft held back naval aviation.

Little attention was given to Germany's naval ambitions. As it was starting virtually from scratch, it was assumed that many years would pass before the Reichsmarine, later renamed the Kriegsmarine, became a serious competitor on the high seas. No great concern was caused by the launch of three 'pocket' battleships, more powerful than any cruiser and faster than most conventional battleships. This was reprehensible but less so than the Admiralty's lack of interest in the unveiling of a new generation of German submarines soon to be under the command of Admiral Karl Doenitz.

The Royal Navy was slow to catch on to the submarine as a war machine of enormous potential, capable of starving an enemy into submission by cutting off food imports and other supplies by sea. In 1939, Britain was importing by sea an annual total of 55 million tons of supplies, including all its oil and half its food and raw materials. The Merchant Navy had around 2,500 ships at sea at any given time. All were vulnerable to U-boat attack.

The only threat to be taken seriously by British strategists was from the air. Advances in aviation enjoyed wide publicity, with big prizes awarded for pilot skill and endurance. Distance and speed records were set and broken with unnerving frequency while indelible images of the horrendous power of aerial bombing had long impinged on the public imagination.

The trend was set by Stanley Baldwin when, as prime minister, he spoke the words that would forever be attached to his name: 'The bomber will always get through.' He added, and this was the message picked up by the rearmament lobby, 'The only defence is in offence, which means that you have to kill more women and children more quickly than the enemy if you want to save yourselves.'[14]

For the RAF, the lesson was to build aerial strength to a point where damage inflicted by an enemy would meet with full retribution. Under Lord Swinton, appointed air minister in 1935, the Wellingtons and Blenheims, the precursors of heavy bombers, were put into production along with the Spitfire and Hurricane fighters. But ambitious plans and targets were one thing, delivery and the creation of a fighting force quite another.

It was the images of what was possible rather than what was practical that caused consternation. Few questioned the speculations of the military pundit Liddell Hart when he invited his readers to:

> Imagine for a moment London, Manchester, Birmingham and half a dozen other great cities simultaneously attacked, the business localities and Fleet Street wrecked, Whitehall a heap of ruins, the slum districts maddened into the impulse to break loose and maraud, the railways cut, factories destroyed. Would not the general will to resist vanish, and what use would be the still determined factions of the nation, without organisation and directions?

Sociologists and psychologists were quick to endorse the nightmare images. Chiefly known for his theory of animism and for psychical research, William McDougall rushed to print with his *Janus: The Conquest of War*:

The developments of the arts of destruction ... especially the development of aircraft, of the explosive bomb and of the poison gases, have made it only too clear that in the next Great War the civilian populations, and especially the populations of the great cities, will be the first and greatest sufferers, that wounds, mutilation and death, terror and famine, will be broadcast among them with awful impartiality; that no woman, no family, no little child, no church, no treasury of art, no museum of priceless antiquities, no shrine of learning and science will be immune; but that in a few days or hours great cities may be levelled with the dust, while their surviving inhabitants scrape for crusts amid mangled bodies of fair women and the ruins of the monuments or art and science.

Fanciful or not, it was a theme taken up by Churchill in his campaign for standing up to aggressors.

We must expect that, under the pressure of continuous air attack upon London, at least 3,000,000 or 4,000,000 people would be driven out into the open country around the metropolis. This vast mass of human beings, numerically far larger than any armies which have been fed and moved in war, without shelter and without food, without sanitation and without special provision for the maintenance of order, would confront the Government of the day with an administrative problem of the first magnitude, and would certainly absorb the energies of our small Army and our Territorial Force.[15]

No one was left in doubt as to the potential aggressor he had in mind. And few were convinced that the RAF was an adequate deterrent.

Coastal Fighter and Bomber Commands were set up in 1935.

A strategic offensive against Germany was part of the Bomber Command brief, but as a distant prospect. The first Bomber Group, known as No. 2, intended primarily for army support, was poorly equipped. As Michael Bowyer points out in his history of Group 2:

> All the 2 Group bombers were still biplanes ... Such bombs as they carried were small, suitable only for counter-insurgency operations, carried in clutches beneath the wings.
>
> Radio equipment was almost non-existent. ... There was no real air traffic control. It was enough that a duty pilot sent off a signal to a destination station that an aircraft was on its way; if he thought it unlikely the telegram would reach the airfield before the aircraft he remained silent on the matter.

With no electronic navigation, night flying was by tracking the stars.

> Also missing was a station meteorological office and at a time when weather conditions mattered so much. A route or destination forecast was available from the Central Meteorological Office in London – provided sufficient warning was given. Alternatively, pilots flew on a 'hope and see' basis.[16]

As for Fighter Command, the transition from wooden biplanes to a force of cantilever monoplanes, Hurricanes and Spitfires, with superior armament and performance, was still largely on the drawing board. In September 1938, the RAF had only five squadrons of Hurricanes and one of Spitfires. Without heating for their guns, the Hurricanes could not fight above 15,000 feet even in summer.

Commanding the skies was essential to the virile image of the Nazi regime. Following the example of Mussolini, who put aeronautical heroes at the forefront of his campaign to win public esteem, Hitler set great store on building Germany's air power. The opening sequence of Leni Riefenstahl's film, *Triumph of the Will*, shows Hitler descending through the clouds in an aeroplane, while her *Day of Freedom* has the popular air ace Ernst Udet dive-bombing a power station.

To get around the terms of the Versailles Treaty, German pilots were trained abroad, while the state airline Lufthansa was set up in a way that made a military adaptation relatively simple. As Lloyd Ifould, an engineer at Le Bourget, then the chief European airport, recorded in March 1935:

> The little freight that was loaded into the Lufthansa machines was all loaded from underneath (as bombs would be loaded) and into the fuselage. The freight compartments of these machines were all designed to take bomb racks, which could be installed in a matter of a few hours.[17]

Lufthansa staff were also suspect.

> Germany had restored conscription, and the Lufthansa, whose staff had now begun to increase, were becoming bolder. For the first time, we witnessed the 'Heil Hitler' salute, a thing we had not seen before, except in the newsreels. Some of the older members of the Lufthansa ground staff, who had been out of Germany for a long time, did not catch on immediately, but it was not long before they succeeded in grasping the idea. Now, the Nazi salute had come to Le Bourget, but that was only the beginning, and still nothing compared to the saluting and heel-clicking that came later.[18]

But while it was essential propaganda for the Luftwaffe to raise fears of air attack, it had neither plans nor capacity for a mass bombing of

London or any other city. Why was this not known or even suspected at the highest level of British government and military planning? The failure of intelligence gives the answer. The destruction of Guernica by aerial bombing in 1937 is a case in point. The German and Italian contribution to the Fascist cause in the Spanish Civil War reinforced the chorus of siren voices, drowning out those who noted that the circumstances of the atrocity were in no way typical. Republican forces had few means of defence against a surprise air attack.

Hitler's congratulations meted out to the German air commander neglected to take into account that the Republican forces had only ancient aircraft, few guns and almost no warning devices to protect their towns which were, in any case, only a few minutes' flying time from enemy airfields. Nor was it pointed out that the German Condor Legion and the Italian Aviazione Legionaria had been deployed chiefly not to attack civilians but to support land operations. Finally, Madrid, though attacked from the air, had not been bombed into submission nor had it been razed to the ground. It was the same with Barcelona, which suffered 230 raids. The casualty figures, though bad enough, were almost certainly exaggerated by the Republicans, eager to demonstrate the savagery of the Nationalist insurrection and by Franco's supporters as a means of discouraging other cities not to resist.

THAT IN BRITAIN the horror of Guernica, accentuated by newsreel footage, was allowed to smother countervailing facts was symptomatic of the poor quality of intelligence that determined government policy. Britain's intelligence services had a record for consistency. For most of the time they were wrong. There were simply too many under-resourced departments with too many reporting lines to too many ill-qualified staff recruited from the old-boy network.

The Secret Intelligence Service, otherwise known as SIS, had suffered a succession of budget cuts since 1918. With little factual backup, its judgements on Germany were little more than guesses on what Hitler would do next. The expectation of more money for intelligence followed Sir John Simon's visit to Berlin in April 1935 when he was told that the German air force had already achieved parity with the RAF. But after a brief attack of Cabinet jitters, other claims to funding were allowed to take precedence. As late as the winter of 1938, the SIS could not even afford wireless sets for its agents.

It did not help that the Foreign Office had no branch of its own exclusively dedicated to intelligence. Voluminous reports of economic data, put together by diplomats who relied chiefly on business contacts, were considered more important than assessments of military potential. As for the three services, each jealously guarding its own preserve, their directors of intelligence were noted more for their bravery in the last war than for their analytical or predictive powers.

In an attempt to bring some sort of order to the system, the Joint Intelligence Committee was set up in 1936. But its members lacked status. Renowned for 'on the one hand, on the other hand' waffle, their reports were quickly filed and forgotten. There was some improvement in 1939 when the chairmanship of the JIC went to Victor Cavendish-Bentinck, a diplomat in his early forties who had served in Paris and in the League of Nations department of the Foreign Office. Of aristocratic stock (in 1980 he succeeded his brother as Duke of Portland), he was able to count Lord William Cavendish-Bentinck, first governor-general of India, among his forebears.

Retaining his JIC job throughout the war, Cavendish-Bentinck was credited with holding together a disparate collection of personalities. These included, for the RAF, Archie Boyle, subsequently head of the Special Operations Executive (SOE) and of security and personnel, a stable if relatively junior member of the team; Frederick

Beaumont-Nesbitt, deputy director of military intelligence at the War Office and Cavendish-Bentinck's predecessor as JIC chairman, a former Guards officer who, in his time as military attaché in Paris, convinced himself that France was unbeatable; and Rear Admiral John Godfrey, director of naval intelligence, a highly opinionated officer whose bee in the bonnet was a fear of German infiltration of Eire.

Their great weakness was in failing to take the true measure of German air power. Adapting arguments to suit their prejudices, they bolstered the irrational fear of a knockout blow on London from mass formations of German bombers. Evidence to the contrary, such as the air attacks in Spain, was ignored or minimised. Likewise, a German land offensive to the west was predicted to be limited to seizing Holland as a taking-off point for an airborne invasion.

Visits by British aeronautical engineers to German factories produced reliable observations on the output of airframes and engines, but adopting the worst-case assumption the Air Ministry gave too much credence to German boasts of industrial efficiency and managerial brilliance that would roll out 2,000 planes a month by 1940. The true figure was close to 780. The actual strength of the Luftwaffe was exaggerated by nearly 20 per cent.

But the egregious error was to assume that the Luftwaffe was ready to engage in an intensive bombing campaign that would take the heart out of London with devastating impact on civilian morale. The proposition had its origin in the imagination of the futurologists but also in the underlying strategy of the RAF under the leadership of Air Chief Marshal Sir Hugh Trenchard who, as chief of the air staff, pressed hard for a bomber force capable of destroying Germany's industrial base.

The fantasy of German air hegemony was kept up in the face of technical evidence later advanced by Sir Arthur (Bomber) Harris that in 1939 the heaviest of German planes were simply 'not equipped for weight carrying' and were 'too small' to deliver to Britain the vast tonnage of high explosives needed for a knockout blow. Moreover, without bases in the Low Countries, the Luftwaffe would have had to sacrifice bomb load to the carrying of enough fuel for the flight from north-west Germany and back. Finally, all the indications were of the German military using the air force not as an independent firepower but as a backup for the highly mechanised army in the field. The emergence of an effective bomber force was held up by opposition from the army generals who wanted air power to support the infantry, and by the shortage of aeronautical designers and engineers.[19] The concept of blitzkrieg was almost entirely land-based.

None of this appears to have filtered through to the Home Office, where plans for civil defence owed more to the doom-laden predictions of novelist and historian H.G. Wells. In his *War in the Air* (1907), written when he was in his early forties, Wells had the imperial powers fighting a war to extinction, taking the world back to a sort of pre-industrial medievalism in which his little man hero found contentment. There was no such happy ending tagged on to *The Shape of Things to Come* (1933), where the only escape from devastation and discord on Earth was the colonisation of space. Written for the screen, where it was billed as *Things to Come*, the movie was released in 1936.

Wells was not alone in propagating doom and destruction. Dismal futurology made for strong sellers in the publishing trade. Titles that occupied station bookstalls included *The Air War of 1936*, *The Gas War of 1940*, *The Poison War* and *War Upon Women*.

Occasionally, the voice of reason was heard above the hubbub. The Austrian-born military strategist Stephen Possony argued convincingly that big cities were too dispersed to be destroyed by bombing and that, in any case, heavy bombers were vulnerable to artillery and fighters.[20] But his words of encouragement were ignored or casually dismissed.

Of the arresting scenes in *Things to Come*, one that stayed long-est with cinemagoers was of the mass of heavy bombers flying in over a supine London. Panic in the streets, according to Wells, was the inevitable sequel. Those who escaped the incendiaries and high explosives were liable to fall victim to poison gas. As foretold by Lord Halsbury in 1933, a single gas bomb 'if dropped on Piccadilly Circus, would kill everybody in an area from Regent's Park to the Thames'. That was close on a million people.

Up to and beyond the opening stages of the European war, it was taken as axiomatic in Whitehall that in the first air attacks, up to 600,000 people would be killed and twice that number injured. Estimates of bomb tonnage were revised at irregular intervals but always on a rising graph. The consensus in 1938 was of a drop of up to 3,500 tons over the first 24 hours. Subsequently and for several weeks the daily weight of attack would average 700 tons. A particular fear was of delayed action bombs, likely to be up to 50 per cent of those dropped, suggested the air staff. As a consequence after a raid even undamaged homes would have to be evacuated, adding yet more confusion to an already chaotic emergency.

Though London was expected to be the main target, other centres of commerce and industry including the biggest ports, particularly on the east coast, were vulnerable. A fifth of the total population, around 9 million people, were at risk. While the use of gas was thought probable, the deployment of biological weapons was thought to be unlikely, though 'we must expect', said the Bacteriological Warfare Committee, 'a serious dislocation of our sanitary system and a result-ant increase of disease'. A committee of psychiatrists, set up by the Ministry of Health in mid-1938, to study mental health at a time of war, suggested that psychiatric cases, brought on by acute panic and hysteria, might exceed physical casualties by three to one.

For the record, and without in any way belittling the human

drama of the blitz, over the entire war there were only 147,000 civilian fatalities or serious casualties, 80,000 of them in London.

ALONG WITH MODEST rearmament and friendly gestures towards the dictators went measures to protect the civil population against an aerial onslaught. As early as 1924, the Home Office was ruminating on what could be done to limit the damage of an air offensive. But little that was constructive emerged until eleven years later when local authorities were invited to plan ahead. On the strict injunction that 'consultation should be made with discretion and that every precaution should be taken to avoid misrepresentation'[21] (that is, costs had to be kept to a minimum), the Air Raids Precaution department of the Home Office, consisting of a staff of just thirteen, offered advice on what was necessary to improve the chances of survival should the bombs fall. An underlying assumption was of the government being ready to adopt emergency powers.

Guided by a consensus that the country was on track to secure a lasting peace, successive home secretaries gave less than half attention to civil defence. As home secretary in Stanley Baldwin's second government from 1924 to 1929, William Joynson-Hicks was too preoccupied with his evangelical opposition to the Church of England Revised Prayer Book and a campaign against depravity in London's nightspots to bother over much about possible air raids.

It was not until 1936 that the call went out for more civil defence volunteers. A particular worry was the shortage of instructors in countermeasures to poison gas, remembered with horror by frontline troops in the Great War and lately used by the Italians in their invasion of Abyssinia. In fact, Britain was ahead of other European countries in preparing against gas warfare. The first circular on civil defence sent to local authorities by the Home Office was primarily about anti-gas equipment, gas-masks and the setting up of a gas school to train instructors, at Falfield in Gloucestershire. A second training unit, at Easingwold near York, opened in late 1937. By then there were some 30 to 40 centres for anti-gas and general air raid precaution training.

Gas-mask output was up to 150,000 a week. Production was centred on a former cotton mill at Blackburn. But numerous firms with related expertise were put under government contract. One of these was Siebe Gorman, a company best known for its diving gear and breathing apparatus. Founded by Augustus Siebe, a German-born engineer who had served as an artillery officer at Waterloo, the Lambeth factory was given over almost entirely to making gas-masks. After a direct hit early in the war, the company moved out to Chessington in Surrey.

To raise public awareness of the risks from gas, the Home Office came up with the quaint idea of sponsoring a display at the Ideal Home Exhibition. Wiser counsels suggested that the public was not yet ready for incorporating a gas-proof room into their dream house.

By mid-1938, around 38 million gas-masks were in storage or had been distributed. But there was still a long way to go. The design for a 'baby-bag' to be fitted over the baby's head, shoulders and arms and tied by a tape round the waist, though approved, was not yet in production. It was the same with the Mickey Mouse mask for children who, it was hoped, would be attracted by the red rubber face-piece, bright eye-pieces and blue container.

Also in short supply were the respirators, anti-gas clothing and steel helmets for ARP volunteers. Other shortages included anti-gas suits (there were too few oilskin manufacturers to meet the demand) and hospital equipment, still to be supplemented by a bulk purchase of stretchers.

With the Air Raid Precautions Act of January 1938, regional coun-cils were set up to encourage local authorities and commerce to take the initiative in creating their own ARP schemes. Across the country, a start was made on locating cellars and basements suitable for conver-sion to air raid shelters. Press and poster advertising urged volunteers to come forward. By June, 200,000 men and women had answered the call. The Post Office produced a scheme for an emergency telephone service and a plan was made for protecting London's docks. A war fever was beginning to take hold.

CHAPTER 3

Reckoning

Czechoslovakia was the strongest and best-governed of the new states created in 1918. But it was a state of many peoples who were seldom at ease with each other. Along with 7.5 million Czechs, there were 3.2 million Germans, 2.3 million Slovaks and smaller numbers of Magyars, Ruthenians and Poles. The Sudeten Germans had a lot to say about unfavourable discrimination but their minority status had been a bone of contention ever since the days when they were part of the Austro-Hungarian empire. In building up their grievances, Hitler had an eye to purloining the heavy industrial centre of Sudetenland with its armament manufacturers, the world's leading exporters of advanced weaponry.

Though Britain had no commitment to Czechoslovakia, France was pledged to protect that country's independence. If German forces crossed the Czech frontier and France retaliated, this was bound to bring Britain into the conflict. Chamberlain was in no doubt as to what he had to do. His task, as he saw it, was to pacify Germany by restraining the bellicose tendencies of Czechoslovakia and France, a twist in defence mentality that was almost certain to reward the aggressor. With the pro-Nazi Sudeten German party under orders from Berlin to stir up trouble, the tough-talking Edouard Daladier, recently installed as French premier, and his rather more passive foreign minister, Georges Bonnet, came to London in April 1938 for talks with their opposite numbers.

The results were inconclusive but Chamberlain made clear his own position when he told American and Canadian journalists that he looked forward to a peaceful solution to the Czech crisis. After a warning from Halifax that an attempted coup in Czechoslovakia, a repeat of what had happened in Austria, might well lead to war, Hitler backed off. But so then did Halifax.

Playing for time, the decision was taken to send a mediator whose mission was to find a solution that would satisfy German aspirations at minimum cost to Czechoslovakia. The chalice was handed to Lord Runciman, a ship-building tycoon and former president of the Board of Trade who was in poor health. Having had his protestations swept aside, he and a small team set off for Prague on August 4th, 1938. Convinced that no peace progress could be made unless Czechoslovakia made substantial concessions, Runciman did not go down well with those called upon to make the sacrifice.

Though he was unaware of it at the time, Runciman was being undermined by the British ambassador in Berlin who was encouraging Hitler to believe that he would get his way. An instruction to Sir Nevile Henderson to make clear Britain's support for Czechoslovakia was studiously ignored. Instead, without consulting the Foreign Office, Henderson was delighted to be invited to a Nuremberg rally where he referred to Hitler as an 'apostle of peace'.

Returning to London to report his lack of success, Runciman was horrified to be told that he was now expected to go to Berlin to deal directly with Hitler. He refused flatly. And so the chalice was passed to Chamberlain who conceived the idea of a top-level appeal to Hitler to join him in instituting a lasting peace. He was not deterred when on September 12th, at Nuremberg, Hitler declared unequivocally that failing the immediate grant of autonomy to the Sudetens he would march.

In his book, *The Thirties*, Malcolm Muggeridge saw through the self-deception of Chamberlain and the feeble nature of the forces that drove him.

> As, in his business days, he had been accustomed to go after a contract in person when less enterprising rivals contented themselves with submitting a written tender, so now he was determined to go after peace in person. A chat with Mussolini or with Hitler, even a friendly nod to Stalin, would make all the difference. Chamber of Commerce Quixote, Knight of the Woeful Countenance, bearing umbrella instead of lance, his chivalry Rotarian, his accoutrements funereal, with Lord Halifax, his Sancho Panza, trotting faithfully beside him, he set forth hopefully to save the world from an impending catastrophe.[1]

A telegram suggesting a face-to-face meeting was well received by Hitler who realised that simply by making the journey Chamberlain was acknowledging his role as a supplicant at the great man's table. Accompanied by Sir Horace Wilson, Chamberlain's special adviser, and Sir William Strang, head of the Foreign Office section responsible for relations with Germany, the prime minister flew to Munich on September 15th, 1938. From there he travelled by special train to Berchtesgaden, made a brief stop at his hotel and then went straight up to Hitler's mountain home at Obersalzberg. The meeting did not start well, as Lord Strang recalled:

> There was a somewhat macabre tea-party at a round table in the room with the great window looking out towards

Austria. The small-talk of statesmen whose only point of contact is an international emergency ... is best left in oblivion. Mr Chamberlain and Hitler then retired for their conference accompanied by the Führer's interpreter alone. It was at Mr Chamberlain's own choice that the talks were held *tête-à-tête*. ... Hitler said that he wanted the Sudeten majority areas to pass to Germany, and that he was prepared to risk a world-war rather than allow the present situation to drag on; but he agreed to hold his hand while Mr Chamberlain consulted his colleagues and the French Government on the principle of the separation of the Sudeten areas. After staying the night in Berchtesgaden, travelling by car with von Ribbentrop to Munich next morning and being entertained by him to a luncheon party there, Mr Chamberlain flew home.[2]

In giving nothing away, Hitler had good reason to believe that Chamberlain already had it in mind to hand over the Sudetens. He had only to add that he would be happy to discuss ways and means. With this diplomatic morsel, Chamberlain returned to London, there to persuade his Cabinet and, subsequently, the French leaders, that all Czech territory where Germans accounted for more than 50 per cent of the population should immediately be incorporated into the Reich.

An ultimatum to President Eduard Benes to accept the carve-up of his country or face the prospect of war without the support of Britain and France had, from Chamberlain's point of view, the desired effect. Back he went to Hitler, this time meeting in the Rhenish town of Bad Godesberg, only to hear that the timetable for the handover was altogether too slow. The Fuehrer wanted instant action, an evacuation by the Czech authorities of German-speaking areas within a week. Angry and disappointed, Chamberlain's protests were rewarded with a small extension of the deadline to October 1st and a promise from Hitler that he had no further territorial demands.

The first reaction in London and Paris was to reject what the *Telegraph* called 'an abject and humiliating capitulation'. Pressed by Halifax who wanted to reject the Godesberg demands, on September 26th Chamberlain sent an emissary to tell Hitler that France and Britain were on-side with the Czechs, who could no longer be advised to hold back on mobilisation.

War seemed to be inevitable and imminent. On September 22nd, the Ministry of Health put out a statement on the BBC:

34 hospitals in the London area have been allotted as clearing stations for air raid casualties, and detailed plans have been prepared for removing between three and four thousand patients by ambulance trains to towns over 50 miles from London. Casualties will be taken to the railway stations in motor coaches converted to carry stretchers.

Three days later, on 'gas-mask Sunday', ARP centres were open for the collection of masks. From pulpits, congregations were urged to comply with Home Office advice. Trench digging in the London parks continued at night under arc lights. Anti-aircraft batteries appeared on Horse Guards Parade and on the Embankment. All police leave was cancelled and the recently formed Auxiliary Territorial Service (ATS) appealed to women to volunteer as drivers. The price of some foods including bacon, butter, cheese, lard and cooking fats was frozen for fourteen days.

In Paris there was near-panic. Six thousand Parisians fled in a week. The aviation minister, certain that 'the destruction of Paris would pass all imagination', sent his family to Brittany and advised others to do the same. Before long, however, the false logic of appeasement was reaffirmed. There could be no war; peace was worth any price. An appeal from Chamberlain to Hitler to allow him one last effort to secure an agreement brought a response in the form of an invitation to meet in Munich. Announcing this to the House of Commons, the prime minister was gratified by an outburst of cheering. Among the few who dissented was Jan Masaryk, the Czech ambassador, who was in the public gallery. Cornering Chamberlain and Halifax in the Foreign Office, he told them: 'If you have sacrificed my nation to preserve the peace of the world, I will be the first to applaud you, but if not, gentlemen, God help your souls.'

Next morning Chamberlain flew to Munich. He was in good humour, telling reporters that he was going in the spirit of a refrain from his childhood: 'If at first you don't succeed, try, try, try again.' In the event, Munich was a humiliating defeat for Britain and France. Hitler, with Mussolini in attendance, got all he demanded. The Sudeten territory was to be surrendered in four stages beginning on October 1st and ending on the 7th. Czechoslovakia lost her frontier defences and the best part of her industrial capacity. The Czech representatives were kept away from the conference until the main business was completed. They were then told to accept the terms as they stood. There was no question of negotiation. Daladier feared the worst but made no objection. 'Everything depends on the English; we must follow them.'

Was it naivety or political calculation that inspired Chamberlain to cover his shame with an attention-grabbing fig leaf? Probably both. Of a certainty, he felt he had something of great value in his joint pledge with Hitler to settle all future disputes by peaceful negotiation and in the promise that their two countries would never again go to war with one another. This was the document the prime minister waved at reporters when he stepped off the plane at Heston airport and later at crowds gathered in Downing Street. It was, declared

Chamberlain, a guarantee of 'peace for our time'. The settlement was 'only a prelude to a larger settlement in which all Europe may find peace'.

The press, by and large, believed him. Lord Rothermere told him, 'You are wonderful'. Writing in the *Sunday Express*, the popular columnist Godfrey Winn offered praise to God and Mr Chamberlain: 'I find no sacrilege, no bathos, in combining these two names.' The following day, *The Times* gave credit to Chamberlain for saving the world from 'the illimitable catastrophe of a general war'. Even the left-wing *Daily Herald* allowed that Hitler had had to abandon the most brutal of the Godesberg terms while adding that the agreement remained 'open to grave criticism'. The *Daily Express* had no doubts. Pushed along by its owner Lord Beaverbrook, on September 30th the paper gave its repetitive verdict on Munich. 'Britain will not be involved in a European war this year or next year either.' The response from the radical journalist Claud Cockburn was to remark that Chamberlain had 'turned all four cheeks' to Hitler.

In the House of Commons, bubbling with praise for the prime minister, the Tory member Henry Raikes declared that his leader 'will go down to history as the greatest European statesman of this or any other time'. George Lansbury, pacifist former Labour leader, gave it as his conviction that there was nothing special about Hitler. He was 'much like any other politician or diplomat one meets'. With Chamberlain invited to Buckingham Palace, the King voiced his 'most heartfelt congratulations on the success of your visit to Munich'. A vast crowd cheered Chamberlain when he and his wife appeared alongside the King and Queen on the palace balcony. Congratulatory letters and telegrams arrived at Downing Street by the sack load along with gifts of fishing rods and umbrellas.

For his peace efforts, Chamberlain acquired an almost saintly image. A contribution from John Masefield, the Poet Laureate, printed in *The Times* described the prime minister as 'divinely led'. Nothing but respect and adoration was due to him. Writing to the *Daily Mirror*, a reader was 'shocked and surprised' to hear in a broadcast from Paris 'what purports to be a new dance called "Le Chamberlain". This dance apparently involves the use of an umbrella, and we think you will agree with us that, in times like these, our beloved Premier should be spared such exhibitions of bad taste.'

One wonders how the correspondent reacted to the song written by the popular band leader, Harry Roy.

> God bless you, Mr Chamberlain,
> We're all mighty proud of you.
> You look swell holding your umbrella,
> All the world loves a wonderful feller – so
> God bless you, Mr Chamberlain.

Chamberlain agreed for his photograph to appear on the cover of the sheet music.

It was left to Churchill to put the boot in. He spoke on the third day of the House of Commons debate. 'We have sustained a total and unmitigated defeat ... a disaster of the first magnitude.' He worried:

> This is only the beginning of the reckoning. This is only the first sip, the first foretaste of a bitter cup which will be proffered to us year by year unless by a supreme recovery of moral health and martial vigour, we arise again and take our stand for freedom as in the olden time.

His reception was hostile, though significantly he was supported by the leader of the opposition. The settlement, said Clement Attlee, was 'one of Britain's greatest diplomatic defeats'. A gallant and democratic people had been 'betrayed and handed over to a ruthless despotism'. Among politicians, there were few other voices of dissent. Halifax had his doubts but while he professed himself willing to fight for the 'great moralities', he put loyalty to Chamberlain before all else. Leslie Hore-Belisha pointed out that a pledge to protect Czech sovereignty, or what was left of it, had no value since it could not be fulfilled. Munich, he argued, was no more than 'a postponement of the evil day'. But he held on to his job as war minister. The only loss to the government was Duff Cooper who resigned as first lord of the admiralty, with a denunciation of Munich as the precursor to 'war with dishonour'.

The voice in the street was not entirely laudatory. Interviewers for Mass-Observation, the organisation set up in 1937 by Tom Harrisson, Charles Madge and Humphrey Jennings to record the opinions of ordinary citizens, found sympathy for the underdog. Said a 30-year-old bus conductor:

What the hell's he [Chamberlain] got the right to go over there and do a dirty trick like that? It'll have the whole world against us now. Who'll trust us? It's like throwing your own kid to the wolves.

And a Scotsman encountered on Trafalgar Square:

The dirty so and so, that's what he is, selling 'em like that. He's done the same to all the others now. Only a ruddy Englishman could act like that. He flies to see Hitler, then he comes back and tells the papers that peace is near. He thinks he's going to keep England out of a war. Let the other fellers fight and he'll sell them the arms to do it, is that the big idea? I'll bet he goes to church like his wife does. They'll never be any use to the working class.

Chamberlain's return from Munich was a setback for civil defence. Enthusiasts were liable to be dismissed as warmongers. Local authorities were only too pleased to cut back on what was now seen by many as panic spending. At national level, the publication of *The Householder's Handbook*, a guide to civil defence, was put on hold.

APPEASEMENT HAD STILL to run its course, though soon the indications were of Nazi virulence intensifying. Over November 9th and 10th came *Kristallnacht*, the night of broken glass, a stage-managed assault on the German Jewish community that for a supposedly civilised country, touched the depths of barbarism.

At around midnight the fires started. By morning 267 synagogues had been destroyed, thousands of Jewish shops and homes devastated, one hundred Jews murdered and many thousands arrested. Ten thousand Jews were herded into Buchenwald and 12,000 into Dachau. By the end of the month some had already died in these camps.

Belatedly, the British government published a White Paper describing the brutality meted out to the inmates of concentration camps. Why had it taken so long to share with the public what had been long known to first-hand observers? The official explanation was that Germany had invited retaliation after an unprecedented propaganda campaign against Britain. In other words, restraint would have been rewarded with suppression of the truth.

The new year started on a buoyant note with Chamberlain expressing the hope that 'it will not only be a peaceful one but a happy one for everybody', adding, 'I can assure you that the government for which I am speaking will do its utmost to make it so'. Matching the prime minister for fatuous sentiments, Hitler had 'but one wish ... to be able to contribute to the general peace of the world'.

In unanimous support of fantasy came the astrologers who were as one in predicting a bright future. Fanciful though it may be to look to the stars for guidance, it was nonetheless true that *Prediction* and *Astrology* were among the high-circulation journals, while newspaper columns on what the day would bring, such as that of Lyndoe in *The People*, were read more avidly than the sports section. Lyndoe was convinced there would be no war. She added that it was only women with nervous dispositions who worried, and they worried too much. If, by some terrible misinterpretation of her readings, the bombs did fall, her safety suggestion was to run up the nearest hill.

Her colleagues kept it up to the end. One of their number, Leonardo Blake, staked all in a book published in the summer of 1939. With self-assurance that can only be marvelled at, he opened his seminal work with a promise to disclose the 'realities behind the great riddles of European events'.

Years of study of the subjects of psychology and astrology have placed in the hands of the writer a key to the happenings on the world stage. The true face of the European situation lies revealed to him. And out of this chaos he sees shining towards him a more hopeful and heartening picture of the future.

The end of the Nazi Party and its Leader is here. The Army Party in Germany will tear down the Swastika flag and unfurl once again the old black, white and red flag of the Kaiser's day as a symbol of the liberation of the nation from economic and moral thraldom. It will prove the nation's saviour, and cause a happy turn in the events of Europe.[3]

On January 10th, 1939, Chamberlain and Halifax set off for Rome for talks with Mussolini who was preening in his unlikely role of peacemaker. This while Italian planes based in Majorca were engaged in daily bombing raids on Spanish cities and 10,000 Italian troops were participating in Franco's Catalan offensive.

Avoiding any reference to Mussolini's proclivity for military glory against weak adversaries and nodding respectfully at references to Italian designs on French sovereignty in Corsica and Tunisia, Chamberlain assured his host that Britain wanted 'close, friendly and even intimate relations' with Italy. He concluded his visit with a tribute to Mussolini's 'guidance and inspiration' that had made Italy 'powerful and progressive'. At home the News Chronicle, one of the rare Fleet Street critics of Chamberlain, was relieved that he had not followed the precedents of his other foreign travels by 'giving something away, usually something belonging to other people'.

At the end of the month, Hitler appeared before the Reichstag to celebrate the 'new sense of German unity'. His speech of two and a half hours singled out Churchill, Eden and other 'warmongers' for stirring up hatred of the German people. He derided the Jews who 'possess nothing except infectious political and physical diseases' and went on to claim that 'National Socialists and Fascist volunteers had gone to help General Franco as part of a crusade against Bolshevism'. All this was regarded by the foreign press as familiar padding for the message they wanted to hear, that Germany 'had no territorial demands against England and France'.

There was one small exception. The Fuehrer wanted a return of the former German colonies, mostly in Africa, confiscated by the victors of the Great War. His words suggested that he intended plundering natural resources to support the German economy. But in Europe, he was content with the existing frontiers in the west, south and north. While, for Polish benefit, the east was added to the official translation, it came too late to allay fears in Poland that it was next in line for Teutonic hammering.

It was no secret that after humbling the Czechs, Hitler had his eye on Danzig (now Gdańsk), a former German seaport designated a Free City under the Versailles Treaty to give the otherwise land-locked Poland an opening to the Baltic. Also in his sights was Memel, another one-time German port that had become the Baltic access for Lithuania. In both regions, Nazi sympathisers were encouraged to take to the streets. In a war of nerves the threat of military action was ever present.

However, for the Chamberlain government and its supporters in the media, the spirit of Munich shone as brightly as ever. For most of the British press, Hitler's Reichstag speech was heard as a peace offering. It was 'polemical in tone', said the *Telegraph*, but allowance had to be made for Hitler's tendency to over-dramatise. The *Express* was more forthright with a repeat of its favourite prediction: 'Hitler says that he expects that there will be peace for a long time. We were right ... There will be no war involving Britain in 1939.' Chamberlain added his own gloss on events. 'It is untrue to say that the policy of appeasement has failed. On the contrary, I believe that it is steadily succeeding.' He kept this up until early March when he told a press conference at 10 Downing Street that an era of peace was about to unfold. Among the comforted was the editor of *Punch*, a mildly satirical weekly magazine, famous for imparting political homilies with its full-page frontispiece cartoons. Chamberlain's good cheer was to inspire Bernard Partridge to draw 'The Ides of March' showing John Bull waking from a nightmare with the nightmare itself escaping through a window. The caption had John Bull sighing with relief. 'Thank God! That's over!' On the day of publication, March 15th, German troops marched into Prague. German domination of Czechoslovakia was now complete.

The Times report of the outrage was matter-of-fact.

German troops under General Blaskowitz crossed the frontier early this morning. Prague was entered a few hours later and is now under German military control, as is all of Bohemia and Moravia.

The people of Prague last night went to bed in a nervous but still hopeful mood. ... The first news that these hopes were unfounded came at 4.30 this morning.

An hour and a half later early-rising civilians heard over the wireless the first official news that their country was under new mastership after 20 years of freedom. At the same moment the first German armoured car reached Melnik, 30 miles from Prague. Immediately a proclamation, bordered in red and bearing the German eagle and swastika which is now familiar to every Czech town and village, was posted on the hoardings. No one was allowed in the streets after 8 p.m. without special permission unless he was a doctor or a railway worker; all popular gatherings were forbidden; and weapons, munitions, and wireless sets were ordered to be surrendered.

These orders were calmly received. In Prague little groups collected silently at street corners to await the incoming troops. It was snowing heavily and no sound could be heard save when a party of Czechs broke the silence to sing their National Anthem. At 9 o'clock in the morning the first motorized column entered Prague.

Workmen going to their jobs looked in astonishment at the grey-uniformed soldiers, since many of them had not heard of the occupation. The little clumps of Czechs who had been waiting for the troops greeted them with whistles and with clenched fists raised. As the soldiers reached the Wenceslas Square, the centre of Prague, at 9.30, they were met by a large number of people, many of them in tears. The Germans, red in the face but maintaining excellent discipline, ignored these demonstrations ... raising their arms in the Nazi salute when isolated Germans ... shouted a welcome.[4]

The Czech people were forced to come to terms with life under military rule. Now aged 100, Vera Hykšová has clear memories of German dictates which included the closing of the university, a ban on dancing and the overnight switch from driving on the left to driving on the right.

Chamberlain was shattered. His absurd belief that he, and he alone, could bring everlasting peace to Europe, was shown to be a mirage. For the first time he saw Hitler for what he truly was. Speaking in Birmingham on March 17th, he shared his apprehension of what would follow the absorption of most of Czechoslovakia into the Reich, with the remainder placed under German 'protection'.

> Every man and woman in this country who remembers the fate of the Jews and the political prisoners in Austria must be filled to-day with distress and foreboding. Who can fail to feel his heart go out in sympathy to the proud and brave people who have so suddenly been subjected to this invasion, whose liberties are curtailed, whose national independence has gone? What has become of this declaration of 'No further territorial ambition'? What has become of the assurance 'We don't want Czechs in the Reich'?

He had one more rhetorical question: 'Is this ... a step in the direction of an attempt to dominate the world by force?'

As if in answer, a week later Hitler ordered the occupation of Memel and demanded that Poland hand over Danzig. At the same time, he repudiated the German–Polish non-aggression pact and forced economic concessions on Rumania. The British reaction was a pledge to defend Poland's independence. According to the foreign office mandarin William Strang:

> The declaration about Poland was an improvisation. It was drafted on the afternoon of March 30 by the Prime Minister with the help of Lord Halifax and Sir Alexander Cadogan [permanent under-secretary for foreign affairs] ... Normally, when any grave new step in foreign policy is in contemplation, its implications, political and military, are thoroughly canvassed by Ministers with their civilian and military advisers. In the case of the Polish declaration, the idea seems to have sprung fully grown from the Ministerial mind. It was designed, no doubt, among other things, to meet what was recognised to be an imperative demand by public opinion that Poland should not be allowed to go the same way as Czechoslovakia.[5]

On the 31st, Britain and Poland signed the Treaty of Mutual Assistance. If either country suffered aggression from a European power, the other signatory would 'at once' give 'all the support and assistance in its power'. What this amounted to was anyone's guess. That afternoon Nevile Henderson had an interview with Hitler who made a vague offer of compromise. But this time Chamberlain refused to take the bait. As the prospect of war began to snowball, even those on the hard right found it impossible to stomach Hitler's treachery.

'His fault is writ large across a startled Europe', wrote Francis Yeats-Brown, up to then a far-right apologist for Hitler, reacting to Hitler's carve-up of Czechoslovakia.

> None of his neighbours trust him. The law of the jungle prevails. With the breaking of his pledge at Munich our recent

hopes of disarmament and reconciliation lie shattered beyond the possibility of a quick repair.[6]

Another disappointed man was George Ward Price, foreign correspondent of the *Daily Mail*. Recognising, at last, that the Nazis had 'done much evil', he declared that 'the possibility of cordial relations has now passed away'.[7] Lord Londonderry still had moments of optimism. Amending his book on Anglo-German relations to justify Hitler's overthrow of Austria's legitimate government, he sent Hitler a copy of *Ourselves and Germany* inscribed with best wishes and hopes for a 'better and lasting understanding between our two countries'.

COME THE REALISATION that the Munich agreement might not be all that it was cracked up to be, civil defence enjoyed a rebirth. Deciding, a little late in the day, that the Home Office ARP department should have its own minister, Chamberlain gave the job to Sir John Anderson who assumed the catch-all title of Lord Privy Seal. A high-flying civil servant by his early thirties, Anderson was an imperturbable administrator with a reputation for seizing on the essentials. As permanent under-secretary at the Home Office from 1922 he was known by his staff as 'Ja Jehovah, the all wise, the all knowing, the all powerful'. To work for him, said one of his close colleagues, was 'at once a pleasure and an education ... Always in obvious control of the situation, patient and decisive, he had the rare faculty of entrusting a task to his subordinates and letting them get on with it in peace.'[8]

There is a caveat to this paean of praise. Anderson was a martinet, one who did not welcome contradiction and was not noted for his sensitivity. As governor of Bengal from 1932, a region of India strong on its nationalist sympathies (Anderson's predecessor narrowly escaped assassination), he gave no quarter to the opponents of British rule. Returning home in 1937, he was elected as an Independent MP for the Scottish Universities, joining the government a few weeks later.

Dry and didactic, Anderson did not shine as a combative politician. In the House of Commons he was inclined to treat members like a class of rather dim schoolchildren. On one occasion a member asked waspishly if the minister thought he was addressing the primitive natives of Bengal. The alternative, when he spoke off the cuff, could lead to such convolutions that a government colleague had to interpose with a translation into plain English. But there was no denying the energy Anderson put into creating a network of civil defence. Whether it was the right policy for the time is another question.

Foremost among Anderson's opponents were the service chiefs who naturally wanted a bigger share of the national budget. They had a good case. In 1938, Germany was spending up to £1,710 million, around a quarter of the country's income, on armaments. For Britain, the figure was £358 million or 7 per cent of national income. The government was able to point out that this represented a 350 per cent increase on 1934 and that expenditure on arms was now higher than that of France.

But there were glaring omissions in the defence structure. The available anti-aircraft guns were barely adequate for London, let alone other cities. The service chiefs wanted more heavy guns and searchlights, arguing that this, together with the completion of the radar chain around Britain, would offer better defence than building shelters and distributing gas-masks. They proved to be right but the prevailing political instinct was for the community to pull together in a campaign for self-protection. Anderson was given his head.

His first move was to create a network of regional commissioners to hold in reserve almost unlimited powers should a war cause the collapse of central government. Among former colleagues who slotted into these new jobs was Harold Scott. As principal officer for the London region, he threw himself into a 'hectic and chaotic' round of improvisation.

> A concrete result of our work was the installation by the Post Office of a battery of telephones with direct lines to the Home Office, the War Office and County Hall. This job was done with a speed which astonished us then, but was to be surpassed in the months ahead. It seemed to me a good idea to distinguish the various lines by telephones of three different colours, red, white and green; but when Lord Brocket, one of the District Commissioners, saw them on his first visit he exclaimed: 'Why on earth have you chosen Mussolini's colours?'[9]

In early 1939, Scott took on a grander title – chief administration officer for the London region – and an enhanced job description.

> I was now responsible for co-ordinating the ARP plans of some forty scheme-making authorities and the protection of nine million people. London's many services, old and new – fire brigade, ambulance, police, stretcher bearers, rescue parties, etc. – had been enormously increased by thousands of volunteers, but they were under the control of some ninety-five different local authorities, and in general the capital's state of preparedness was, according to the ARP Department, 'deplorably behind-hand'. Some metropolitan boroughs had made good progress, others seemed to be paralysed ... no general plan had been agreed upon, still less put into effect.[10]

Scott called together the town clerks of the metropolitan boroughs who agreed to an administrative network allowing for the County of London to be split into five groups, with Middlesex and the urban parts of Essex, Kent and Surrey making four more groups. Each of the ARP services – ambulance, fire and so on – were given their own chiefs. It was a pattern that, before long, was to be replicated over the country.

London's civil defence headquarters was set up in the Geological Museum in South Kensington. On the face of it, it was an odd choice; the museum walls were almost entirely of glass. But the building was steel-framed with plenty of space along two galleries. On the ground floor, soon protected by a fire wall, a control room with gas-proof doors was installed.

> It was here that the Post Office engineers showed what they could really do. In no time at all, it seemed, the control room was linked by direct telephone lines with the group centres, New Scotland Yard, the headquarters of the fire and ambulance services, and the Home Security War Room in the Home Office basement. As an additional precaution the lines were in triplicate leaving the building in different directions, so that if one was knocked out we could still rely on the others. We always knew that this first control room was a temporary affair, and that although it would protect the staff against near-misses, it could not withstand a direct hit; but it was the quickest way of providing for immediate and urgent needs.[11]

The favoured protection for buildings under threat from bombing was the stacking of sandbags against the outer walls. But demand outpaced supply. Two hundred and seventy-five million bags were on order, a quantity that required the entire output of sacking from the Scottish jute industry. And this only allowed for the barricading of essential buildings. An order for a further 200 million bags from India

increased the supply to around 12 million a week by March 1939. At
the start of the war the total order from India and Dundee stood at
525 million. As Harold Scott recalled:

> I asked the Geological Survey (our involuntary hosts in
> Exhibition Road) to select some twenty sites, well distributed
> throughout the Region, where sand could be readily exca-
> vated. This was done very quickly and accurately; only once
> did we fail to find sand where they had indicated, and that was
> because the excavation was made on the wrong side of the
> road! Meanwhile I arranged for the hiring of every available
> mechanical excavator within fifty miles of London, dividing
> this task force between the sites selected by the Survey, and
> the public was told that it could take away as much sand as it
> could carry. There was an overwhelming response from both
> public bodies and private citizens; a special corps of telepho-
> nists was on duty day and night giving advice and information
> on Operation Sand, as it would no doubt have been called in
> the later jargon of the war; and millions of yards of sand were
> distributed at a cost which worked out at less than a shilling
> a yard.[12]

In Hyde Park, the site of the 1851 Great Exhibition was excavated for
sand quarrying to a depth of 40 feet, revealing the concrete founda-
tions of the original Crystal Palace. This left a huge crater, later to
overflow with rubble from bombed buildings. The crater reappeared
when the rubble was carried off to East Anglia to make the runways
for American Superfortresses.

On Hampstead Heath the sand-diggers created a miniature Cheddar Gorge, which glowed in the sunshine of that

wonderful autumn in warm lines of ochre, orange and red. I went up one morning to see the work in progress. Up from the Vale of Health roared and rocked a continuous stream of three, five and ten ton lorries, and then amongst them appeared a small Austin car with a tiny trailer attached. Beside the driver sat his small daughter. When their turn came they drew up beside the giant grab, received a great dollop of sand on their trailer, and drove happily away to fortify their home against the wrath to come.[13]

In a nationwide mailing, householders were delivered a handout on *The Protection of Your Home Against Air Raids*. Among 'things to do' was the choice of a refuge room to be protected against gas and made ready for occupation during a raid.

> This room would be the householder's or shopkeeper's 'first line of defence because a respirator cannot protect the other parts of your body from dangerous liquids, such as "mustard gas"'. It should be in the cellar or basement, if this could be made reasonably gas-proof and secure against flooding; other-wise it might be any room on any floor below the top floor.[14]

Any room within solid walls was said to be safer than being in the open.

> If war broke out and air raids took place, the head of the household's first duty after hearing the warning would be to send all under his care, with their respirators, to the refuge-room; and he should keep them there until he heard the 'raiders passed' and had satisfied himself that the neighbour-hood was free from gas.[15]

The follow-up was a series of four-page pamphlets. Their effectiveness was reduced by clumsy composition and by the apparent inability of those responsible for public information to recognise that their intended readership might not be entirely of the literate and prosperous middle class. Ordinary families were quickly lost in the verbiage and superfluous advice. What possible help was it to a family living in a small tenement to be told to clear the top floor of all inflammables? The leaflet on coping with incendiaries warned: 'If you throw a bucket of water on a burning incendiary bomb, it will explode and throw burning fragments in all directions.' The same publication added: 'Water is the best means of putting out a fire caused by an incendiary bomb.' It was not exactly contradictory but the widespread conclusion that an incendiary could be made harmless by a good dousing was hardly surprising.

The core of civil defence was the domestic shelter. The policy was based on Anderson's belief that dispersal, everybody to be protected in their own homes, was the best defence against the expected hail of bombs. The household shelter that Anderson gave his name to was the brainchild of engineers William Patterson and Oscar Kerrison. Intended to take up to six people at a pinch, the Anderson shelter consisted of fourteen galvanised corrugated steel panels. Six curved panels, bolted together at the top, had three straight sheets on either side and one at each end, one of them serving as a door. Putting together the structure, digging it into the garden and adding a light covering of soil, was the responsibility of the householder. Those who were elderly or infirm or who lacked basic practical skills were expected to call on neighbours to help them do the job.

The first Anderson was built in a garden in Islington in February 1939 but the design for the shelter was well in hand before the start of the year. It came in for heavy criticism. Widely seen as uncomfortable, cramped and generally unfit for purpose (it could not possibly survive a direct hit; at best it offered protection against flying debris), the family shelter was no use at all to those who lived in flats or in houses without gardens.

The favoured alternative was not to build up but to dig down. A popular campaign for deep shelters was accompanied by a variety of schemes for providing security while overcoming Whitehall objections that furnishing large numbers of people underground would create insurmountable problems of crowd control with the risk of more injuries caused by pushing and shoving than by high explosive. Deep shelters, and this was at the centre of the dispute, would also be more expensive than the distribution of Andersons and the conversion of domestic cellars.

Some of the projects advanced by architects and engineers were eye-wateringly expensive. At the top end, the eccentric and egocentric scientist, J.B.S. Haldane, proposed a 780-mile system of tunnels, 60 feet down, to hold 4.4 million Londoners. Irrespective of cost, time did not allow for such a massive undertaking. But other schemes were within the scope of enterprise and economics. A system of tunnel shelters under St Pancras promised bomb-proof protection for a densely populated borough at a smaller cost than any other type of shelter. A similar proposal from Finsbury Council suggested overcoming the problem of access by installing a spiral ramp turning about a central column. But this and other bright ideas did not find favour with Anderson who, in April 1939, told Parliament that the government saw no grounds for changing course.

The German option for building large concrete blocks above ground was not even considered. Known as *hochbunkers*, these shelters of reinforced concrete, designed to take up to 500 people, were reckoned to be bomb-proof. Certainly, most of them survived the war and can still be seen in urban areas where they have been converted to office blocks or apartments or used for storage. Demolition proved to be too costly.

That the *hochbunkers* did the job was a tribute to German engineering that begs the question as to whether 'dispersal' really was the best policy.

Those with money to spare made their own arrangements. *The Times* for January 3rd, 1939 carried an advertisement for 'Bombproof Air-Raid Shelters, made to measure by Glazier Sons in Savile Row' and designed by a 'pre-eminent technical expert who has made a careful study of the actual conditions of aerial warfare in Barcelona'.

Professing himself unfazed by the emergency, the drama critic James Agate nonetheless paid for a garden dug-out, made to his specifications.

> Its internal measurements are fifteen feet long by six feet wide by eight feet high. Concreted one foot thick throughout, with concrete roof and five foot of clay on top. Cost £100.[16]

As Agate soon discovered, there was no guarantee against flooding.

To make gas protection more user-friendly, gas-masks were awarded pet names. In London a mask was known as a Dicky-bird, Canary or Nose-bag. In Barrow-in-Furness a child was found crying because he had 'forgotten his 'Itler'. Children took to their masks far more readily than anyone, and went on carrying them after their parents had given them up. From Newcastle:

> Just before he went to bed, Ian (aged 9) reminded us that he would not be at home for his birthday on October 25. We promised to remember it, and asked him what he would like for a present. He thought for a while, and then said he would like a bag for his gas-mask. I gave him the one Mother had bought for me and sent him happy to bed.[17]

But the gas-mask was *not* fun. It made the wearer look sub-human, something out of a horror movie; the smell of rubber was pervading and disgusting and there could be no concession to claustrophobia. The prospect of wearing a gas-mask, possibly for hours on end, was for some more depressing than the thought of an actual gas attack.

It was a terrible irony that the fear of gas and of another war led some to the use of gas to put an end to it all. Having collected his gas-mask, William Rumbell, a 27-year-old sales clerk in Brixton was heard to cry out, 'Well, that means war' before turning on the gas in his room. The coroner decided that Rumbell was suffering from extreme anxiety neuroses brought on by the European crisis.[18]

Retired people and those of the older generation were the first to give up carrying their masks, probably because they were not under compulsion from employers. Factory and office workers were told always to have their masks at the ready. A survey of passers-by on Westminster Bridge in November 1938 found that gas-masks were carried only by 24 per cent of the men and 39 per cent of the women. By December, 20,000 masks had been handed in to London Transport's lost property office.

The rectangular cardboard boxes for gas-masks – clumsy, ugly and liable to fall to pieces if caught in the rain – inspired fashion designers to create stylish models to suit the wealthier purse. Women's magazines advised on gas-mask gentrification. A story in the *Daily Mirror* told of a bride 'carrying her gas-mask in a dainty satchel which matched her wedding gown'. Marion Rees set aside an evening to make a

> utilitarian, albeit attractive cover for my gas-mask, on the assumption that even a gas-mask box can and should look smart. For the price of 8d I bought half a yard of pale blue

rubber sheeting and some surgical plaster, and the parents were most impressed with the result.[19]

Marion reflected on a 'strange evening occupation'.

A DRESS REHEARSAL for civil defence was provided by the Irish Republican Army. Mid-January 1939 saw the start of the S-Plan, a series of attacks on the British mainland. On the 15th, a poster campaign in Irish cities called for a 'supreme effort' to force Britain 'to withdraw her institutions and representatives of all kinds from Ireland'. The following day, there were explosions at electricity, gas and water mains in London, Liverpool and Manchester. As the round-up of suspects began, injuries were caused by bombs planted at Leicester Square and Tottenham Court Road tube stations.

That there was no panic was reassuring for the emergency services. A Prevention of Violence Bill, rushed through Parliament, allowed for the police to fingerprint and register, and, if necessary, deport Irish people they had reason to suspect.

The most serious attack came in August with an explosion in Coventry's crowded Broadgate. Five shoppers were killed and several injured. A bomb had been planted in the basket of an errand boy's bicycle. The Irishmen found guilty of the Coventry murders were condemned to death in December. By then, Irish taoiseach Éamon de Valera, mindful of the Republic's declaration of strict neutrality, had declared the IRA an illegal organisation.

As war minister, Hore-Belisha pressed for general conscription; Chamberlain prevaricated. Had not his predecessor as prime minister pledged never to introduce conscription in peacetime? But changed circumstances persuaded him to change policy, if half-heartedly. The Military Training Bill of April 1939 put all males between the ages of 20 and 22 on notice of six months' compulsory military service. Conscription proper had to wait until the outbreak of war. But voluntary recruitment was stepped up with the result that by midsummer over 300,000 had joined the armed forces. When the war came, the regular army was some 400,000 strong with about the same number in the Territorial Army.

While efforts were stepped up to bolster the armed forces and to protect the home front, the politicians and diplomats cast about for new ways of containing the Nazi lust for glory.

If Hitler could not be appeased, he could, perhaps, be deterred. An idea that had gained currency was for an Anglo-French alliance with the Soviet Union to create a barrier to the east while Britain and France stood guard over the west. This enticing vision had strong appeal in the Labour party, where pacifists and the seekers after Marxist enlightenment shared common ground. Though in the government ranks hostility to Bolshevism was endemic, there was an undeniable attraction in a grand alliance taking in all countries, big or small, threatened by Germany. Support came from Robert Vansittart, chief diplomatic adviser to foreign secretary Anthony Eden and a passionate anti-appeaser, and from Churchill who welcomed any strengthening of the coalition against Nazism.

The kick-start to negotiations was the Anglo-French commitment to Poland, hard enough to enforce in normal circumstances but impossible in the face of a hostile or even neutral Soviet Union. There were encouraging signals from Maksim Litvinov, Soviet foreign minister until he was replaced by Vyacheslav Molotov in May 1939, and by Ivan Maisky, Soviet ambassador in London. Neither side had to be reminded of Hitler's implacable hatred of communism or of his designs for encroaching on Russian territory.

But the obstacles were formidable and, in the end, insurmountable. Britain and France were hamstrung by the lack of support of

the countries they were seeking to defend. Poland and its neighbours were none too keen on enlisting Russian aid if this meant
the Red Army marching across their borders. It was no secret that
Stalin's expansionist ambitions matched those of his Teutonic rival.
Conversely, Stalin had no intention of entering an agreement that
required the Soviet Union to divert German pressure from the west.
If the Red Army was to be called into play, Stalin needed guarantees
that Britain and France would pull their weight.

These sentiments were fully reciprocated. What assurances
were there that Stalin would not hold back from battle in the hope
that the Allies and Germany would fight it out until both sides were
exhausted? This was the unanswerable question put by those who
loathed communism as much as, if not more than Nazism.

For double-dealing as for sadistic brutality, Hitler and Stalin were
a match for each other. Though the details were slow to emerge, it
was known that, from 1936 to 1938, on Stalin's orders hundreds of
thousands (it eventually ran to millions) of peasants and their families
had died resisting collectivisation. The subsequent round-up of 'unre-
liable' party members, dragged off to execution or to remote labour
camps, soon extended to the highest ranks of the Red Army. The
purge reinforced the case against Stalin who, even assuming he could
be trusted, was thought to be militarily incapable of conducting a war.

Setting aside all the reservations, there was no question that if
there was to be any prospect of a deal, Stalin needed careful handling.
Yet, in contrast to his treatment of Hitler, Chamberlain seemed to go
out of his way to alienate the Soviet leader. It was bad enough, from
Stalin's point of view, that he had not been invited to Munich (Halifax
claimed, ingenuously, that there was no time to extend an invitation)
but the rebuff was made all the more galling by Stalin's suspicion
that the Munich non-aggression pact cooked up by Chamberlain was
directed against Russia. In return for peace in the west, Hitler was to

be given a free hand in the east. It is unlikely that Chamberlain had in mind anything quite as Machiavellian. But with Stalin the suspicion was all.

That Chamberlain had little faith in a successful outcome to the talks with Stalin was made evident by the low-key delegation he sent to Moscow. Instead of Halifax who refused to go, saying he was too much in demand at home, it fell to Sir William Seeds, the British ambassador in Moscow, to act as his understudy. In support went William Strang, a Foreign Office veteran of Munich and other encounters with the dictators. But whatever Strang's qualities, he was *not* foreign minister. He was accompanied by a military mission led by the none too distinguished and fancifully named Admiral Sir Reginald Plunkett-Ernle-Erle-Drax. With no power of decision, Drax was to become the punch-bag for Russian demands to know what precisely Britain and France would bring to a military alliance.

The delegation took its time getting to Moscow. Flying was not thought to be practical, while a warship, said Halifax, 'would have the effect of attaching too much importance to the mission'. The only alternative was a slow passenger steamer – though an exasperated General 'Pug' Ismay suggested that they might try going by bicycle. It was not until August 12th, 1939 that negotiations began in earnest. That little of substance was covered in the opening rounds led to a feeling that Molotov, ever the stone-faced, cold-eyed diplomat, was stalling. Which was, indeed, the case. While the talks dragged on, Stalin was distracted by unexpected but not unwelcome blandishments from Berlin. The enticing vision opened up of a deal with Germany for the two countries to carve up Poland while allowing Hitler to have his war in the west and for Stalin to tighten his hold on the Baltic states.

None of this filtered through to London where optimistic soundings from Downing Street encouraged the press to talk up the chances of a Soviet pact. In the *Daily Express*, the glad news was of a protocol all but ready for signature. But, as usual, the Beaverbrook pundits were wide of the mark.

Meanwhile, the Nazi hold tightened on Danzig. Equipped with arms, German nationalists were eager to demonstrate their strength. Nazi propaganda raised the stakes; Danzig was no longer enough. Polish Silesia and the whole of the Polish Corridor – which gave Poland access to the sea, cutting off East Prussia from the rest of Germany – were now earmarked for absorption into the Reich.

The reaction from Britain and France was to dispense more guarantees against aggression. After Poland, and in response to Italy's annexation of Albania, offers of protection were extended to Rumania, Greece and Turkey, this prompting the gag, 'A guarantee a day keeps Hitler away'. Left unspoken was the sure knowledge that in the absence of a commitment from the Soviet Union, the only means by which Britain and France could fulfil their obligations was to attack Germany from the west. And neither power was ready for that.

For Chamberlain, appeasement still offered the best escape route. In early June, Halifax assured the House of Lords that he was doing his best to persuade Germany that his government was ready to consider all legitimate demands on the way to a peaceful settlement. What these demands might be, he wisely refrained from spelling out. However, there could be no doubt that his olive branch was heavy with fruit ripe for picking.

Hitler was quick to catch the message. Britain and France were not prepared to stand up for their friends. In Bayreuth to meet Dr Otto Dietrich, the commanding voice of the Reich press, Leonard Mosley, a roving reporter for American and British papers, had an unexpected encounter with Hitler.

Dietrich, when he saw Hitler, tried to bundle me from the room, but Hitler stopped him and demanded that I should come forward and be introduced. He was in a good mood; he made a couple of jokes about the English Press when he knew who I was, and then banteringly asked why British journalists in Germany wrote so much about the threat of war. 'There will be no war,' he said. 'Don't you agree?' This, mark you, was the summer of 1939.

I said that there would be no war if the rights of Poland and the Free City of Danzig were not infringed.

Hitler slapped his thigh, and laughed. 'Even if they are, there will be no war,' he said. 'There was no war over the Sudetenland, nor over Czechoslovakia. There will be no war over Danzig.'

[...] I remember quoting my friends in London and saying: 'The conditions are different, Herr Hitler. Almost a year has passed since Munich was signed. Then Britain and France were unprepared. We had no troops, nor arms, nor planes. Now we have had almost a year to get ready ... and this time we shall keep our pledges if Poland's rights are infringed.'

He turned on me sarcastically then. I remember his pale face growing ruddy with passion, and his stubby forefinger with its bitten fingernail jabbing towards me, as he said: 'A year to prepare! What foolishness is that! The position of Britain and France today is worse – far worse – than in September, 1938. There will be no war, because you are less in a position to go to war now than you were a year ago. In that year you have achieved less than nothing. You have made things worse, in fact. You have built up your Army? Your Air Force? Your Navy? For every ship you have put on the stocks I have laid down one as well. For every plane you have built I have built twenty. For every tank you have made, I have constructed a hundred, and a hundred guns to your single cannon. And for every man you have put in your Army I have conscripted a thousand, and every one is trained and has a gun. A year to prepare! You are worse off than you ever were! You will not go to war!'[20]

Downing Street was not short of warnings of the way things were going but Chamberlain remained unperturbed. As German troops gathered on the Polish border, he approved the adjournment of Parliament for its summer break and departed for a three-week fishing holiday in Scotland.

CHAPTER 4

Preparing for the Worst

With the Civil Defence Act of July 1939, a detailed plan for civil defence began to take shape. Certain contingencies had already been made. Ration books for 45 million people were waiting for distribution, though as yet there was no decision on what was to be rationed and in what circumstances. By early August, 1 million Anderson shelters had been sent to householders, many of them, probably the majority, still to be erected.

While the combined strength of the civil defence organisation was close to 1.5 million, there were shortages of basic equipment and training was inadequate. A long-standing problem for civil defence was the dearth of qualified instructors. Even those who were technically proficient were not always equipped with the knowledge to persuade a sceptical public that it was for their own good that precautions had to be taken. The question 'why' elicited some odd responses. A meeting called to promote the use of gas-masks had the speaker assuring his audience that the 'terrible danger' they faced was coming 'not from Germany' but from Holland, Belgium and France. The reaction, said a reporter, was 'slight bewilderment and then some laughter'.[1]

Where were the plans to cope with the widely anticipated disruption caused by mass bombing?

The measures to help protect civilian society against a new form of warfare were not directed by a 'General Staff'. No Cabinet committee maintained a continuous watch over the social services. No research was conducted into the effects of bombing on the apparatus of civilian life. No comprehensive study was made of the social consequences that might flow from the kind of war that the Government expected. Inadequate factual knowledge and an inadequate endeavour to acquire it, a deep ignorance of social relationships and a shallow interest in social research – these things were later to handicap the work of Government Departments.[2]

Even the introduction of the Civil Defence Act led to no more than a skeleton scheme for shelters for the homeless and emergency stations for providing food and hot drinks. While twelve new hospitals were planned, medical and first-aid provision did not come close to matching the dire predictions of the number of bomb casualties.

It needed something dramatic to break the cycle of complacency. It came on August 23rd, 1939 with the news that given the choice between an Anglo-French alliance and a deal with Germany, Stalin had decided that Germany had more to offer. The small compensation for the German–Soviet non-aggression pact was that Admiral Drax and William Strang had the satisfaction of being allowed to return home. Drax made it perfectly plain that his first visit to Moscow was also his last.

A sense of urgency at last took hold of the British government. While the finishing touches were put to a military alliance with Poland, a hastily recalled Parliament voted near-unanimous approval to an Emergency Powers Defence Bill.

With this one abrupt move, Britain became a dictatorship, a benevolent dictatorship for the most part but a dictatorship nonetheless. Parliamentary elections were suspended, as was *habeas corpus*, the ancient protection against imprisonment without trial. The state assumed unchallengeable power to lock up any person thought to be a risk to public safety. Property was liable to requisition; it might be a building but was just as likely to be any means of transportation on land or sea. The right of entry to private property was extended from the police to almost any government employee. All letters overseas were to be censored.

Sir Samuel Hoare, home secretary until the outbreak of war, promised that the measures would be applied 'with moderation, toleration and commonsense' but many of the new regulations (hundreds were published within days) were so vague as to incite abuse by over-zealous or vindictive officials.

'Living in London is like being an inmate of a reformatory school', wrote Charles Ritchie:

> Everywhere you turn you run into some regulation designed for your own protection. The Government is like the School Matron with her keys jangling at her waist. She orders you about, good-humouredly enough, but all the same, in no uncertain terms. You need look no further to know what British fascism would be like. Nothing but acute physical danger can make such a regime bearable.[3]

On August 25th, the day after emergency powers were adopted, all service leave was stopped and ARP organisations were put on the alert. War minister Hore-Belisha wanted an immediate call-up of 300,000 men of the Territorial Army but Chamberlain put the cap on 35,000. This allowed for coastal defences and anti-aircraft units to be made ready. A week later, mobilisation was extended to 145,000 men of the Army Reserve.

While all the evidence was of a makeshift system of civil defence, no one could doubt the enthusiasm of those involved. R.A. Levinge was a volunteer in the Royal Observer Corps responsible for watching out for enemy aircraft. Based in Bristol, he was head observer for Group 23.

One week before war was declared the Observer Corps was called out. We had no warning that we might be required to 'stand to' unless or until a state of war was about to be proclaimed or we should not have gone away from home for some hours. As it was we had decided to spend the day at Odiham [in Hampshire] because we wanted to see as many different types of aircraft flying as possible and we thought that around Odiham was as good a place as anywhere. Such was the keenness to learn about aircraft that nearly all our free time was spent in trying to see them or searching through *The Aeroplane* or *Flight*. It proved to be a hobby that could be turned to a very valuable use.

We got back about tea-time and during the evening received the code word 'Readiness'. As this was not used for Exercises we knew at once that it was the real thing. The Chief got the equipment together and went straight to the Post Site to connect up the telephone, while I was dispatched to find as many of the crew as I could. They all lived fairly near the Post but just at first I was not very successful at finding them – either they had just gone out for the evening or, in some cases, they were working on a late shift. However, I came upon Observer B. Haydon who was doing some hoeing. I explained my errand. He was a man of few words, and putting

his hoe away at once, he just said 'I'll be there' – and he was
– in a very few minutes.

He and Captain Levinge were the only two members of Group 23
to be on duty at the beginning of the war and who were also there
at the finish. What to wear on duty was always a contentious issue.

During the first autumn of the war we received a parcel of
knitted comforts in R.A.F. blue, which were extremely welcome. The colour alone was a great 'boost to morale' as it
made us feel that we really were in close relationship with the
Royal Air Force and that we really mattered. Included in the
parcel were Balaclava helmets, which on the face of it looked
excellent, but we found in practice that by covering up our
ears, we could not hear so well, so we had to lay them by for
off-duty periods and make do with scarves and pullovers.

Our first item of uniform was an issue of what were called
'Zee Kee' coats in R.A.F. blue with shiny black cuffs and an
interlining of yellow oil skin which became extremely stiff in
cold weather! They were very welcome but the general effect
of tin hat, 'Zee Kee' coat and civilian trousers or stockings
showing underneath, must have been a bit incongruous!

We found that one of the best things to wear on the head in
wet weather was the old black Sou'wester hat like those worn
by lifeboat crews. They really were excellent for the job. The
long backs prevented rain running down the neck, which of
course it would do with devilish delight from a beret.

The Emergency Powers Act was the call to action for the regional
commissioners. For Harold Scott, whose powers extended over
greater London:

Those last few days of August seem a nightmare. Lock, stock and barrel our staff and papers were moved to the war head-quarters in Exhibition Road, and irrespective of his or her normal duties everyone lent a hand in shifting files and equipment, so that not a moment should be lost. Arrangements had already been made for sleeping and eating on the prem-ises, and from then onwards a twenty-four hour watch was kept. Our day began at seven and ended after midnight. The builders were still installing the equipment for ventilating the control room and an emergency lighting plant, and for three nights my deputy, Hughes-Gibb, and I slept (more or less) on camp beds beside the machinery, surrounded by wires, pipes, and bricks: through a hole in the wall which was to take the ventilation shaft we could see the sky as we lay in bed. But soon our little community settled down to a regular routine, as far as that was possible for men living on the brink of war.[4]

Elsewhere in the country, where there were vacancies, the role of commissioner invariably went to a civil servant or a high-ranking retired army officer. They were paid generously, up to £2,500 a year or around £150,000 in today's money.

Hundreds of thousands of *papier-mâché* coffins were ordered and outdoor swimming pools were emptied to receive corpses. Tents were hired by the Ministry of Health to provide over 10,000 extra beds for air-raid casualties. A severe winter brought an end to this improvisation. Those that were not blown over were soon removed because, it was said, their sharp whiteness caused distress among local residents.

The demand for blankets was overwhelming. In early 1939, the government had committed to supplying 4,200,000 blankets and 1,470,000 mattresses or beds to support a large-scale evacuation. But that was only the start and it was a bad start at that. By late August, only 29,000 blankets were available for evacuees. The first order for camp beds was not even placed until August 15th. Other large orders for beds, mattresses and pillows, along with 260,000 nightshirts for hospital patients, followed later in the month.

Another 100,000 blankets came from cutting up stocks of men's overcoats, a decision that came to be regretted as the cold weather began to bite. A national broadcast appeal helped to bring in 789,000 blankets and 20,000 camp beds by the time the national evacuation got under way. Local authorities complained of the absence of instructions and advice. A Home Office request to set up emergency feeding stations and 'temporary shelter of some kind' for the homeless was not circulated until after the outbreak of war.

With the approach of September, air-raid wardens and casualty and rescue volunteers reported for duty in their thousands. Public shelters and trenches were opened under the supervision of police or wardens. The requisitioning of vehicles suitable for ambulances and other forms of rescue back-up was accelerated along with the sandbagging and shutting of public buildings. Factory sirens and hooters that might have been mistaken for air-raid warnings were silenced.

In readiness for air-raid casualties, hospital beds were cleared of patients not judged to be in need of urgent medical attention. These included sufferers of contagious tuberculosis and patients in an early, operable stage of cancer. Pregnant women were kept at home. In London, two-thirds of maternity beds were held back for the war injured.

Constance Siggers in south London was one of the many with a seriously ill relative. After church on September 3rd, she visited her father in the local hospital but said nothing about the onset of war. A week later, he was discharged. His daughter did the best she could to look after him but without medical aid his condition worsened and within the month he was dead.

'Surely never before', wrote a hospital almoner, 'has a nation inflicted such untold suffering on itself as a precaution against potential suffering ... war or no war, there could not fail to be civilian sick ... Why should it have been considered less disastrous for anyone to die untreated of cancer, appendicitis or pneumonia than as a result of a bomb?'

The government was not entirely to blame for this mismatch of resources. There was evidence of voluntary hospitals, those in the private sector, and municipal hospitals finding it irresistible to save on limited funds by clearing beds while being paid for keeping them empty. It was later calculated that at the start of the war close on 250,000 people in need of treatment had been denied admission to hospital. After six years of war, taking into account the blitz of 1940–41 and the flying bombs, the total number of air-raid casualties treated in hospital was less than 40 per cent of those turned out of their beds in 1939.

THAT A BLACKOUT would be imposed immediately on the outbreak of war was regarded as inevitable. Any sort of lighting, particularly in urban areas, might invite the attention of enemy bombers. The first of a series of leaflets describing how doors and windows could be made light-proof by close-fitting blinds, old blankets or sheets of thick paper, was posted to householders in July.

But until the war started, no one knew how the blackout would work in practice. A trial exercise held in London and south-east England in mid-August was made farcical by the out-of-towners who turned out in strength to experience the novelty of bumping into each other, and maybe taking a few liberties, in crowded, darkened streets.

In the early hours of the morning, reported *The Times*, there were 'almost rush-hour conditions' in Piccadilly. But RAF observer planes sent up to assess the effectiveness of lights-out judged the dummy-run to have been a success.

A nationwide blackout was enforced from sunset on September 1st. It was to be nearly six years before there was any light relief to the hours of darkness.

Among the curiosities thrown up by the blackout was the suspension of the driving test, which meant that learners were let loose on the roads in hazardous conditions. More constructively and for the first time, cyclists had to carry a low-voltage rear red light. In February 1940, a speed limit of 20 miles per hour was introduced for all built-up areas.

Lieutenant A.J. Noble of the Queen's Own Cameron Highlanders found that an army uniform was no protection against diligent air-raid wardens.

As it was a little time before petrol rationing was introduced, I was able and allowed to drive my little car north. I had fitted the regulation mask on one headlight and taken the bulb out of the other. All was well during the daylight, but night fell while crossing the Yorkshire moors west of Catterick. I was stopped umpteen times by air-raid wardens at the various tiny villages telling me that I was showing too much light. Just outside Brough I was told I could not go on and must await daylight. This was too much, and as I was in uniform I said I just had to reach Inverness next morning. With many exhortations to take care and douse my one light if I heard aircraft noises, I was allowed to proceed.

Railway timetables were disrupted, with delays and cancellations part of every traveller's catalogue of complaints. After dusk, finding a seat in a carriage with only a thin beam from a boxed-in light to show the way was a challenge that led to many angry exchanges.

A raft of crime novels in the early part of the war relied on the blackout as a plot device for nefarious activities. But there is no evidence of a steep rise in serious crime until the blitz of 1940–41 gave the chance to looters. Rather, in 1939 and early 1940 it was petty crime that took off – stealing from vegetable patches, pickpocketing and vice. Male and female prostitution thrived.

Before long, the symbols of war were everywhere. The tops of pillar boxes were given a coat of yellowish gas-detector paint. Blinds, curtains and paint had to be bought to prepare for the blackout; windows and fanlights screened with cardboard and brown paper. White stripes were put down the centre of roads and kerbs were painted with alternate white squares to help cope with poor visibility. Watchmen in the docks were provided with conical steel 'pepper pot' shelters, as were the sentries at Buckingham Palace.

In the countryside where street lighting was a rarity, householders with whitewashed cottages were told to give them a coat of mud-coloured paint to make them less visible to enemy bombers. The removal of signposts with the intention of confusing enemy infiltrators was frustrating for strangers on legitimate business. There was the story of an army officer who asked a rustic to help him find his unit. He named a village.

'I can't tell you that.'
Pointing to a spot on the map, 'What about this place?'
'I can't tell you that.'
'You don't know much, do you?'
'I know more than you do. I b'aint lost.'

The custom of putting the name of towns on the top of gas holders as a guide to flyers was hastily reversed.

IT DID NOT take much imagination to assume that a German air attack, if and when it came, would aim first at central London in the hope of disrupting central government and breaking communications with the rest of the country. The first instinct was to create a new base for essential decision-making somewhere outside the danger area. Accordingly, plans were made for the exodus of the Cabinet, Parliament and some 16,000 civil servants critical to the war effort to the suburbs of south-west London. What was known as the 'black move' was intended to take place over three or four days after the outbreak of war. The follow-up or 'yellow move' would involve 44,000 less essential support staff. For accommodation, some 220 hotels and 30 schools along with a motley collection of other buildings in the west Midlands and north-west were requisitioned.

The Cabinet then had second thoughts. While ministers and their senior advisers cautioned against a move that was bound to interrupt the smooth running of government, others warned of the unfavourable impact on public opinion if the country's leaders were seen to be scuttling out of the centre of London.

The compromise was to push ahead with the yellow move. At the same time, the Bank of England took itself off to the Hampshire village of Overton after dispatching 2,000 tons of its gold to Canada; the Post Office's senior managers decamped to Harrogate, while the BBC and its senior staff moved to a stately home near Evesham.

In London, meanwhile, General Ismay, secretary to the Committee of Imperial Defence and soon to be Churchill's chief of staff, presided over an informal, high-powered sub-committee to decide on secure premises for those charged with the direction of a war.

The cellars beneath the large block of Government offices which in those days housed the Ministry of Health, Office of Works and Board of Trade were selected for our purpose. They were cleared of archives and air-conditioned, and their roofs were shored up by lengths of crude timber. Steel would have been preferable, but this was all required for other more urgent purposes. The principal features of the stronghold were a small room for the Chiefs of Staff, a larger room for the Cabinet, and between the two a still larger room, called the Map Room, in which the latest information on all aspects of the war situation was to be available at all hours of the day and night. It was connected by telephone with the Admiralty, the War Office, the Air Ministry, the Ministry of Home Security and the Foreign Office, and the telephones were to be manned on a twenty-four-hour basis by retired officers of the three Services, who would be specially ear-marked for this duty. In the event, all these officers reported for duty on the day before the outbreak of war, and the Map Room functioned from that date, night and day, without a break, until Japan surrendered.[5]

Now a fixture on the tourist trail, the War Rooms were not even half ready when the war started and were still short of completion when Churchill took power in May 1940. It was Churchill who ordered the structure to be topped by three to four feet of concrete. Even then, though no one liked to mention it, it was unlikely that the War Rooms would have survived a direct hit. But, Ismay recalled,

[I]t was at least proof against noise, and enabled the Cabinet to hold their meetings there undisturbed by the clatter of bombs and anti-aircraft artillery fire. The only interruptions to their deliberations that I can recall were due to a very different cause. Whenever the Duty Officer in the Map Room reported that a very heavy air-raid on London was in progress, the Prime Minister used to insist on an adjournment in order that we all might watch the proceedings from the Air Ministry roof. It made an admirable, though not very safe, grandstand.[6]

While Chamberlain was prime minister, the Cabinet met only once in the War Rooms. That was in October 1939. In December, the name was changed from Central War Rooms to Cabinet War Rooms.

THE BEST OF the nation's cultural heritage was removed from public gaze, packaged and sent to remote places for safe storage. The 30-year-old director of the National Gallery in London, Kenneth Clark, supervised the dismantling of the displays.

> We chose places in the west of Britain which were not at all likely to be bombed and where all the pictures could be arranged in such a way that we could inspect them easily and see that they were not coming to any harm.
>
> We decided to take the pictures there by rail rather than by road because it really is much smoother and more certain. The only difficulty was that three of our biggest pictures would not go through any of the tunnels, even if slung quite low on the lines on what is called a well-waggon, and to meet this difficulty a member of our staff who is a mathematician thought of that old idea which used to be such a nuisance to us at school, called the theorem of Pythagoras, and he constructed a case by which these big pictures were tilted slightly on their side and the upright part of the case was just low enough to pass through all the tunnels.[7]

Journey's end for the paintings was a deep quarry near Blaenau Ffestiniog in the heart of Snowdonia. The twelfth-century stained glass in Canterbury Cathedral and the Seven Sisters window in York Minster were among the church treasures to be squirrelled away.

Stately homes in rural seclusion and hotels in holiday spots were liable to be purloined by the state without notice. The headquarters staff of vital industries were among those who found themselves posted to out-of-the-way places. For Gerald Lacey, a senior manager with the British Aluminium Company, the order to prepare to move came a week before war was declared. He and two colleagues made their way to Shrewsbury to reconnoitre the Raven Hotel, earmarked to be the headquarters of Aluminium Control. It was all to be done undercover.

> We arrived at separate times as though joining one another on holiday and carefully surveyed the hotel for accommodation, without giving the management any idea of what was afoot.

The order to requisition came on Friday, September 1st.

> When we informed the manager that his hotel was to be taken over he collapsed in his chair. To give some idea of the planning, we had all visitors in the hotel out by 9.30 a.m. on Saturday. Post Office telephone engineers arrived to fit the rooms with telephones for office work. 7,000 sets of instructions and licence application forms were delivered from storage in a British Aluminium Company works in the Midlands. ... Users of aluminium were astonished to receive instructions so soon after war was declared. Licence applications and a stream of enquiries were being dealt with before the week was out.

In the days following, more staff arrived to be billeted in Shrewsbury. Senior staff lived and worked in the Raven Hotel. Before long, a reorganisation prompted by the ever-increasing demands of the aircraft industry had Gerald Lacey move to Banbury as Light Metals Controller based at Alcan Aluminium (UK) Ltd.

> By the end of the first year the work of the Light Metals Control had greatly increased with the need to coordinate all the different forms of metal against the Aircraft Programme and the introduction of new aircraft. Military and Naval requirements had also to be coordinated while civil demands had to be seriously curtailed and were ultimately confined to no more than 5% of the total available supplies. No other allied country, except perhaps Russia, reduced civil uses so drastically.

The production of incendiary bombs came within Lacey's brief. At the time of the blitz, there was a stock of about a million incendiaries.

> Churchill gave the order 'throw 500,000 on Cologne', a memorable raid. The next day he ordered another 500,000 to be thrown on Dusseldorf, and we were practically out of stock. This led to a frantic demand for more bombs and as a result the Control had to organise the setting up of no less than four automatic magnesium casting foundries to make the finally agreed programme of 4,500,000 bombs a month!

The stock left at the end of the war provided a source of magnesium.

> Bombs were dismantled and the magnesium bodies melted down and re-alloyed for making magnesium alloy castings for various uses including motor and aircraft construction.

The 'yellow move' from Whitehall dispatched some departments of the Admiralty to Bath, the Ministry of Food to Colwyn Bay, and the production section of the Air Ministry to Harrogate. Premises large enough for accommodation and office space were hot in demand. Told by the Admiralty that it was about to be requisitioned, Malvern College in Worcestershire (bizarrely about as far away from the sea as it is possible to get in the British Isles) found an alternative home in Blenheim Palace. In the summer of 1940, when they were joined by Canadian troops, the boys returned to their first home, which was no longer on the government list of desirable properties. Not long afterwards, Blenheim was taken over by MI5.

By a neat irony, Brocket Hall in Hertfordshire, the country seat of the second Lord Brocket, a Nazi sympathiser, was handed over to the Red Cross as a maternity home for evacuees from London's East End. Mothers gave birth in the Ribbentrop Bedroom.[8]

Barrage balloons began to appear over London. Three times the size of a cricket pitch, they were described variously as 'little elephants', 'giant cigars', 'big whales', 'great motionless blowflies' and, later, as 'fat Jerry sausages'. An observer of a romantic turn of mind was mesmerised by the sight of barrage balloons against the setting sun. He called them 'golden asteroids'. Half-filled with hydrogen, the bottom half left to inflate as the balloon ascended, these deterrents to enemy dive bombers were put up and hauled down on steel cables by British Balloon Command. On the first day of the war, 40 balloons were hovering over central London.

Barrage balloons were good for morale but of little practical use. The assumption that they would destroy low-flying aircraft was true enough but low-flying aircraft were not much in evidence. Over the period of war, balloons did more damage to friendly aircraft than to enemy attackers, which were chiefly high-flying bombers. Even so, by mid-1940, some 1,400 balloons were floating over the country, a third of them protecting London.

CHAPTER 5

The Descent to War

B ritain's belated resolve to stand up to Nazi bullying was a shot in the arm for the French government. Still clinging to his pacifist principles, foreign minister Georges Bonnet found himself outvoted in cabinet when he tried to argue that the guarantee to Poland was an empty threat. Prime minister Edouard Daladier demanded and got an assurance from the military command that it was ready to take on the might of a German offensive. Partial mobilisation was ordered on August 27th, 1939. Another Munich was not to be tolerated.

The apparent intransigence of Britain and France presented Hitler with a dilemma. It came as a surprise to him that his compact with the Soviet Union had not had the desired effect of weakening the resolution of his enemies. His original plan was for the invasion of Poland two days after Russia came in on side. The army was ready to move and there were German forces in Danzig ready to take control when the word was given. Still not fully mobilised, Poland was vulnerable to a bold offensive.

On the afternoon of August 25th, Hitler gave the order to attack at 4.30 the following morning. But a few hours later, still anticipating an Anglo-French cave-in, he changed his mind. Instead, he played what he thought was his trump card against the soft-centred Chamberlain. Sir Nevile Henderson was summoned to deliver a message of friendship to Britain. If the Polish question was settled to his satisfaction, Hitler was prepared to make 'a large comprehensive offer'. This would require some limited deal over colonies but would guarantee the future existence of the British empire and finally lead to general disarmament. He added the irrevocable determination of Germany never again to enter into conflict with Russia.

As an appeaser who outdid his political masters in his readiness to accommodate Germany, Henderson was quick to take Hitler's offer at face value. He flew immediately to London to deliver the news to Downing Street. He was taken aback when Chamberlain and Halifax were not overly impressed. Across the political spectrum, disillusionment had gone too deep. While the left was in disarray over Soviet treachery, the right was dismayed by Nazi readiness to forsake its vaunted role as the bulwark against Bolshevism. If anything, Allied support for Poland was strengthened by the Nazi–Soviet pact.

Even so, the response Henderson carried back to Berlin left the way open for Hitler to return to the negotiating table. He was assured that the British government was anxious to assist in finding a solution to satisfy Germany and Poland. But failure to reach a just settlement would wreck the chances of a wider understanding and might plunge the nations into war, 'a calamity without parallel in history'.

Hitler's counter tactic, after an ill-tempered meeting with Henderson, was to appear to be reasonable by acceding to direct negotiations while racking up the pressure with a demand that a Polish representative with full powers to negotiate should arrive in Berlin by the end of the very next day. What amounted to an ultimatum was ignored in London. To agree would have been tantamount to a Polish surrender. Even Chamberlain could see that. Instead, on the evening of the 30th, Henderson, who was not standing up well to the tension, delivered a reproof couched in a suggestion that the German government should adhere to normal diplomatic procedure by 'inviting the Polish ambassador to call and handing proposals to him for transmission to Warsaw'.

This was not what Hitler wanted to hear. Fearing the humiliation of backing down and trapped by his own military timetable, he gambled on destiny. On the early morning of September 1st, bombs fell on Warsaw and German forces crossed the Polish frontier.

Hore-Belisha issued orders for mobilisation of the whole army, while Lord Chatfield, First Lord of the Admiralty, and Sir Kingsley Wood, minister for air, issued similar orders to the Royal Navy and the Royal Air Force. But neither Britain nor France declared war immediately. An attempt by Mussolini to get in on the act by offering himself as an honest broker persuaded Bonnet that another talking-shop might yet avert catastrophe. Though hardened by the Munich humiliation, Halifax weighed in with a plea to his Cabinet colleagues to give Mussolini a chance. The idea foundered on news from Rome that Mussolini had abandoned his enterprise as soon as he heard that Germany had marched into Poland.

Chamberlain, like Hitler, was now caught up in the tide of events. The man of peace was being driven inexorably towards war. At the Cabinet meeting on the afternoon of September 2nd it was agreed that an ultimatum to Germany should expire at midnight. But when it came to the crunch, Chamberlain made one last attempt to resist the inevitable.

That evening when he faced the House of Commons, MPs expected to hear a declaration of war or that a declaration was imminent. Instead, the prime minister opined that, even now, if Hitler agreed to withdraw his troops from Poland, he would re-embark on a diplomatic shuttle to win the peace. He was received in silence. When Arthur Greenwood rose to speak for Labour in the absence of Clement Attlee, Conservative anti-appeaser Leo Amery shouted across to him, 'Speak for England, Arthur'.

The call was taken up in all parts of the House. Though not a great orator, Greenwood's quiet manner was all the more effective in delivering a damning verdict on the government's prevarication. Chamberlain, he declared, would have one chance to recover his dignity and Britain's self-respect when the Commons reconvened the following day.

> 'And I must put this point to him. Every minute's delay now means the loss of life, imperilling our nation's interests and the very foundations of our national honour.'

There could be no backing down. Chamberlain was isolated in his own Cabinet. Halifax was the first to insist on an end to prevarication. His colleagues agreed. Even Kingsley Wood, the most dove-like of ministers, spoke out against further delays. But this overdue unity of purpose was achieved more in regret than with real enthusiasm for the cause. The British ultimatum delivered at 9.00am on September 3rd was followed at noon by a similarly couched French ultimatum. By the end of the day both countries were at war with Germany.

There were no jingoistic demonstrations. The scenes of jubilation that marked August 1914 were entirely absent a quarter of a century later. In Berlin, when Hitler drove to the Reichstag, the usual crowds of well-wishers were conspicuously absent. With the mood of resignation in Paris the boulevard cafes were quiet. Looking back on those days, the maverick Tory MP Robert Boothby wrote: 'We tumbled into Armageddon without heart, without songs.'

Charles Carter was a junior clerk at the publisher Methuen, then based in Essex Street just off Aldwych.

We were told that the firm would close down until further notice. We left work early, wondering when we should meet again. Miss Caddell was very upset, her mother being in hospital and her brother called-up suddenly, nobody knowing where he was gone. She said she could hardly believe it. I felt very sorry for her.

In the evening I was going to the Beethoven Prom, and I felt so unwell that I merely wandered along Shaftesbury Avenue and Charing Cross Road. Everywhere seemed sandbagged, and in front of Prince's Theatre was a great heap of sand, and dust carts and volunteers packing and transporting it. I sat on an Embankment seat, and watched a host of barrage balloons ascending ominously. Then to Queen's Hall.

The place was almost empty, and I was able to sit on a seat all the time. At 7.45 there was nobody standing: then came 37 people – I counted them – and fewer than a hundred were standing when the concert started. They did the Seventh Symphony and the song-cycle 'An die ferne Geliebte': this latter somehow very affecting at this time.

I left at the interval, and emerged into a darkened Regent Street. All street lights were extinguished, motors had dimmed headlights, and buses had no lights at all inside. The bus conductors had to feel and fumble and guess at the form of the money handled. Thus I got to Bloomsbury, and then to Leyton by 555 trolleybus; and in many places not one light was visible – I never saw such blackness. So I wondered how long it would be before street lights were lighted once more.

While there were those who succumbed to a sense of futility, delivering to Downing Street thousands of letters appealing to Chamberlain to stop the war, for most people the worry and sadness were secondary to a determination to get the job done. A Gallup poll found 89 per cent of its sample believing that the fight was to the finish, that 77 per cent opposed any immediate discussion of peace proposals and that 84 per cent believed in eventual victory over Germany.

On the evening of September 3rd, J.B. Priestley was due to broadcast the first episode of his upbeat novel, *Let the People Sing*. 'I groped my way to Broadcasting House through an appalling blackness ... I found myself among sandbags, bayonets, nurses in uniform.' He fought off depression with hopes that he would live to see a better world.[1]

POLAND FELL TO a brilliantly mounted blitzkrieg, the first in modern warfare. Fourteen mechanised or partially mechanised German divisions leading 40 infantry divisions swept across the Polish plain, conveniently flat and easy going for a mobile invader. The Luftwaffe bombed the Polish air force before it could get off the ground and smashed the country's railway network. The help expected from Britain and France did not arrive. Not a single rifle or bomb was sent to Poland. A miserly £8 million credit was offered by Britain as long as it was spent on British goods.

On September 17th, the Red Army invaded Poland from the east. Warsaw held out for ten days after the government had fled to Rumania. The Polish army fought on until October 5th, partly in expectation that Britain and France would mount an attack in the west powerful enough to stop Hitler in his tracks. It was not to be. The French army made a few 'probing' assaults on German defences while mobilisation geared up at a lumbering pace and heavy artillery, deemed essential for a full-blown offensive, was brought out of storage.

No bombers were sent to Germany, ostensibly for fear of alienating the sympathy of neutral America. But in truth, the RAF was simply not ready. As air minister, Kingsley Wood came in for stick from those who wanted to get on with the fighting. The story went round that when Leo Amery called for incendiaries to be dropped on German forests, Wood protested a violation of private property: 'Why, you'll be asking me to bomb Essex next.' There is no evidence that he said any such thing but the anecdote, widely circulated, reflected the weak fighting spirit of the government.

In common with the entire country, ministers waited for the bombs. But the enemy did not oblige, the Luftwaffe did not fill the sky and no bombs fell. Brooding over a 'waste of dull desolation', junior diplomat Charles Ritchie wrote in his diary:

London is waiting for the first raid like an anxious hostess who has made all the preparations to receive formidable guests – but the guests do not seem to be going to turn up.[2]

CHAPTER 6

Britain on the Move

The government and people were convinced that it would not be long before the bombing started. Two days before the declaration of war, the signal was given for the mass evacuation of women and children from city centres. But by then a general exodus was already under way. Among those who could afford the luxury of choice, the growing expectation of war prompted an early migration from areas thought to be vulnerable to attack. While there was no panic rush from London, a steady stream of people left by road and rail. Hotels in 'safe resorts' were soon reporting 'no vacancies'.

To ease the traffic congestion, Scotland Yard advised on the trouble-free routes out of London. There was also an official designation of safe towns such as Bath, said to be 'immune from all air raid dangers', while Aldwick Bay, near Bognor, was in the even happier position of being 'immune from the international situation'. Estate agents were quick to adapt their sales pitch. Properties that hitherto had been a drag on the market because of inaccessibility were now promoted as five-star attractions. 'Remotely placed' and 'remote and inaccessible' were now positive selling points. In demand too were houses with deep cellars or concrete garages that might double as air-raid shelters.

Helpful advice on sales jargon was provided by a newspaper columnist who found that a 'renovated cottage' meant two bathrooms while an 'old-world' village meant two pubs. In his own local he spotted a faded print of John Bull standing on the cliffs of Dover, straddle-legged with his hands behind him, viewing the preparations for invasion across the Channel and saying 'You may all be damned!' The print was dated October 23rd, 1803.

Among the rental oddities on offer as wartime accommodation was a fully-furnished motor yacht, to sleep seven, on Lake Windermere. For those on limited means there were caravans, 'sixteen feet of concentrated comfort on wheels', in remote beauty spots in north Wales. And for the really hard up, converted buses and railway carriages could be sited on rural outposts. Seaside hotels touted for long-term residents seeking retirement or those who 'cannot take an active part in the war effort' or who were otherwise seeking peace and security away from the noise of battle.

Some recommendations, official or otherwise, for getting away from it all turned out to be none too sensible. Folkestone, soon to be in range of enemy guns across the Channel, was hardly 'safe', while Sark, destined to experience German occupation, was most certainly not 'a haven of safety in the Channel Islands'.

In all, between June and the first week of September 1939, around 2 million people abandoned London and other large cities without official help or encouragement. On September 1st it was reported from Southampton that 5,000 passengers had sailed for America in 48 hours.

Keeping track of those on the move was a complication for the authorities. Employed by Wembley Borough Council to chase up on

householders who had not paid their rates, George Beardmore found
the job harder than he expected.

> The number of well-to-do people who have just upped and
> gone is astonishing. At one house I found a back door open,
> walked inside, and a *Mary Celeste* situation presented itself:
> breakfast-things unwashed, a half-smoked cigarette dipped
> in tea to put it out, fruit going mouldy in a bowl, and a mys-
> terious note on the gas-stove that read: 'Grandma Highgate
> Ponds 5.30'. Made me laugh. A neighbour told me over the
> fence: 'You from the Council? I thought so. They've gone to
> somewhere in Bedford.' But another house I tried had so obvi-
> ously been broken into that I dialled 999.[1]

Among the voluntary evacuees from London was Valerie Ranzetta,
who took her two children to the home of a family friend in
Cambridge. She did not go willingly.

> I was unhappy about this, but, like everyone, expected air-raids
> to begin almost immediately. I had never had any illusions
> about the Germans and the spirit of war. I had lived in London
> during the Great War, and seen much. All right, we would go,
> leaving my husband behind to carry on, and to 'dig a shelter'
> for us if we decided to return. The car came round at four a.m.
> the following morning. I couldn't even summon up a smile
> as I got in, with the children following, and waved good-bye
> to Father. It had all happened so quickly. There were a thou-
> sand things still unsaid between us, because even working
> in the City had its hazards, with the admirable fire-watching
> rotas already allocated. Good-bye, good-bye, but *why*? All we
> had ever wanted from life was a decent living-wage for the

breadwinner, and a place to make a home for our children. Who *were* the people who thrived on war, the grabbers of money, or the munition manufacturers? Not that it mattered much to us. We just had to *endure*.

The welcome in Cambridge was not what Valerie expected:

If we had deliberately chosen the wrong time for our arrival we could not have succeeded more! There was a family wedding going on, and no one at the house. Our hired-driver-cum-friend, probably feeling as empty and as queasy as we all did after that tedious journey, took us to the church and left us there, saying he had an urgent appointment in London, *would we be all right*? We *had* to be. Someone ushered us into the hall where the jubilant reception was in full swing. Alas, they had already eaten. … We could not find Aunt Em, our target. It was ten years since we had met, anyway, and I wasn't sure whether I would recognise her among the noisy crowd. The children were scared. They imagined we were in an alien country. … When I took them outside to the lavatory to be violently sick, I found Aunt Em. She was almost casual. I think they were tougher than we 'townies'. She simply nodded when I told her that the children had been ill, and said, '*It'll do 'em good!*' She gave a swift glance round, saying that she must attend to her guests, that it was 'awkward' coming just then (she meant *us*) then she was off, pointing vaguely towards a plate of pastries nearby and a huge jug of pale lemonade.

We knew nobody there except Aunt Em and her daughter, Annie, who was the bride, anyway, and unapproachable because of her swarming admirers. The children ate a cake, drank some lemonade, then were all sick again, so we just sat quietly on a bench in the corner near the silent harmonium and waited.

When, at last, the guests departed, Valerie's children were asleep.

Aunt Em came rushing in from outside, laughing, to say that she'd forgotten us, what with getting Annie and her husband off to their new farm, that she'd evidently mixed up our wire, telling her that we were on our way, with all the wedding telegrams, and they'd all been so *excited*, and it had been a *wonderful* wedding. She had seen our woebegone faces, perhaps, because she sobered up, and asked about London, and whether people were afraid the bombing would start straightaway. She didn't wait for an answer, but whisked us off home to her small cottage, in an old cart, lent by her brother, for the occasion. I didn't care. I would have travelled in a hearse if it led somewhere, to a bath, and a bed.

After six weeks of mother and children sharing a bed and getting sick on water from the garden well, the Ranzetta family returned to London. They were not the first or the last to decide that the risk of bombardment was preferable to the tedium and hardships of country life.

Irene Boston was in the final stages of pregnancy when plans were made for her and her three children all under seven, and the newborn baby, to move from London to south Wales. They were to share the home of the mother of a university friend.

When we arrived our benefactor was horrified when she realised the baby was only 3 days old. However, we were taken in, but the only space left in the house was in a reconditioned loft room where the sky showed through in one part. The house was overflowing with refugees, mostly from London. There were no other small children. My hostess at once sought a doctor to give me a checkover, and the only one in the village she could get was a very old retired medico, blind in one eye and obviously poorly in the other, as, when he bent over me to see all was well, he said 'I see you have had your appendix out!' I was overcome with laughter as the 'scar' was only a pleat in my ample abdominal wrapping for a 10lb. son.

Within a week we were found two rooms with a kindly family connected with the railway. They had no children of their own, and during the three months I stayed there, I turned my thoughts to facing the future alone with the family.

Many businesses made their own arrangements for moving their staff to a haven outside the target areas.

As a seventeen-year-old when the war started, Wanda Handscombe was a typist with a firm of wholesale chemists on the Clerkenwell Road.

Mid-August a memorandum was sent round all the offices stating that Mr Sanger had decided that his country house at Purley, nr Pangbourne in Berkshire would be used as an office and accommodation for any of the staff that wished to be transferred in the event of war. Clerkenwell Road was a very dreary place and I, with several girls of my own age, were agog at the chance of working in what seemed then a very pleasant place. My parents were only too pleased that I should be out of London, as my brother who was then 16, was only waiting for the chance to become of age so that he could join the Navy, so my parents thought at least one of us would be safe. In those days we worked a six-day week and on Sept. 2nd, the Saturday we were told at work should war break out during the weekend we were to report on the Monday morning at Clerkenwell Road with a minimum of luggage, identity cards and of course our gas-masks.

Monday morning saw me on my way to Purley on the back of a lorry with fifty or so other girls and women, plus office equipment and our few bits and pieces; it seemed like a glorious adventure at the time, but at 17½ one does not take life too seriously and ignorance of the horrors of war played a big part too. When we arrived at Purley Park I remember it was a very hot day and everyone was directed to different rooms with jobs to do. It was the smell of new wool blankets that stays in my mind, a feeling of home-sickness when it got dark, wondering how things were going at home. I stayed there 1½ years and came home at the tail end of the blitz.

Among the institutions that were best prepared for emergency were the private sector schools. With contacts in safe areas, many of the vulnerable were relocated to new and often more congenial surroundings. The North London Collegiate School joined Luton High School. For the schoolgirls it was a great adventure worthy of an Angela Brazil novel.

On Monday the 28th of August we turned up at school laden with changes of underclothes and barley-sugar. We went up to our formrooms, heartily greeting our friends again … Only a little more than a third of the school was present. We sat in the half empty hall and were told by Miss Drummond that the order to evacuate might come through at any moment and we must always be ready.

So, all that week, we came to school in the morning after fond farewells and the hurried making of sandwiches, and all that week, until the fateful Friday, we returned home in the evening and ate our sandwiches for supper ...

On Thursday the uncertainty was ended – Friday was to be the day. The barley-sugar was hastily replenished and we said goodbye in earnest ... We marched in twos to Kentish Town Station, feeling intensely like a Sunday children's outing, or a caravan of camels. We were heartily cheered on our way by the inhabitants of Camden Town who stood at their front gates gazing sympathetically upon us and murmuring 'Cheer up, ducky' ...

We stood on the platform for about twenty minutes, feeling rather subdued and wishing that our rucksacks were not quite so heavy ... The train finally stopped at Luton, which to most of us was an unknown quantity ...

After eating our sandwiches we were examined medically and given rations for the next twenty-four hours, condensed milk, biscuits, chocolate and corned beef (one tin for girls, two for mistresses, who apparently needed extra nourishment). Then the billeting began.

The next few days were spent in getting accustomed to our strange surroundings ... We went round the museum, and learned the history of the town, and blistered our hands filling sandbags at the Emergency Hospital.

Then came the welcome news that we could share the building of the Luton High School and at last get on with our work in earnest. A time-table was drawn up, and arrangements made to play games in the park. So here we are, living a strange new life, which we are beginning to like.[2]

While so many were abandoning their homes, others returning from overseas postings were only too happy to get back to their roots. After five years' service in Malaya, Jim Potter set out from Singapore on August 25th.

> We reached Bombay and were not cheered up to find it was a 'dry' port! The passengers were depressed, to say the least, at the thought that their hard earned leave was likely to be spoilt by the war. One friend of mine on board was placed in a dilemma. He had a wife and two children and had the opportunity of two good jobs awaiting him: one in England and one in Malaya. Should he risk the lives of his wife and two children in the expected wholesale bombing of England or return with his family to the comparative safety and peace of Malaya? In the event he stayed in England and avoided captivity under the Japanese …

As soon as war was declared the look-out for enemy submarines was intensified.

> Every male passenger was once in every eight hours on duty for an hour at a time. … The ship adopted a zig zagging course and we were out of sight of land for two whole weeks. Boat drill was practised daily and we carried our life jackets at all times. Strict precautions were taken to prevent lights showing at night. In the tropics this made cabins very hot and stuffy.
>
> After a week in Cape Town for repairs we left for Freetown, zig zagging again. Convoys were collecting at Freetown, but we were fast enough to travel on alone. … As we reached the dangerous waters of the approach to the English Channel, where a number of ships had already been sunk, we attained

25 knots with the whole ship rattling. We arrived safely in mid October seven weeks and a day after leaving Singapore.

With her husband and two-year-old daughter, Kate Wilks sailed from East Africa at the end of August. They had been at sea three days when war was declared.

By this time my husband was getting worried, in case we would be separated, so he went to the barbers shop, and bought two old fashioned tobacco pouches, ones that you roll up, and were more or less waterproof. He then went to the Purser, to have his money returned, divided the notes in two lots, one for me, the other for himself, and rolled them up in the pouches. He also got a small bottle of brandy, very small indeed, and said to me, I don't know where you might land up, but if you have some money, this might help.

There were depth charges and smoke screens for much of the time and there was some damage done to our ship by a depth charge. In spite of all this the Captain still had the children's tea party and there was the usual large cake, which was really wonderful. Instead of all the lovely iced decorations the cook had decorated it with bit of veg, making a beautiful flower display.

After tea there were no fun and games on deck but members of the crew started to play with the children, which was very unusual. We found out afterwards that we had had a terrific smoke screen round us. It was a blessing that the mothers and children didn't know anything about it.

Then there was trouble with the children going down with Prickly Heat. Poor mites, they looked a terrible sight. We had a port-hole cabin, but when they had to be closed for the duration and blacked out, we were the unlucky ones, as the other cabins had electric fans. The heat was terrific when we reached the tropics, and the poor children were so unhappy. I can't remember how long the trip took, but we eventually landed then went on to Nairobi, where to my surprise the hotel was crowded with soldiers. One of them came up to me and asked if he could pick my daughter up and cuddle her, as she reminded him of his little girl left behind in England.

A Royal Marine officer on the cruiser *Orion*, Major J.H. Moxham was looking forward to a farewell party in Kingston, Jamaica before sailing for home.

That party was suddenly called off and we were ordered to sea, cruising off the Miami coast. We were in Cruising Stations, which involved one third of the guns permanently manned and in three watches. I spent four hours out of every twelve in the gun control tower at the top of the mast. At night we darkened the ship but kept navigation lights burning.

On the third night I had the first watch (20.00–midnight). At about eleven o'clock a signalman climbed up the mast, opened the hatch and handed me a signal. It read 'Admiralty to General – commence hostilities against Germany'. It made me feel I ought to get cracking, but all that happened was we put the navigation lights out and went on as before.

We stayed at sea for three months. Every so often we received a report that a German merchantman had left a nearby port. We increased to full speed but our quarry always got the tip and sneaked back. Shadowed by a US destroyer, U.S.S. *Schenk*, we exchanged friendly signals from time to time.

Once, when chasing, we closed Miami and the local boat-men made a small fortune taking holidaymakers around us at ten dollars a time – see the British Navy at War.

Interrupted holidays ended abruptly. Lianne Bridgford and two friends had just one day in Cornwall before the call came.

What had been a full hotel slowly emptied. My friends had to return north immediately – being members of the St Johns Ambulance Brigade. What should I do? My home was in Sussex, my family was on holiday in the north. Should I make my way home and stay alone till they joined me? Supposing they couldn't join me – what then? I didn't fancy being in a house, within a ¼ of a mile of the beach – alone – who knows what might land on that beach. I finally decided to stay put till I'd been in touch with the family. Trying to pretend that nothing had really happened, I went off with my surf board. It was the eeriest bathe I'd ever had – almost the entire coast-line to myself and each time I waded back I couldn't help but wonder if a German U-Boat would pop up and use me for target practice.

A Territorial officer who had spent time in Warsaw, Herbert Lloyd-Johnes was called up in May 1939 to be part of an advisory military mission to Poland. Sensitivities were such that he was not allowed to fly, since this would have meant crossing German airspace. Instead, he embarked on the *Shropshire*, a passenger liner packed with colonial service personnel on their way back to the Far and Middle East. He slept in a lifeboat. Armed with a false passport which made him out to be a musician (he could not play a note) and still holding on to his bowler hat, Lloyd-Johnes disembarked at Alexandria to be put on a plane to Athens. From there he made his way up the coast by boat and then on by train. When he eventually crossed the Polish frontier it was to hear that Germany had invaded.

> Our appearance in uniform created excitement, as the unfortunate population mistook us for an advance party of an allied army, and I was compelled to make impromptu speeches at various stations. We moved up towards Deblin near the Vistula, but could hear nothing of our mission. Trains packed with refugees from Warsaw and the north passed us frequently and the roads were crowded with vehicles moving east. We set up our wireless but could make very little contact. The German air force quartered the whole country shooting up refugees and even firing on people minding the cattle. The Polish troops we met were in good heart, but it was obvious that their army was nineteenth century, relying largely on cavalry and horse drawn transport. ...
>
> For food we lived on the country and the hospitality and kindness of the local population. After several days near Deblin we realised we must retreat to the east if capture was to be avoided. We moved back and eventually contacted the rest of the Mission at Brest-Litovsk. ... We suffered air attacks and the wife of the Passport Control Officer at Warsaw was killed.

Near Tarnopol, Lloyd-Johnes was left with two volunteer signallers to bring back the wirelesses and other stores to the frontier.

> At a small station between Tarnopol and Trembowla we lost our engine and were stranded for a night and a day. To avoid the attention of German planes we hid in a potato field. I was

not getting seriously alarmed, but after repeated requests to Trembowla, a light engine was sent up and took us down to that town.

I should have been even more alarmed had I known that Russian troops had already entered Tarnopol the morning we left. […] That evening our carriages were attached to an ammunition train, the last train to leave and we arrived in Kolymaya where an officer had been left by the Mission to meet us if we were able to make it.

We were then driven to the Mission H.Q. in the mountains of the Bukovina where I met our C.O. for the first time and learnt of the Russian invasion. I was glad I had not known how close I had been sandwiched between the Russians and the Germans. We moved towards the frontier, fires were burning behind us and the feeling of great disaster was around us. Officers and men were discarding their weapons in heaps. I changed into a mufti and took my turn at the frontier in a friend's car. We saw the Polish President and the Government cross the frontier bridge and then we followed, but our car broke down and we were pushed from behind into safety.

As a member of a mission to the French air force, William Yool spent the last week before the war in Versailles.

Our arrival had not worked out as planned. The French had arranged for us to be accommodated in a small hotel, but it was soon clear that we were far from being welcome guests. It was still nominally the height of the tourist season, and the thought that a European war was only too likely in a matter of days had either not crossed the proprietor's mind or, if it had, he was not going to allow such a detail to affect his trade.

Tourists paid full rates. We were to be billeted on him for a few francs a day. He clearly considered such a proposal an insult. In retrospect I can't altogether blame him, infuriating though his attitude was at the time. After an interminable argument, we decided to cut the Gordian knot by going to another hotel, and paying our own expenses.

By a coincidence the French had decided to move out to their wartime headquarters on the very Sunday on which war was declared. It was while lunching in a small wayside café near St Jean les deux Jumeaux, where the joint headquarters was to be located, that we heard on the wireless that Britain had declared war, to be followed in a few hours by the French.

St Jean is on the Marne, a few miles east of Meaux, and the site of the French Air headquarters there had been decided upon many months before the war started. They were to be housed in a modern monastery at the end of the village, and we were given a not so modern building hard by which had been part of the monastery. But what a part!

Never have I seen so much dust in any building, and even after we had been in it for several months puffs of grey dust arose whenever a window or door was banged. Numerous cupboards held piles of musty papers and one felt that it would not have been surprising to come across an equivalent of the Sinai Codex at any moment.

The ruthless methods of a nation in the throes of a general mobilisation were well illustrated in St Jean. The village was in the *Zone des Armées* and hence subject to military law. In order to provide accommodation for the joint headquarters and ourselves, all the local inhabitants, including the monks, had been evacuated at a moment's notice and it was literally a deserted village in which we found ourselves.

The houses had been left fully furnished with most of the previous occupants' goods and chattels still in place. What had happened to the inhabitants we never found out, and although we did not actually find kettles boiling on the hob or half-eaten meals on the tables there was a *Mary Celeste* air about it all.

The buildings allotted to us included a summer villa occupying a lovely position on the high ground to the south of the village. The main living room had a large picture window entirely filling one end. There was a wonderful view to the north through the window of the Marne valley and the peaceful French countryside stretching in the distance, where the twin towers of the ancient abbey at Soissons could be seen on the horizon about twenty miles away.

One of Yool's principal memories of those times was of the long working day of the French peasant.

Shortly after our arrival the beet harvest was in full swing, and, from long before daylight to long after dark every day, the jingling of the horses' harness and the creaking axles of the farm carts could be heard from the fields surrounding the villa.

Another poignant memory was of the incessant rumble throughout the nights of the slow-moving trains taking the troops to the front. But the immediate worry was of setting up communications.

Before leaving England we had been told that when we moved into the headquarters at St Jean we should find a direct telephone connection to the Air Ministry. So after luncheon on this peaceful Sunday, having formally taken over our quarters in the morning, we started to look for this telephone line.

The main building and its surroundings were in a state of chaos, lorries arriving with cupboards, papers, and various stores and being unloaded, with crowds of men bustling in and out of the buildings and getting in each other's way with their loads. No one seemed to be in control and confusion appeared to be general.

Eventually we found our way into a large room where the telephone exchange was in process of being installed. The room was a mass of wires, with numerous excitable Frenchmen dashing about in seemingly uncontrolled disorder.

The prospects of establishing communication with the Air Ministry from the midst of this chaos appeared remote, but at length we espied a corporal in French Air Force uniform who seemed to be in charge of the proceedings. Approaching him we enquired tentatively about our line. At first our French did not seem to make much impression, but suddenly a look of comprehension dawned on his face.

He produced a portable field telephone of ancient pattern and dashed into the maze of wires, which to us looked as though they were in inextricable confusion. Seizing two of the wires he clipped his ancient instrument to them and turned the handle vigorously. Then turning to us with a look of triumph on his face he shouted 'Air Ministree', and gave me the instrument. The 'miracle' had happened.

CHAPTER 7

Women and Children First

The wholesale evacuation of women and children had first appeared on the agenda of the Committee of Imperial Defence in 1931. At this point, the chief consideration was to guard against panic flight. Such was the fear of mass bombing, it was assumed that from London alone, 3.5 million or 75 per cent of the population would have to be relocated to safe areas. But while there was much talk of the need for a blueprint, it was not until mid-1938 that the Home Office began to face up to the hard questions such as how to maintain a balance between saving families and keeping up an industrial production essential to the war effort. The broad plan was for Britain to be divided into evacuation, neutral and reception areas, the boundaries set by estimates of probable targets. Just how easy it was to get it wrong is suggested by the designation of three cities, Plymouth, Bristol and Swansea, later heavily bombed, as safe areas suitable for evacuation. Neutral areas could neither take nor send evacuees. Then again, if priority was to be given to mothers with young children, where were these migrants to be accommodated?

House-to-house checks by volunteers identified 'surplus accommodation' for 4.8 million people, but this gross over-estimate was almost certainly accounted for by untrained assessors hearing what they wanted to hear. The reality was a housing shortage in country areas where existing accommodation was just as likely to be sub-standard as in towns. Provision for receiving and accommodating evacuees did not appear on any local authority budget.

The hope that rural households would put out a welcome mat was an unsafe assumption, given the middle-class angst at having what a county councillor described as 'the dregs of London' dumped on their doorsteps. Or to quote a not untypical Devon farmer: 'We don't want 'em here and we can't do with 'em.'

The order was given on August 31st, 1939 for evacuation to start the following day. Nearly 1.5 million mothers and children took part in what the minister of health called 'an exodus bigger than that of Moses'. It included 826,959 unaccompanied schoolchildren, 523,670 mothers with pre-schoolchildren and 12,705 expectant mothers. Over three days, 12,000 volunteer helpers supervised embarkation on to 3,000 buses and 4,000 special trains. When it was all over, the gentle-men in Whitehall, setting aside their maps, timetables and slide rules, were able to give themselves a pat on the back for an administration job well done. The fault lines were easily forgotten, as too was the most important question – not whether the evacuation was done well or badly but whether it should have been done at all.

Whether or not to leave home was a matter for family choice. The take-up varied across the country. The government's call to 'get the children away' met with a 35 per cent response from those eligible in London but only 24 per cent in Liverpool. Manchester did better than Portsmouth and Southampton, while Leeds was twice as successful as Sheffield. When the numbers came to be counted, the only safe generalisation was that poorer families with limited education were most likely to accept instructions – not always sensitively expressed – to evacuate. In total only half the expected numbers turned up at the assembly points, a fact which may help to explain why the administration was smoother than might otherwise have been expected.

With exquisite timing, the compilation of the 1939 Register – when, on September 29th, 65,000 enumerators visited every house in England and Wales to put together a national profile – took place well *after* the start of the evacuation. Not surprisingly, what was dubbed *The Wartime Domesday Book* showed that just under 2 per cent of London's population was under the age of ten as against a national average of 14 per cent, while 8 per cent was aged ten to nineteen against 16 per cent nationally. A demonstration of the impact made by evacuation shows up in the gender split in the big cities. In London it was 60 per cent male to 40 per cent female, compared to 47 per cent to 53 per cent nationally.

Among the oddities thrown up was the identity of a Birmingham jewellery case-maker who had the misfortune to be named Hermann Goering. The places most heavily loaded with retirees and with those who had taken themselves off to safe areas were Tavistock, Glastonbury, Looe, Newquay, Woodstock, Brixham, Torpoint, Knighton, Herne Bay and Dawlish.

Overall, and hardly a surprise, the data collected on 40 million individuals reveals a socially conservative, class-bound manufacturing nation.

It is said that the 1939 Register gave an essential framework to the allocation of ration books and identity cards and to the management of conscription and reserved occupations. But with so many changed addresses in the second half of 1939, how much more valuable the survey would have been had it been carried out earlier in the year.

CAME THE DAY of the evacuation, urban railway stations were alive with the sound of chattering children. After being held on standby for over a week, parents, teachers and the army of volunteer helpers were keen to get going. Their charges, identified by armbands or labels tied round their necks, were equally impatient and liable to be fretful. The logic of the exercise was not always apparent to those in the reception areas. Living in Worthing, Joan Strange heard on the radio news that London schoolchildren were to be evacuated the following day (September 1st).

> Worthing is to expect 13,000. Terrible, as it makes war seem nearer. Surely it *can't* happen? It's dreadful to think that the 'victors' will be those who use most effectively the most diabolical instruments of death as quickly as possible ... The papers are very depressing – all the pictures are of soldiers – sandbags – ARP city girls evacuating from their offices – guns, aeroplanes and so on.

A few days later:

> Worthing, being a safe zone, has had to billet over 10,000 evacuees from London. On Saturday afternoon Schofield and I helped billet some Bermondsey blind people. We both felt how terrible it was that so much money, time and trouble was taken to help these poor, old, blind people, while we sent healthy, young, virile people to be killed.[1]

The best-laid plans fell to inadequate provision at the start of the journey or at the end or at some point in between. Some trains had carriages without corridors which also meant they were without lavatories. This caused problems for 400 mothers and children under five who were sent from Liverpool to Pwllheli, a distance of some 120 miles. On a non-corridor train from Paddington to Somerset, the guard was persuaded to allow an emergency stop at Wantage in Berkshire.

The quality of the reception for evacuees depended on the efficiency and generosity of local authorities. Some, a minority, were ready with transport laid on to outlying areas, talks to prospective foster parents on children from different backgrounds, and plans for slotting the newcomers into appropriate schools. The prospect for most children was much grimmer. Lined up in a church or village hall, they were viewed by hostile or, at best, reluctant householders who were invited to take their pick. An evacuation officer at West Hartlepool described 'scenes reminiscent of a cross between an early Roman slave market and Selfridges' bargain basement'.

Children who were neatly dressed and scrubbed clean had the best chance of finding a hospitable billet. Out of luck were the offspring of families where the breadwinner was on a low wage or no wage at all. They came without a change of clothing in shoddy footwear showing all the signs of living hand-to-mouth. Where hostels were provided there was invariably a shortage of beds, blankets and cooking equipment. Councils blamed the government for its parsimony. It was not until six days before the outbreak of war that local authorities were permitted to incur 'such expenditure as is necessary for the reception of evacuated persons'.

The privations extended to the adult escorts. Mrs. K.H. Elsmore, a teacher at a school in Southampton, accompanied her pupils to Milford-on-Sea.

Official instructions were issued forbidding large numbers of children congregating at one place, and as no schooling had as yet been organised, we spent many hours in warm sunshine on the beach, or blackberry picking. As the children had not expected to have sea bathing, the costumes for this were very unconventional.

After three days my friend and I were billeted at a guest

house with broken furniture and poor food, but we were eventually able to go to a family who wished to have teachers, and for the remainder of the time we lived in a friendly home.

Schooling for our pupils was arranged later by alternating morning and afternoon sessions with the local school. At some time in these early days it became apparent that the small tooth comb had to be used (against lice), in spite of careful medical examinations taken before evacuation. The other Domestic Science teacher and myself were the unlucky ones to deal with this. We purchased cheap white overalls and yards of white calico with which to cover our heads completely, and bottles of disinfectant. This was one aspect of it all we never imagined would be our lot, but in cramped and somewhat unhygienic conditions, we managed to deal with this unpleasant task, cheering each other as best we could.

When others were dealing with more or less normal lessons, permission was given to the Domestic Science teachers to provide a midday dinner for our pupils.

Mrs Elsmore paid tribute to members of the Women's Institute who fitted out their hall with large gas stoves and cooking utensils. The senior girls took turns with the cooking but all the serving, cleaning away and dish-washing was done by voluntary helpers.

Yet more critical to the general administration was the work of the Women's Voluntary Service. Led by the Marchioness of Reading, widow of a one-time viceroy of India, the WVS was set up in 1938 at the behest of the home secretary who put out a call for 'large numbers of women ... for first aid, ambulance drivers, for clerical work' and to act as wardens – though, in the event, the public face of the ARP was almost exclusively male. Even in dire emergency, having lone women out on the streets was beyond the pale.

Lady Reading was a *grande dame* whose autocratic tendencies led
to many social misjudgements but her organising talents were never
in doubt. With a regional structure soon in place the WVS had over
a thousand centres and over 300,000 members, mostly middle-aged,
middle-class housewives, by the summer of 1939. When the evacuation got under way the WVS was an active participant in almost every
reception committee, with a vital role in finding billets, organising
transport and providing food and extra clothing.

In Huntingdonshire, now a rural division of Cambridgeshire, the
WVS took on the brunt of the responsibility for relocating around
6,000 evacuees from across London.

The morning after war was declared, the WVS began providing meals at the Corn Exchange and on the following
day 128 mothers and children were reported to be eating
there. Palliasses were ready to be stuffed with straw, some
emergency clothing was in stock and facilities were soon in
place for those with special needs, such as the sick, young
children – there was a 'short-stay home for toddlers' – and
women who were pregnant or had just given birth. Empty
houses were found 'for mothers or children who could not
be billeted in the ordinary way' and, according to a write-up
from mid-October 1939, 'buyers have combed out second-
hand shops for miles in search of furniture, or have laid
in stocks of new goods before these disappeared from the
market'. A social centre for evacuated mothers and children
was quickly up and running in Huntingdon, and there and
in the neighbouring town of St Ives bathing and laundry
facilities were made available for the newcomers. ... A social
worker was hired to support young single women, including nurses, evacuated teachers, hostel staff and teenage

schoolgirls away from home, and to arrange suitable rec-
reations. Communal feeding centres for evacuees were
opened in both Huntingdon and St Ives; such centres (and
they cropped up in many other places) usually provided hot
mid-day dinners and thereby avoided forcing 'foster mothers'
and others accommodating strangers to take on additional
cooking burdens.[2]

At Hinchingbrooke Castle, near Huntingdon, the Earl and Countess
of Sandwich shared their home with a Dockland Settlements nursery
school from Canning Town.

But smooth administration was a rarity. The town of Dagenham
was evacuated by coastal shipping. When the steamers arrived at
Yarmouth, Lowestoft and Felixstowe, the reception committees were
shocked by the numbers of children offloaded. Schools were converted into temporary hostels where the guests, children and adults,
slept on beds of straw and lived on milk, apples and cheese for several
days before billets could be found.[3] Patience soon ran out and tolerant
understanding soon gave way to angry prejudice.

It might have been otherwise had the bombs fallen. The community spirit of pulling together to meet a national catastrophe must
surely have overcome the problems of social disruption. As it was, a
plan that was not intended to operate in peaceful conditions came
up against a lack of resources and an excess of ill-feeling caused by
what was soon judged to be a pointless exercise.

Douglas Whitehead and his cousin Dennis were among the lucky
ones. They started their evacuation adventure from Lyndhurst Grove
primary school in south-east London.

It seemed that the order to prepare to march off spread more
quickly among the parents in their homes than among the

children in the playgrounds, for, by the time the classes had been grouped together and heads had been counted, all the adults in the borough (or so it seemed) had gathered round the iron gates of the school and along the route to the station. It was like the Coronation all over again, except that the procession emerging like a serpent from the school gates, burdened with luggage and indignantly labelled felt far from regal. Nevertheless, the crowd, waving and photographing, might have come straight from the events of 1937.

On the train, Douglas and Dennis shared a compartment and a tube of Rolo with six other boys.

There was Bates who died in a road accident a few months later, and Harris who went home at the height of the blitz and was killed the same night. There was Ken Richards, son of a theatrical family who had just been on holiday to Germany and was regarded as worldly-wise. He joined his parents in Liverpool in 1940.

The first stop was Sevenoaks in Kent where the children were put on buses for the three-mile journey to the village of Seal by the North Downs. It was there that they began to discover how the other half lived.

At the school, ladies of obviously refined backgrounds took charge, and the children, waiting in the playground, were intrigued when they each received a paper carrier bag containing many wonderful goodies such as chocolate, corned beef and biscuits. ... By the time the distribution had finished a number of cars, driven by more 'posh' ladies, some of whom were obviously WVS, had arrived, and, a few at a time, the children were whisked away. Where they went to, no-one seemed to know. ... Far more exciting was the prospect of a ride in a motor car, a rare treat for most in those days. ... It was driven by a refined young lady in tweeds who remarked, quite casually, 'Oh yes, my husband gave it to me as a birthday present'. A car for a birthday present!

The two boys were dropped off at a large double-fronted house at the end of a short terrace of cottages.

The door was opened by a very upright, grey haired lady of middle age. 'These are your evacuees, Miss Greagsbey,' said the car owner.

It was the start of an idyllic year when the boys discovered the pleasures of the countryside.

Bushes covered in black-berries growing by the very roadside, and real acorns on real oak trees, and fallow deer roaming wild in Knole Park. Much of this was seen on the rambles organised to keep the evacuees amused and to allow their foster parents to catch up on domestic duties. There was no sign of school work, though the rambles were led by a retired teacher. It even seemed huge fun when he conducted air raid practices, roaring 'Scatter!', while the children ran off and lay prone in the bracken, giggling.

It was not generally thus. Settling in to new homes was liable to open a chapter of disasters. At the start, dissent was held in check by warnings that an attack, if not immediate, could happen at any time. But as the weeks and months passed there were signs of another sort of disaster in the making.

> In many parts of Britain, children went for months without education and medical supervision; the school dental service closed down, eye defects were uncorrected and children remained in need of glasses, speech defect classes were suspended, the special schools for handicapped children, cripples and heart cases were disastrously affected, maternity and child welfare clinics were commandeered for civil defence purposes, sick people were unable to get into hospital and the number of children receiving school meals dropped steeply. Even the milk industry faced a minor crisis owing to the disorganisation of the urban market for milk (a consequence of evacuation), and a sharp fall in the consumption of milk at schools. By the end of 1939, for instance, the quantity of milk used in schools had fallen by over a third in England and Wales, and by nearly half in Scotland.[4]

Rural householders were loud in their complaints at being landed with ungrateful or, even worse, unclean denizens of city life. For their part, the uninvited guests were soon bored by the quiet of the countryside, though there were cases where tough young boys from the slums took easily and enthusiastically to farm work. Looking on the bright side, officials spoke of the beneficial effects of fresh country air, with boys and girls from deprived backgrounds losing their pale complexions and putting on weight.

But the downside could not be denied. Class differences were highlighted when London Cockneys had to adapt to middle-class manners. A friend of the drama critic James Agate wrote to him from the country: 'There are six evacuated children in our house.

My wife and I hate them so much that we have decided to take away something from them for Christmas!'

From York came a report of evacuees from Durham:

> Though provided with knife, fork and spoon, they insist on eating everything with their fingers. Further, they refuse to keep in bed. They will sleep under it, or anywhere else on the floor; but beds, they say, are for dead people – and they aren't going to be laid out yet.

The anti-hero of Evelyn Waugh's novel of the early part of the war, *Put Out More Flags*, had the profitable idea of semi-adopting a primitive family of migrants whom he landed on unsuspected retired couples until they paid to have him take them away. Like all the best fiction, it was uncomfortably close to the truth.

There were frequent complaints from the less well-off who had little enough accommodation of their own that while they were expected to take in evacuees, those with large houses and large incomes were by-passed by the billeting authorities.

In some areas, opposition to billeting reached the verge of mutiny. In January 1940 a party of schoolchildren evacuated from London to Woking were sent back because no billets could be found for them. At once the Ministry of Health said that if the local council did not use its compulsory billeting powers the ministry would assume control. The council made another appeal to its householders, with little effect. Residents interviewed by the *Woking News* said they were unable to go out to tea because of the children, that children ought to be kept in hostels, that 'we did not have all this fuss in the last war when the Zeppelins bombed London', that 'you can't put a pint in a pint pot when it's half-full', that Woking was too convenient for sponging parents to visit, that meters and telephone boxes had been rifled by children, and that the town was already sheltering a large number of privately-educated families.

There were happier stories of the upper classes reaching out. Sir John Hammerton, who kept a diary of the first sixteen months of the war, tells of two East End boys billeted in a country mansion waiting impatiently for their breakfast.

At the top of the table sat the elderly *Châtelaine* and behind her stood the butler. When it looked as if they were going to be late for school, one of the lads said to the butler: 'When's that bloody breakfast coming?' The old lady said: 'I'm so glad you have said that. I have been wanting to say it for years.'[5]

If there is a stretching of the truth here, we might blame the newspapers where prizes were offered for the best evacuee stories. These usually revolved on the mismatch of deprived children and their middle-class foster parents. One of the most quoted was that of a couple who found their two billeted youngsters lying at the extreme edges of the bed with an empty space between them. When asked why, they said, 'Well, where are youse yins going to sleep?'

To this must be added that working-class families were just as likely, if not more likely, to have children billeted on them. There were still misunderstandings but these generally related to city children being unfamiliar with the countryside. 'The house I am in is a very nice place,' wrote a child to his parents, 'only there's a manure heap on the roof'; a reasonable conclusion for one who had never before seen thatch.

There are stories of relationships forged for a lifetime. Barbara Martin and her school friend Margaret had to take pot luck when they were evacuated to Horsham in Sussex.

At the gate a lady in a mauve coat was just leaving with her bicycle. We were 'handed over' and Miss Ireland, who was apparently our wartime foster mother, turned and led us into the house. Introductions were brief, we were shown our room, and then invited to explore the garden by ourselves. About an acre, a small orchard, a huge lawn, trees at the bottom and to our joy the River Arun. Only shallow, but ten minutes later Margaret was soaking wet and muddy having fallen in because I wanted to know how deep it was. We laughed, but then, what if *she* turned us out, where would we go? Rather scared we returned to the house and were greeted with only understanding, a bowl of hot water and soap, and a suggestion to get cleaned up before Mr Ireland (he was Miss Ireland's uncle and she was his housekeeper-companion – he had lost his wife a few months previously) arrived home for lunch in a few minutes.

And so began for Margaret 11 months and for me 20 months of happiness with our wartime 'Uncle' and 'Auntie'. No fuss, no spoiling, but the security of being members of their family, sharing the chores, sharing their pleasures, and knowing we were loved and wanted.

It's true our formal schooling suffered – through nobody's fault during most of this time we were about 70 boys and girls from 6 to 16 altogether in the St John Ambulance Hall, but we gained another and more valuable education in living with our foster family.

It came as a surprise to the Home Office to find that so few of the 4 million city dwellers who qualified for evacuation had taken advantage of the scheme. Even more of a surprise to the organisers was the speed with which disillusionment set in, causing a mass return to the danger zones. No matter how often it was said that the bombs might fall at any moment, dire predictions were no cure for homesickness. By Christmas, in the London and Liverpool areas, about two-thirds of the evacuated children were back with their parents, while 80 per cent of mothers with infants had returned home. Elsewhere the figure was never less than one half. It turned out that the proportion of children returning to the poor areas of east London was higher than that to the better-off districts of west London.

Dealing as they did with people as if they were units on a balance sheet, the bureaucrats were unable to grasp the possible traumatic effect of being sent away from the family circle, in most cases for the first time in a child's life.

> The whole of the child's life, its hopes and fears, its dependence for affection and social development on the checks and balances of home life, and all the deep emotional ties that bound it to its parents, were suddenly disrupted. From the first day of September 1939 evacuation ceased to be a problem of administrative planning. It became instead a multitude of problems in human relationships.[6]

By the end of December, over 1 million children had been without education, health services, school meals and milk for over four months. Eileen Potter, an evacuation officer with the London County Council, argued convincingly that the 'neglect of education may prove a greater danger to civilisation than the falling of a few bombs'.[7]

The extent of the crisis is revealed in a report sent in by the inspector of education in Devon.

> The main difficulty here is the mother. She has been put into a completely new environment away from the freedom and

responsibilities of her own home. There is a lack of organisation and definite objective in her life. She has no husband to care for and more often than not she is accepted as a necessity, but not welcomed in the billeting household. It follows that all sorts of restrictions will prevail both for her and for her children. Living in a billet is almost equivalent to being cooped up in part of a house. The children, who need activity and interest, are confined to one, or perhaps two, rooms. They cannot run in and out about the house, as the householder expects them to stay in their own quarters. Free use of the garden is very often resented. It is very difficult for the mother to clean the rooms with the children there all the time. More difficult still for her to get the necessary washing done, and not at all easy to cook, as she will have her children running around the kitchen. These conditions create a very bad psychological disturbance both for mothers and children. They become difficult, the children cry and are irritable, and the nervous energy of the mother is sapped. …

And this from the Hertfordshire inspector of education:

Hostesses do not as a rule consider the payment by the government of 5s. a week for the mother and 3s. for the child as covering more than the bare bedroom accommodation and the result was that the evacuees found themselves virtually homeless during the day, with no facilities for bathing the children, for washing or ironing their clothes, or even for providing them with a properly cooked meal. In many cases they were expected to do these things in their bedroom. It is known that one mother takes her child once a week by workman's train to London for a real bath, another takes all her washing back once a fortnight to be done at the public wash house in her own neighbourhood. The children themselves have very little done for them. There are a few toys for which they can scramble and fight, there is a very small gravelled yard where they can play between the perambulators. Indoors there are no small chairs or tables and no beds for rest or sleep. There is no peace or confidence here for the children to build upon. They are out-of-hand, nervous and fretful, lacking sleep, proper nourishing food, regular milk and medical attention, and they are for the most part under-clothed.[8]

THERE WAS ONE group of young evacuees who could not return home however much they missed their parents. These were the mostly Jewish children of the *Kindertransporte*, sent away to Britain by their families in Germany and Czechoslovakia as a last resort against Nazi persecution.

The *Kindertransporte* had its origins in late 1938 when a deputation of Jewish notables, led by Viscount Samuel, called on the home secretary, Sir Samuel Hoare. Hoare was a Quaker with a Quaker's conscience. He knew something of refugee problems and sympathised with their plight. When Viscount Samuel urged the admission of an unspecified number of youngsters, promising that they would not be a charge on public funds and that all of them would eventually re-emigrate, Hoare responded sympathetically. Persuading his Cabinet colleagues to share his concern was more problematic. Nervous of creating problems in Palestine – the only practical second step for the young émigrés – Chamberlain adopted 'a rather negative tone'. But, the following day, when the subject came up at a Cabinet meeting, Halifax provided an argument strong enough to counterbalance the Palestinian factor. He voiced concern that not enough was being done to persuade America that Britain was worth supporting. With a European war increasingly likely, it was time, as Halifax put it, for 'a lead which would force the United States to take some positive action'. That Britain might act as a 'temporary refuge' for those fleeing Nazi oppression was an obvious first thought and Hoare was asked to draft a statement on government action 'to deal with the Jewish problem'.

An open-door policy was still considered impracticable but there was room for compromise on an offer to make special provision for young people. On the morning of November 21st, 1938, just a few hours before a critical House of Commons debate on refugee policy, Hoare met Sir Wyndham Deedes, chairman of the Inter-Aid Committee. Among the ideas discussed was the formation of a new organisation to cope with the rush of applications that would inevitably follow a relaxation of the immigration laws. This organisation was to be called the Movement for the Care of Children from Germany, soon to be known simply as the Refugee Children's Movement (RCM).

In the subsequent Commons debate Hoare gave a clear commitment 'to facilitate entry for all child refugees whose maintenance could be guaranteed either through their own funds or by other individuals'. To ease the bureaucratic process a special travel document, to be issued in London, removed the need for passports or visas.

So began an exodus from German territories that was to save 10,000 children in the ten months up to the outbreak of war. The children came over in groups of between 100 and 600, mostly despatched from Berlin or Vienna by train to the Dutch border, where refugee workers fed them sweets and cheered them up before taking them to the Hook of Holland to be ferried across to Harwich.

A target of 10,000 was adopted by the government as the maximum that could be supported by voluntary effort. Attempts in the United States to emulate the British with a bill to admit 20,000 European children did not get beyond a congressional committee. One of the arguments raised against the proposal held that accepting children without their parents was contrary to the laws of God.

Vera Coppard left Berlin in May 1939. She was thirteen.

> Mother couldn't bear to come to the station. I went with my father. There was a terrible scene when they were shouting out the names of the children. There was one woman who was very agitated and when her children were not on the list she became hysterical. The guards hit her with clubs and knocked her to the ground. Then we were handed on to the platform. I just had time to say goodbye to my father. My former nanny, who had married one of father's patients, managed to get on to the platform, I don't know how. She threw oranges through the carriage window.
>
> The journey was terrible. At stations all along the way, parents had gathered to catch a last glimpse of their children. I'm glad my family didn't do that.

Vera went to a Quaker school in Cornwall and a short time later to a school in Letchworth. Meanwhile, her mother was arrested in Berlin.

> She was a very attractive woman and the senior Nazi officer who interrogated her took a liking to her and said that he would have her released if she would go to bed with him. She said that if he could get tickets to England for herself and her husband she would do what he wanted. But when the tickets came through she sent a message saying that she was ill and that she was going to the mountains to convalesce. Instead she went straight to the airport and flew to England.

She was followed by Vera's father who arrived on September 1st. Denied recognition as a doctor, he was taken on as a cleaner at the Cumberland Hotel. Then he was allowed to work as a medical orderly in Newquay Hospital, looking after soldiers who were injured in the First World War.

By then the *Kindertransporte* were well under way. The first transports had arrived in the early days of December 1938. The *De Praag* docked at Harwich on the 2nd with over 200 children, mostly survivors of a Berlin orphanage burnt down by stormtroopers. Ten days later a transport arrived from Vienna with another 200 children. Thereafter there were at least two children's transports a week until the movement reached its peak in June and July 1939, with transports arriving daily and all but overwhelming the organisers. Bea Green, from Munich, remembers her escape:

We spend what is left of the night in some big hall in Frankfurt where a lot more children join us and then we're off to the Hook van Holland. We come to the border of Holland and before leaving Germany we have to show our passports with the letter 'J' stamped on the front page in red. Also I have been given another name. I am now Maria Beate Sarah Siegel. I rather like it. I think it's nice that all the other girls are also called Sarah. The border guards look at our passports. I am a bit nervous because my mother has hidden a couple of extra ten mark notes wrapped up in one of my sandwiches. It's all right. The border guard is not interested in my sandwiches. More puffing and hissing of the engine and we are in Holland.

At our first stop there a team of big and very kind ladies comes on to the train with fresh orange juice and very white bread and butter. The bread is soft and delicious. I am surprised that the ladies are so very kind. I don't know any of them. The train moves on and I see my first windmill. I am pleased that they are real and not just in story books. I must tell my mother, I think. And then it hits me – I won't be seeing her to tell her these things.

It's night time when we get to the ship. We sleep in bunks and arrive in Harwich at dawn. I cannot find all my luggage. I have more cases than originally stipulated. I don't know why the Munich authorities let me take more. I have to use my English now to ask an official about these cases. I wish I didn't have to. But I find them in another hall and feel triumphant and – and tired, both. A little girl cries and keeps repeating 'Mutti, Mutti'. I put my arm round her and tell her she'll see her soon. Then we have to get on to our train bound for London, Liverpool Street. Funny name, I think: *Lebeteich*.

Memories of early days are of bewilderment at strange sights – small houses in different colours, front gardens, buses but no trams, pennies and half-crowns, lattice windows, open fires and smoking chimneys. Driven through Harwich on a double-decker bus, itself a new experience, a girl on the lower deck found herself looking out at a bookshop window. She recognised just one title among the books on display – *Mein Kampf*. My God, she thought, what have I come to?

The children were from Berlin, Hamburg, Munich, Frankfurt, Düsseldorf, Vienna and Prague. A few had relatives in Britain ready to take them in, but the rest went to hostels or were farmed out to foster parents or boarding schools. It was a new beginning with a new language; the start of a mounting succession of powerful and often bewildering demands on their capacity to adapt and survive.

With the approach of hostilities, two to three thousand of them had to be dispatched from urban Britain into the countryside, their second dramatic upheaval within months. Fourteen hostels were evacuated *en masse*. No child could be expected to welcome evacuation but for refugee children the experience was particularly painful. Even those who had arrived in early 1939 or before did not as yet have complete command of English and this made communication with their new and sometimes reluctant hosts difficult. In rural areas the heavy regional accents added to the problem. Those who suffered most were children placed in remote districts where strangers were automatically suspect. Magda Chadwick experienced this thinly veiled hostility:

> Having a smattering of English, I went to the Lake District near Grange-over-Sands (Cartmel). We went to the village hall and you stood there and people came and chose you. If your face fitted. They let brothers and sisters stay together and I stood with two sisters who were very kind to me. They asked if we were a family and I said, 'No, but I would like to be with them'. So the two girls went to a couple of spinsters who said that the farm next door needed a girl. But they got me there to be a housemaid. They asked me to wash the kitchen floor. I said I had never done it and I wasn't going to start.
>
> I lived in the farmhouse. The country wasn't my style. I am a town person. There were no mod cons. The two sisters had a croquet lawn at their place – it was luck of the draw. *I* had to deliver the milk. In the dark, carrying two milk cans, I walked right into the wall because there was no light and I didn't know where I was going.

Young refugees who had to wait for a suitable foster home to be found for them were put into hostels or housed at two former holiday camps, one at Dovercourt, a small seaside town just along the coast from Harwich, the other further away at Pakefield, near Lowestoft.

Holiday camps were part of the mass leisure movement of the 1920s and 1930s. Inspired by the campaign for annual paid holidays, 'luxury' camps provided family holidays – 'a week's holiday for a week's pay' – for an all-in price. The two pioneers were Harry Warner and Billy Butlin who prided themselves on giving value for money, and certainly better value than the average seaside boarding house. Before long, most popular coastal resorts had a holiday camp on its outskirts. Some were of massive size. The Butlin's at Skegness was able to accommodate 4,000 guests a week.[9]

The model for a typical holiday camp – with its lines of wooden chalets and commodious dining rooms with kitchens designed for mass catering – caught the interest of the armed forces and of the Home Office, the latter in search of accommodation for evacuees. In January 1939, a Camps Bill providing for 50 wartime evacuation centres was approved by Parliament. Harry Warner and Billy Butlin were hired by the Ministry of Supply to advise on building military and civilian camps. Objections from class-conscious local residents and from hoteliers fearful of losing business were summarily rejected and planning regulations overridden. In working for the government, the two holiday camp entrepreneurs held on to their business sense, negotiating to buy the new sites from the state once the war was over.

Dovercourt is the best documented of the holiday camps taken over for young refugees. An Essex coastal village in the 1930s (now part of Harwich), Dovercourt was favoured as a retirement home for those who enjoyed stiff breezes and bracing walks. From the seafront up to a mile inland was an uninterrupted expanse of tall grass and fern, the delight of ramblers. In the wet months it could turn into a quagmire.

Lines of tiny chalets were fronted by pebble-dash walls and mock Tudor porches, copies of the latest fashion in middle-class suburbia.

The hint of quality did not allow for heating and surface drainage, but neither were strictly essential in the summer months.

When the first *Kindertransport* arrived at Dovercourt, it was cold but dry. The children's immediate reaction was a sense of relief at having arrived somewhere. Then there was the excitement of finding out about this strange miniature town with its open view of the North Sea over the mud flats.

Celia Lee's first impression of Dovercourt was roses. 'I couldn't believe it: roses in wintertime! It made a strong impact on me. What a beautiful country.' Others remember the green of the countryside.

In the way children have of promoting the incidental to matters of vital importance, settling in was a flurry of inconsequential activity. When Johnny Blunt was given his pocket money, he immediately went off and bought a tin of pineapple.

That was my first purchase in England. But how to open it? One of the other boys had a penknife and it took us about half an hour to get at the pineapple. But it was worth it.

There was curiosity and wonderment at those features of life that went unremarked by the natives but to foreigners were so eccentric, and so quintessentially British, like porridge and kippers for breakfast, 'a peculiar liquid which looked like coffee, tasted like poison and was said to be tea', and bottles of HP sauce and vinegar on the dining table.

The greatest deprivation was German sausage, made more intense for one boy who had brought a whole salami all the way from Vienna only to have it thrown away by a Dovercourt helper 'because it didn't smell right'.

A reporter visiting Dovercourt a week after arrival of the first *Kindertransport* had nothing but praise for the organisation.

Everybody I saw was dressed in the warmest clothes ... and all the children are given plenty of blankets to keep them warm at night ... Some were playing table tennis, some darts (it was amusing to watch their efforts at this game, which was entirely new to them) ... In a side room there were several surrounding a piano which was being played by a youngster of about ten.

But it did not take a sharp journalistic instinct to realise that for refugees – particularly young refugees – life could never be that simple.

Closer observation revealed here a group of three little girls, one with a doll clutched to her, seated quite silently in a corner, and there a boy rubbing his eyes furtively.

In the weeks ahead the loneliness would intensify.

For the first time in its history, Dovercourt was news. Though some newspapers harped on the theme of 'charity begins at home', the general line was to stress the benefits of taking in such 'lively, sturdily-built and intelligent' children. *Picture Post* thought the young refugees would be a credit to Britain:

They will be trained ... to become farmers and farm-workers, artisans, plumbers, builders, electricians. Many of the girls will become nurses, maids or farm assistants.

Around Christmas the cold became so intense that children slept in their sweaters or coats. 'Four of us shared a double bed,' recalls Margot Barnes. 'When one said "turn" we all turned.' There were nights when stone hot-water bottles left out on the floor froze solid. Top blankets were nearly always damp.

In the last weeks of December, Pakefield had to be evacuated. Two hundred and fifty children were moved to St Felix's Girls' School in Southwold, where the staff gave up their holiday to help look after their guests. The luxury of single cubicles and warm beds lasted until the end of the first week of January when the regular boarders returned. Then it was back to Lowestoft and a new set of problems.

After the snow came the rain. One night the water in the gullies flooded over into the chalets. Children were carried shoulder-high to the road, where a bus took them to a seafront hotel. They spent the night sleeping on the ballroom floor. After that it was boys only at Pakefield. The girls went to Dovercourt. Not that conditions there were very much better. The chalets on the lower ground nearest the beach were liable to flood and more than once young children had to be lifted from their beds in the middle of the night.

Parcels of food and clothing started arriving at Dovercourt. There were shoes and coats from Marks & Spencer, the National Sporting Club sent a pair of boxing gloves, and an Essex butcher provided beef sausages for all, once a week. Free tickets at the Harwich Electric Cinema provided a welcome diversion from camp routine, not to mention a painless method of learning English. News of Dovercourt travelled abroad. One day a trunk-load of winter woollens turned up, a gift from Johannesburg where a news item in the local paper had inspired a ladies' circle to start knitting.

But however welcome, such generosity did not help solve the central problem which was to find suitable homes for the children. Every Sunday, prospective foster parents gathered at Dovercourt to view the inmates. It was a distressing ritual but, given the pressure to move the children out of the camp so that others could take their places, nobody was able to come up with a better alternative to 'the market'.

CHAPTER 8

At the Edge

Having lost the peace, Chamberlain now put his mind to losing the war. Few could visualise him leading the nation into battle, yet Chamberlain seems not to have suffered any self-doubt. With a thumping parliamentary majority and surrounded by acolytes who could hardly deny him without denying themselves, he proceeded almost as if the declaration of war was simply a hitch in the natural order of things.

A modest reshuffling of the administration in September 1939 was noteworthy for returning Churchill to his old job as First Lord of the Admiralty. Chamberlain could not abide Churchill. He thought him arrogant (the old saying about the pot and the kettle springs to mind) and bombastic. Taking issue with Churchill, he said, was 'like arguing with a brass band'. The puritan in Chamberlain was repelled by a hard drinker (Churchill was no alcoholic, said the scientist and writer C.P. Snow, because no alcoholic could drink that much) and a free spender who enjoyed the company of disreputable characters for whom wealth was the primary virtue. But Chamberlain recognised a skilled parliamentarian who might challenge him for the premiership. It was better, he calculated, to bind Churchill into government where he would be restrained by the ties of office from roaming the back benches stirring up disaffection.

Churchill was balanced by the retention of Chamberlain's three closest allies in appeasement – Halifax at the Foreign Office, Sir John Simon at the Treasury and Sir Samuel Hoare who moved from the Home Office to the open-ended role of Lord Privy Seal. Succeeding him as home secretary was Sir John Anderson who doubled as minister for home security. Anderson was now the undisputed home front supremo, a minister with almost unfettered control over everyday life, from the imposition of the blackout and the distribution of shelters to the management of the evacuation. It was Anderson's policy of dispersal that remained the guiding principle of civilian security. Even when it was seen to fail, as with the evacuation, Anderson never wavered in his conviction that protection against air attack was his overriding priority. If the blitz, from September 1940 to May 1941, would in some measure prove a justification for Anderson's perception of home security, it nonetheless remains true that, relying on faulty intelligence and the fanciful notions of military futurologists, much if not most of the effort put into protecting the homeland could more usefully have been directed towards the armed forces.

Anderson felt in no way constrained by the new ministries created, not least because they were more form than substance. The Ministry of Information and the Ministry of Food will reappear later in this story but in their early stages, neither was well led. The Ministry of Supply, set up in April 1939 to bring some sort of order to the procurement of arms, was headed by an undistinguished former transport minister, the uninspired and uninspiring Leslie Bergin. To complicate matters, a Cabinet sub-committee for military coordination, chaired by the recently retired Admiral of the Fleet, Lord Chatfield, fell victim to service in-fighting. Not strong enough to make his voice heard above the din, Chatfield lasted until March 1940.

With nine members, the War Cabinet was too large for purpose. It was further weakened by Chamberlain's refusal to countenance bringing the Labour and Liberal parties into a coalition. Moreover, Churchill was quick to point out, the administration was loaded with too many elderly time-servers. The average age of the Cabinet was only one year short of the state pension. Brought in as a minister without portfolio, Lord Hankey had served as secretary to the War Cabinet in the Great War.

Experience counted, but where was the energy and imagination? Complacency was more the rule. In conversation with James Garvin, editor of *The Observer*, Sir John Simon could see no point in disturbing the even tenor of the Treasury by having an economic minister take charge of long-term planning.

Churchill could not quite believe the self-satisfied attitude of his colleagues. He made a particular point of the failings of the munitions industry. In a report to the Cabinet, he drew the contrast between two wars with Germany.

In the first year of the last war, July, 1914, to July, 1915, the new workers drafted into the metal industries amounted to 20% of those already there ... Now ... only 11% have been added in the last ten months. ... Although 350,000 boys leave school each year, there is an increase of only 25,000 in the number of males under 21 employed in metal industries. Moreover, the proportion of women and young persons has only increased from 26.6% to 27.6%. In the engineering, motor and aircraft group we now have only one woman for every 12 men. During the last war the ratio of women to men in the metal industries increased from one woman for every 10 men to one woman for every 3 men.

With so much work to be done, unemployment nonetheless remained high, at about a million throughout the first six months of the war.

If Chamberlain had hoped to contain Churchill by bringing him into government, he must have been disappointed. Making his voice heard in every department, Churchill marked himself out as a leader in waiting with his nationwide appeal for 'the wholehearted concurrence of scores of millions of men and women, whose cooperation is indispensable and whose comradeship and brotherhood are indispensable; the only foundation upon which the trial and tribulation of modern war can be endured and surmounted'.

In the dark days ahead, 'the storms of war may blow and the lands may be lashed with the fury of its gales, but in our own hearts ... there is peace. Our hands may be active, but our consciences are at rest.'

According to Mass-Observation, the opinion-gathering organisation, the public warmed to Churchill's rhetoric.

'Churchill gave us a good fruity speech this evening.'

'Winston's wonderful talk.'

'Heard Winston's speech. Very good. Think he ought to be Prime Minister. Think his reference to P.M. very "sporty" in view of the fact that every one knows pig-headed Neville kept him out of the Cabinet. ...'

'Thought his definition of what we are fighting for was put plainer than we had had it before ...'[1]

A belligerent note, tempered by civilised values, was never far from Churchill's speeches.

The Royal Navy has immediately attacked the U-boats, and is hunting them night and day – I will not say without mercy – because God forbid we should ever part company with that; but at any rate with zeal, and not altogether without relish ...

Now we have begun: now we are going on; now, with the help of God, and with the conviction that we are the defenders of civilisation and freedom, we are going on, and we are going to go on to the end ...

I do not under-rate what lies before us; but I must say this: I cannot doubt we have the strength to carry a good cause forward, and to break down the barriers which stand between the wage-earning masses of every land and a free and more abundant daily life.

One can almost feel Chamberlain and Halifax squirming with embarrassment. Chamberlain could do nothing about Churchill but he was able to dispose of another bullish minister who habitually spoke out of turn. Leslie Hore-Belisha had had his successes as war minister but his attempts to modernise the army had brought him up against the diehards whose idea of leadership was to speak with a plum in the mouth and to dress properly for dinner.

The muttering against Hore-Belisha climaxed with the Pillbox Affair, when the army chiefs accused the war minister of disloyalty when he criticised the defences being built by the British Expeditionary Force (BEF) in France. Hore-Belisha could be aggressively pushy and was disinclined to humour the senior army officers. General Edmund Ironside, appointed Chief of the Imperial General Staff in 1939, a job he did not want and for which he was ill-prepared, was one of Hore-Belisha's fiercest critics.

Nothing could have gone right with a man like that at the

head of the War Office. He took up so much time over his own political life and future and over trivialities that we never got down to the real business. I am usually the most steady-going individual, but I several times lost my temper with Belisha. At times he showed the temperament of a prima-donna in a temper.[2]

The thought of Ironside as a 'steady-going individual' took some swallowing. A mercurial character, six feet four, one-time rugby international and heavyweight boxer, he was himself often accused of prima-donna-ish behaviour. A personal assistant to Ironside, Ralph Arnold marvelled at an overwhelming presence. At their first meeting,

> The door opened and an enormous man came into the room, red-banded cap pushed on to the back of his grizzled head, field boots gleaming, row after row of medal ribbons on his tunic, and a bulging black brief-case gripped in one enormous hand.[3]

Without question, Hore-Belisha found Ironside hard to handle. He had more trouble with the very superior Lord Gort as commander of the BEF in France. Appointed to that role to get him out of the War Office where he had performed inadequately as Chief of the Imperial General Staff, Hore-Belisha said of him that he was 'utterly brainless and unable to grasp the simplest problem'. Gort was quick to use the Pillbox Affair as a means of discrediting his political boss.

Underlying the hostility to Hore-Belisha was anti-Semitic xenophobia, of which the army had a thick vein. This came out in all its nastiness in *Truth*, a weekly news sheet owned by Sir Joseph Ball, a Chamberlain cheerleader who endorsed the anti-Semitic sentiment that was felt if not openly voiced in government. Hore-Belisha was replaced by the aristocratic and malleable Oliver Stanley.

Hore-Belisha's dismissal, officially and euphemistically dubbed a resignation, caused a press furore. For commentators who had long given Chamberlain the benefit of the doubt, the departure of one of the few ministers who gave any semblance of leadership served as an indictment of the entire government and the way the war was being fought. Even the editor of *The Times*, though staying loyal to Chamberlain, found 'nothing to enthuse' about in the prime minister's rearranging of the deckchairs. That Sir Samuel Hoare was now put in charge of the Air Ministry was regarded as almost laughable.

There were moments when, talking to friendly journalists, Hore-Belisha must have seen himself leading a parliamentary revolt that would clear the way for a new administration, with himself in prime position, capable of taking the war into enemy territory. But come the day of his resignation address to the House of Commons, either his courage failed him or he came to realise that the bunch of nodders and winkers who comprised the bulk of the parliamentary Tory party would not accept a Jew in Downing Street or anywhere close to it. Having rejected a demotion to the Board of Trade and failed to inspire the back benches, the tide of gossip and rumour against the former war minister was allowed to flow uninterrupted, carrying its victim into political oblivion.

But Hore-Belisha had served his purpose insofar as, following his departure, the normally loyal press began to doubt that Chamberlain was the best man in a crisis.

There were circles where a good word for Hitler could still be heard. In his last report as British ambassador in Berlin, delivered seventeen days after the start of the war, Sir Nevile Henderson asserted unblushingly:

It would be idle to deny the great achievements of the man who restored to the German nation its self-respect and its disciplined orderliness. The tyrannical methods which were employed within Germany itself to obtain this result were detestable, but were Germany's own concern. Many of Herr Hitler's social reforms, in spite of their complete disregard of personal liberty of thought, word or deed, were on highly democratic lines.[4]

Letters urging that Hitler be given a free hand to allow Germany to attack the Soviet Union were still arriving in Downing Street and at the Foreign Office.

Halifax had high hopes of Mussolini interceding to achieve a negotiated peace or at least a ceasefire using the Italian ambassador Giuseppe Bastianini as the go-between. It came to nothing. Meanwhile, Halifax was besieged by leading lights of international business eager to give service as intermediaries. So much hot air; so much wasted breath.

YET NEITHER CHAMBERLAIN nor Halifax was convinced that the declaration of war was irreversible. Both were persuaded that peace could be achieved before western Europe joined the shooting match that Germany had embarked on in Poland to the east. Appeasement was not dead, just dozing. That it might be reawakened was based on the hope that a Royal Navy blockade of Germany reinforced by sanctions against countries and companies trading with Germany would cripple the Nazi economy. Political backup was supposed to be provided by the Ministry of Economic Warfare, presided over by Sir Ronald Cross, a lightweight Tory MP who had held junior ministerial jobs before his elevation. That he failed dismally in efforts to limit German access to vital war supplies, notably oil and gas, was not altogether his fault. Chamberlain put too much faith on intelligence reports that the German economy was 'brittle' and lacked 'the hidden reserves of the 1914–18 war'.

While all German imports and exports, even in neutral ships, were to be treated as contraband, German trade with Russia and eastern Europe was able to continue uninterrupted. In the spring of 1940, the War Cabinet was warned that the German economy was standing up to war pressures surprisingly well. Oil stocks were maintained at a high level by imports from Russia and Rumania, while supplies of high-grade iron ore were kept up by trade with the Scandinavian neutrals.

In April 1940 the War Cabinet was reflecting on an intelligence assessment of a German economy that was 'not comfortable' but giving little hope that within a year the 'discomfort will have greatly increased'. For the blockade to be effective, increased pressure would have to be put on all nineteen neutral countries exporting to Germany, an acceleration of the war even assuming that it was practical, and that was liable to reduce the chances of further economic and financial support from America 'without which we do not consider we could continue the war with any chance of success'.

At this stage in the war, the United States was still an unknown quantity. President Franklin D. Roosevelt was keen to be onside in the defence of democracy. But he was up against formidable stumbling blocks. US public opinion and most of the political establishment were overwhelmingly isolationist. Having reluctantly approved the neutrality law which forbade American intervention in any conflict that did not pose a direct threat to the homeland, Roosevelt had lobbied hard for a compromise whereby a distinction could be made between aggressors and their victims, arguing that the neutrality laws were, in effect, giving support to the aggressors. After the broken promises of Munich, said Roosevelt, all the small states of Europe were under threat. Was nothing to be done to save them from subjugation? He made clear his own view that 'We cannot forever let past, without effective protest, acts of aggression against sister nations'.

In April 1939, with a reminder to his critics that 'the next generation will so narrow the oceans separating us from the Old World that our customs and our actions will necessarily be involved with hers whether we like it or not', Roosevelt had made a direct appeal to Hitler and Mussolini to observe the decencies of international relations and to give assurance:

> That your armed forces will not attack or invade the territory or possessions of the following independent nations – Finland, Estonia, Latvia, Sweden, Norway, Denmark, the Netherlands, Belgium, Great Britain and Ireland, France, Portugal, Spain, Switzerland, Liechtenstein, Luxemburg, Poland, Hungary, Roumania, Yugoslavia, Russia, Bulgaria, Greece, Turkey, Iraq, the Arabias, Syria, Palestine, Egypt, and Iran.

The suggestion was for such guarantees to last for at least ten years but 'a quarter of a century if we dare look that far ahead'. He concluded:

> I think you will not misunderstand the spirit of frankness in which I send you this message. Heads of great governments in this hour are literally responsible for the fate of humanity in the coming years. They cannot fail to hear the prayers of their peoples to be protected from the foreseeable chaos of war. History will hold them accountable for the lives and happiness of all – even unto the least. I hope that your answer will make it possible for humanity to lose fear and regain security for many years to come.

Roosevelt's message was enthusiastically endorsed by the democracies, though the president came in for criticism for treating the dictators as equals open to persuasion and for pushing for an international conference to reduce the 'crushing burden of armament'. That route had been tried to exhaustion. But it is too easy to assume naivety. Roosevelt was addressing himself as much to his own people as to the dictators by emphasising the peril that Europe was facing. That he achieved that objective is proved by the, predictably, hostile reaction from Germany and Italy and by the adverse comment the dictators received in the American press. It did not go down well when Hitler described the US as a 'mongrel society' populated by 'Jews, blacks and inferior Slavs'.

Isolationism remained strong but from here on in, Roosevelt was able to move towards supplying Britain and France with the armaments they needed to fight the war. Not least of the positive results of the peace message was the start of a close, if sometimes discordant, relationship between Roosevelt and Churchill. In October 1939, Congress approved an amendment to the neutrality laws allowing for the export of arms on a 'cash and carry' basis as long as they were carried in non-American ships with money paid up-front. The legislation was signed by the president on November 4th.

Having delivered what he confidently assumed to be good news, Roosevelt was surprised when it was not followed immediately by a rush of orders for all manner of advanced military hardware. But Chamberlain was not yet ready for a full-blooded arms race. It was not until March 1940 – when it was clear that the German economy was not about to collapse – that the first order was lodged for an American-built aircraft. Chamberlain had to swallow his innate distaste for what he regarded as American meddling. But he had yet to be convinced that an all-out war was inevitable.

CHAPTER 9

War of Words

If wearing down the German economy to the point where white flags would appear was hopelessly unrealistic, equally improbable of success was Chamberlain's second line of offence, that of persuading the German people to overthrow Hitler in favour of a leader opposed to further risky military adventures. Hermann Goering, commander of its Luftwaffe, overlord of the German economy and much else besides, was the favoured successor.

In the first week of the war, Chamberlain wrote to his sister with the optimism born of naivety that the time for 'discussing peace terms' might not be far off. He detected:

> ... such a widespread desire to avoid war and it so deeply rooted that it surely must find expressions somehow. Of course the difficulty is Hitler himself. Until he disappears and his system collapses there can be no peace. But what I hope for is not a military victory. I very much doubt the feasibility of that – but a collapse of the German home front. For that it is necessary to convince the Germans that they cannot win.

Speaking on a French radio station, Chamberlain gave his message to the German people that 'our quarrel is not with them but with the Nazi regime'.

To encourage Germany's disaffected, Britain embarked on one of the most absurd initiatives known to modern warfare. In what was dubbed the 'confetti war', the RAF spent the best part of September 1939 showering the German people with propaganda leaflets. The first load, packed into brown paper parcels, 6 million leaflets in all, was dropped on the night of September 3rd–4th. The message was headed, 'A Warning from Britain to the German People'. The nature of the message had been a source of contention in Whitehall for at least a year. Sir Horace Wilson, head of the civil service, was the first to cast doubts on the 'utility of a pamphlet ... [which] ... may prove to be quite unsuitable when the time comes'. He added, sensibly: 'The minds of the people of Germany, like the minds of our people, will be too much occupied with the excitements attendant upon the event to pay much attention to leaflets.'

Against Wilson's advice, Operation Nickel went ahead with ten Whitley medium bombers from 51 and 58 Squadrons. Their target area was the densely populated Ruhr industrial region, known for its socialist, anti-fascist leanings. The message was as much a justification of appeasement as an appeal to reason.

German Men and Women: The Government of the Reich have with cold deliberation forced war upon Great Britain. They have done so knowing that it must involve mankind in a calamity worse than that of 1914. The assurance of peaceful intentions the Führer gave to you and to the world in April have proved as worthless as his words at the Sportspalast last September, when he said: 'We have no more territorial claims to make in Europe. ...' Never has government ordered subjects to their death with less excuse. This war is utterly unnecessary. Germany was in no way threatened or deprived of justice.

Was she not allowed to re-enter the Rhineland, to achieve the Anschluss, and to take back the Sudeten Germans in peace? Neither we nor any other nation would have sought to limit her advance so long as she did not violate independent non-German peoples.

Every German ambition – just to others – might have been satisfied through friendly negotiations.

We have no enmity against you, the German people. ... You have not the means to sustain protracted warfare. Despite crushing taxation, you are on the verge of bankruptcy. Our resources and those of our Allies, in men, arms and supplies are immense. We are too strong to break by blows and would wear you down inexorably.

You, the German people, can, if you will, insist on peace at any time.

Later variations on the theme raised the stakes.

Never has a government condemned its subjects to death for less reason. This war is completely unnecessary. German lands and German rights are threatened by no one. ... All Germany's endeavours – if they had been just to others – could have been settled by peaceful means.

Your government has condemned you to slaughter, misery and the privations of war, in order to win what you could never hope for. ... Censorship holds the spirit of the German people prisoner in a concentration camp ... We have no enmity towards you, the German people.

Nazi censorship has concealed from you the fact that you do not possess the means to sustain a long war ... You are on the verge of bankruptcy. We and our allies possess enormous reserves of manpower, armaments and supplies ... We can fight you pitilessly to the end.

The mixed communiqué, offering friendship while threatening vengeance on a grand scale, led to muddled thinking on the part of Field Marshal Lord Milne, one-time Chief of the Imperial General Staff. He told an audience: 'The Germans who matter, those under forty years of age, have been brought up in the belief that Great Britain is their hereditary enemy. Nothing but a sound thrashing will convince them of that error.'

Churchill was contemptuous of the confetti war: 'We contented ourselves with dropping pamphlets to rouse the Germans to a higher morality.' Noël Coward, working in Paris on a propaganda liaison job with the French, said that if it was the policy of His Majesty's Government to bore the Germans to death he didn't think we had enough time. 'For this', Coward recalled, 'I was reprimanded'.

The futility of Operation Nickel suggests a bureaucratic cast of mind which sees a job, in this case compiling the texts of the leaflets and printing it in sufficient quantities, as an end in itself without worrying too much about the consequences. A few moments of constructive thought should have told the perpetrators of this fiasco that while there were several home-grown plots to dispose of Hitler, the German people were not about to rise up against their leader on the say-so of a hostile foreign power. The confetti war soon became the butt of every comic and cartoonist. The Peterborough column in the *Daily Telegraph* gave readers a tongue-in-cheek report of one of the 'leaflet' planes returning to base two hours before it was due. The pilot's commanding officer demanded an explanation.

'Well, Sir,' the young officer replied, 'I flew over enemy territory as instructed and tipped out the parcels over the side.'

'Do you mean you dropped them out still roped in bundles?' said the C.O. in an anxious voice.

'Yes, Sir.'

'Good God, man, you might have killed somebody!'

Another tall tale was of the leaflet plane that arrived back many hours
overdue. When asked why he had taken so long, the pilot told his CO
that to ensure safe delivery, he had posted each leaflet through the
letter box. While a naval version went:

> Lieutenant-Commander reports to the Captain on the bridge
> of a destroyer: 'The ship's engines have stopped, sir.'
>
> Captain: 'I know. There's an enemy U-boat about.'
>
> Lieutenant-Commander: 'Are you going to depth-charge
> her, sir?'
>
> Captain: 'No, I'm sending down a diver with leaflets.'

To add to the farce, journalists were told by the censors that they
could not quote from the leaflets on the grounds that 'We are not
allowed to disclose information that might be of value to the enemy'.

This is not to say that bombarding Germany with propaganda
was a soft option for the RAF. An Air Ministry booklet, published in
1941, pointed out the risks:

> The direction and strength of the wind and the height at which
> the aircraft is flying assume much greater importance when
> leaflets are to be dropped. The leaflet, lighter than the bomb,
> is carried by the wind. Our bombers are not equipped for
> their discharge and they had to be dropped by hand through

the fire-chute. The leaflets are packed in bundles secured by a piece of string. On one occasion the dropper cut the string binding the bundles just after they had been stowed in the aircraft. As it was taking off, a sudden draught papered its entire interior with leaflets which completely obscured the pilot's view. He had to make a blind take-off using only his instruments.

The compensation for the RAF, so it was said, was the valuable experience gained from venturing into enemy territory.

But if the RAF was capable of penetrating German air space, why, instead of leaflets, could not a few bombs be dropped on the Ruhr industries? Chamberlain was shocked by the idea that civilians might be put at risk. He told the Commons: 'His Majesty's Government will never resort to the deliberate attack on women, children and other civilians for purposes of mere terrorism.' As it happened, the war had to advance six months before the first British bomb fell on a German land target, and that was the seaplane base at Hoernum on the thinly populated north German island of Sylt.

FROM HIS VANTAGE point at the Foreign Office, Halifax was not averse to forceful measures to supplant Hitler – though, pre-war, he had drawn the line at assassination. There was at least one serious offer to do the deed. It came from Colonel F.N. Mason-Macfarlane, a military attaché in Berlin. When war seemed inevitable he proposed taking a shot at Hitler with a high-powered sporting rifle. He was ideally placed to make good on his scheme. His second-floor apartment was opposite the reviewing stand where Hitler would take the salute at the military parade to mark his birthday. An excellent shot, Mason-Macfarlane was confident that from his balcony, the Fuehrer would present an easy target. Halifax was appalled. 'We have not yet reached that stage ... where we have to use assassination as a substitute for diplomacy.'[1] Mason-Macfarlane was recalled to London and sacked.

A military insider's joke at year end was of a Commonwealth officer, at a loss in Whitehall, asking directions of a British colleague.

'On which side is the War Office?'
'We think on ours but you can never be quite sure.'

Muddle and confusion were the order of the day. Time and again the aversion to entanglements across the Channel left critical decisions on hold. The result was an over-reliance on the French army to hold off a German land attack. Though strong in numbers, there was no enthusiasm in Paris for taking the offensive. Instead, faith was put on the Maginot Line, a fortified barrier running from the Rhine to the southernmost point of Belgium. That the line did nothing to guard against a repetition of the German advance through Belgium in 1914, was a charge that went unanswered. It was enough that the Maginot Line looked to be impenetrable.

In supreme command, General Maurice Gamelin, colourless and complacent, set the tone for discredited orthodoxy. 'We need tanks', he wrote to prime minister Daladier, 'but you cannot hope to achieve a real breakthrough with tanks ... As to air, it will not play the part you expect ... It will be a flash in the pan.' Infantry was the dominant arm; the tank should support it.

There was then much scrambling around at the War Office to put together a force that might strengthen the French backbone while persuading Hitler that he could not sustain an attack in the west.

In early September 1939 five infantry divisions with 50 light tanks crossed the Channel. What amounted to an advance party of the

British Expeditionary Force (BEF) was ill-trained and ill-equipped, with not even enough maps of the terrain they were supposed to defend. Critically, there appeared to be no understanding of the blitz-krieg strategy so successfully adopted by Germany against Poland. A War Office booklet on the 'Order of Battle of the Germany Army' came with the stern injunction that it should 'not be taken into front line trenches'.

Predictably, the news that British troops were on the move was incompetently, almost comically, mishandled. As the *Daily Express* foreign correspondent, Geoffrey Cox was in France to witness their arrival. But there were obstacles to filing his story.

> Some genius in the French High Command had decided that the moment war broke out all telephonic and telegraphic communications between France and Britain, except for official traffic, should be cut off. But to avoid antagonising the Americans, the lines to the United States were kept open, though liable to censorship. This produced the absurd situation that the journalists of two countries allied in a common struggle could not communicate directly with their offices, but had to do so via a third neutral country – the United States – many of whose citizens (and presumably of its telephone and telegraph operators) were hostile to the Allies. Instead of being able to write a story out fully, and telephoning it, down to the last comma, to London, we now had to resort to the cruder method of cables, and send messages via Cable and Wireless to our offices in New York, for relay to London.[2]

There were further complications. The official line in London was to withhold any reference to the operation until it was complete. In the event, the French released the news prematurely before all the troops were across the Channel. The War Office then lifted the embargo. At about the same time, Cox's dispatch, with excellent eye-witness accounts of troops disembarking at Cherbourg and Villennes, landed on the desk of the combative *Express* editor, Arthur Christiansen. The entire front page was handed over to the story. Other pages also gave prominence to the news but without the added flavour of a first-hand account. So it was that when the War Office changed its mind, declaring that all publicity should be prohibited, Christiansen went in fighting.

While he was at odds with the War Office, Scotland Yard got in on the act with orders from a War Office official to seize any papers that contained offending articles. Police were to be seen in Fleet Street and even at railway stations where they confiscated the morning editions already on sale.

Refusing to back down, Christiansen faced up to a police inspector who was 'wearing a World War I DCM ribbon and carrying a tin hat and gas-mask', while shouting down the telephone at the night staff at the War Office. Then came another release from the French Director of Information that made the second embargo yet more futile. Another change of mind allowed the presses to roll, with the *Express* able to claim the first scoop of the war.

By mid-October there were 160,000 British troops in France. A further eight divisions preparing to join them doubled BEF strength, but this was a modest contribution set against the 104 French divisions deployed along the western front. Requisitioned civilian vehicles helped to make up for the shortage of transport but poor servicing and the lack of spares remained a problem. The only tanks were lightweight and designed primarily for reconnaissance.

Army transport planes were noted for their scarcity and for their vintage. Joining the BEF in October, the war correspondent James

Lansdale Hodson had an eight-hour wait on a drizzly day at Heston before taking off.

> The plane was not one of our latest. 'You had this in the last war?', I asked the mechanic. 'No, the 1870 war,' he answered.[3]

Commanding BEF's II Corps, General Alan Brooke, soon to be Chief of the General Staff under Churchill, found it hard to believe that so little had been done to prepare for battle, as he confided to his diary in November:

> On arrival in this country and for the first 2 months the Corps was quite unfit for war, practically in every aspect. Even now our anti-tank gunners are untrained and a large proportion of our artillery have never fired either their equipment or type of smoke shell that they are armed with. To send untrained troops into modern war is courting disaster such as befell the Poles. I only hope that we may now be left in peace for the next 2 to 3 months to complete the required readiness for war.[4]

Most of those to be brought to readiness for front-line fighting were recent conscripts. From the first day of the war all men aged between 18 and 41 were made liable for military service, the youngest to be summoned first and single men before married men.

The length of service was for the duration of hostilities or 'so long as His Majesty may require'. Those called up were able to state their preference for service, over half of the first intake of 200,000 men opting for either the Royal Navy or, more frequently, for the Royal Air Force. This was not to say that their wishes were granted. The majority went into the army where the need for manpower was greatest.

The RAF had the best pick of recruits. Heavily touted in the press and in 'Boy's Own' stories, the blue uniform promised a life of romantic adventure with clean, man-to-man combat high above the clouds. The thoughts of the writer H.V. Morton ran on these lines as he watched a group of happy young flyers preparing for take-off.

> In a minute or so they were several hundred feet overhead. War's attraction for youth, I thought, is that years of slogging and dreary routine and subservience to age are instantly abolished, and a man finds his feet among his contemporaries in the full spring-time of life. It is rather as though a doctor, a barrister or an accountant could reach eminence in his profession in twelve months.[5]

A sense of power, possessed of fictional heroes, was another attraction.

> Can you imagine a boy of twenty or so, encased in a machine moving six times as fast as an express train ... making no more than a minute pressure with his two thumbs on his joystick (ironic phrase) and instantly blowing his enemy to eternity.[6]

A long list of exemptions from military service included lighthouse keepers, fishhook makers, shirt-sleeve makers, scissors makers, ice-cream sellers and *chefs de cuisine*. (Heaven forfend that the service in first-class restaurants should be allowed to deteriorate.) For several occupations, age limits were imposed. Thus, to avoid putting on uniform, a basket maker, bedstead maker, French polisher, accountant or trade union official had to be over the age of 30. Curiously, the age for exemption was five years lower for jobbing gardeners and for administrative and executive grade employees of the BBC. On the creative side of broadcasting and in the entertainment industry generally, there were no exceptions to the call-up.

Several jobs listed as vital for the home front have long since vanished. What, for example, are we to make of a 'holder-on', aka a 'holder-up hand'? At a time when horse-drawn vehicles were more common than the combustion engine, he was the assistant to a blacksmith, one who held the hot metal rivets while they were hammered into place.

Pacifists had a claim to exemption but they had to prove their good faith. Over the entire war, 60,000 men and 1,000 women testified to pacifist beliefs. Some 3,000 were given unconditional exemption while around 18,000 applications were turned down. The remainder were absolved from fighting if they were willing to serve in the military as non-combatants or be directed towards civilian work.

Across the country, tribunals were set up to assess the character of those claiming to be conscientious objectors. Reporting for Columbia Broadcasting, American journalist Ed Murrow attended a London tribunal where he declared the proceedings were as open and fair as could be expected.

The council chamber of Fulham Town Hall looks like a courtroom. Five elderly men sit behind a bench: a judge, a prominent member of a university, a senior civil servant, the secretary of a trade union, and a city alderman. They all wear plain clothes and appear to be eminently respectable gentlemen. The little gallery at the back of the room is crowded with a variety of persons. Most of them are leaning forward. The atmosphere is just between that of a church and a courtroom. Down on the floor – all alone – looking up at the five men, is a boy. He is twenty years and seven months old. He is small and wiry, with sandy hair, an Irishman if there ever

September 5th, 1939: A butcher painting a meat registration notice on the window of his shop: 'Register Here Now And Be Sure Of A Good Supply Of Meat'.

Fox Photos/Getty Images

September 11th, 1939: Soldiers in Cheshire helping with the harvest where farmhands have been called up for military service.

Nick Yapp/Fox Photos/Getty Images

David Low, the New Zealander whose anti-appeasement cartoons in the *Evening Standard* gave as much offence in Downing Street as they did in the Reichstag.

Felix Man/Picture Post/Getty Images

September 16th, 1939: A British wartime poster appearing in the streets of London.

H.F. Davis/Topical Press Agency/Getty Images

December 15th, 1939: Prime Minister Neville Chamberlain inspects
a 25-pounder field gun at Bachy, near Lille in northern France.

Imperial War Museum

The sandbagged structure used to protect the statue of Eros in Piccadilly Circus in London, December 1939.

Imperial War Museum

1940: Signposts removed from their positions in Kent, to confound
the enemy in the event of a German invasion.

Val Doone/Getty Images

ARP workers digging trenches for air-raid shelters in St James's Park, London.

Topical Press Agency/Getty Images

An Austin Therm balloon car. The bag on the roof is full of coal gas, used to fuel the car, thus saving petrol. Gas made from coal was not on ration and saved precious imported oil supplies.

London Express / Getty Images

An Essex farmer has his herd of black cows painted with white stripes in case they should wander on the road after dusk, so that they will be visible to motorists during the blackout.

Imperial War Museum

A poster recruiting women into the war effort:
'ARP Looks To You', issued by the
Women's Voluntary Services.

Imperial War Museum

Women in civil defence:
a female member of
the Auxiliary Fire Service.

Imperial War Museum

An instructional poster providing guidance on good practice during an air raid.

Imperial War Museum

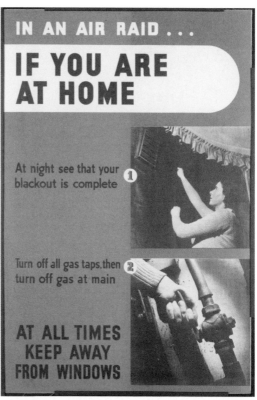

April 1940: A heap of scrap iron collected from householders to help in the salvage of waste products, in Malden and Coombe, Surrey.

J. A. Hampton/Topical Press Agency/Getty Images

A propaganda poster encouraging mothers to leave their evacuated children in the countryside.
Imperial War Museum

Evacuees return home to London: villagers saying goodbye to the children they adopted for the war.
Imperial War Museum

was one. He has been drafted and has asked for exemption as a conscientious objector. The five men on the bench decide what to do with him. Why doesn't he want to fight? Because to him it would be murder. War settles nothing. Four of his cousins were killed fighting in the Irish troubles and nothing was settled. The questions and answers are informal. The boy is given plenty of time to formulate his answers. Would his conscience permit him to continue in a factory? It would. There is a whispered conversation on the bench, and the judge tells him that he will be registered as a conscientious objector and need not go to war. And up in the gallery an elderly lady leans in her chair and relaxes.

The next applicant, 'a fat, dark-haired boy', was treated less sympathetically.

He works in a shell factory and is prepared to go on working there but doesn't want to fight. He doesn't like war. Another conference on the bench. The young munitions worker is not a true conscientious objector and he must go to the army.

Possibly because he was more lucid, an Oxford student had better luck with a fairly weak argument.

He says that he is willing to defend Britain, but he doesn't believe that this is a defensive war. Rather than wreck the world he would submit to German domination. He quotes Chamberlain as saying that the war is being fought in defence of small nations and goes on to say that he is not interested in the small nations and is prepared to go to jail rather than fight. His case takes twenty minutes before it is decided he needn't fight.

Almost certain to be granted exemption were the Christian pacifists with a record of speaking out against violence.

> Next comes a boy with long hair and a thin face. For two years he has been a full-time worker in a religious sect, preaching and distributing pamphlets. He refuses to don a uniform and take an oath because he says he recognises only the authority of God. The university professor asks his interpretation of Christ's attitude to war. The boy replies in a steady voice, using many quotations from the Bible. The judge asks the objector if he feels no responsibility to the state. 'Certainly,' says the boy, 'but I refuse to kill or accept the authority of anyone but God.' The discussion is fascinating – this youngster against the five men who are trying to determine what is in his mind and trying to test the validity of his conscience. After nearly half an hour he is asked if he would work on a farm as a civilian. This he agrees to do; agrees, that is, provided that he can continue to preach.[7]

Talking to the tribunal members, Murrow was unable to extract a definition of conscience. 'But all agreed that a British subject should have the right to say what his conscience dictates before he is forced to fight.'

By the same token, the word of God was frequently invoked to counter the argument for pacifism. Presiding over a tribunal in Newcastle, Judge Richardson gave it as his conviction 'that if Christ appeared today he would approve of this war'. When quoted widely in the press and in the House of Commons, the judge apologised for intemperate remarks after a 'long and tiring day'. Richardson came back into the news with his wish that all conscientious objectors could be packed off to a desert island, a sentiment echoed by Sheriff Brown who told applicants to one of the Scottish tribunals: 'We will call you the new contemptibles.'

That such outbursts were rare says much for British toleration, a contrast to the dictatorships where pacificism was equated with degeneracy. By the end of 1939, 14,995 of those called up had registered as conscientious objectors. But the tribunals had heard only 4,812 cases of which 849 were rejected.

A blanket exemption covered all of Northern Ireland where the threat of unrest persuaded the government that compulsion was not worth the trouble. Against this, the armed forces gained 38,000 volunteers from the province.

The medical tests for recruits were perfunctory but nonetheless revealing. The two lowest categories, those capable of very limited duties (known in the army as 'excused breathing') and those unsuitable for any form of service, accounted for 8.3 per cent of the number examined. For the age group 36 and over, the figure rose to 35.2 per cent, a disturbing indication of the nation's level of fitness.

BY THE END of 1939, over 1.5 million men were in uniform. There were those who couldn't wait to join up. David Butcher was 25 and single.

For years, I had made up my mind that as soon as the war started, I would volunteer for the army. On the Friday, 1st September I went to work as usual, in Huddersfield, and then heard news of the German invasion of Poland. Being certain that this was it, I told a friend and colleague that I would go home – to Southall, Middlesex – on the Sunday, and gave my landlady a very short notice, which she accepted with good grace.

I left my office keys and a letter of resignation in the office on the Saturday and packed a suit-case that evening. I was halfway home from Huddersfield having a snack lunch in a pub when I heard Chamberlain's broadcast, and the declaration of war.

Equally determined to do his bit was my late father-in-law, Morris Fulton, a Scotsman who, having graduated from the University of Georgia School of Medicine, was a resident of surgery at the University Hospital.

The day after war was declared I went back to Britain. When I arrived there, I found that no American medical degrees were accepted by Britain – certainly by 1940 they were delighted to have them – but in 1939 they were not. So I took the British London exams and entered the R.A.M.C. [Royal Army Medical Corps] in November, 1939.

Another eager recruit was Dave Marsh who became a gunner in the Bedfordshire Yeomanry.

The war was a splendid release for young men of my age – we were fed to the teeth with study and the grim business of earning a living. I was one who threw aside my studies without any hesitation, although as a surveyor I could doubtless have obtained deferment, and rushed off to a new excitement. Unhappily, 3 out of 5 of my friends never returned, but we had no thoughts about this, at least none strong enough to disturb us at all seriously.

The strict adherence to the class divide was an irritation for recruits who had been told, 'we are all in this together'. A particular grouse was directed at any publican, and there were many, who reserved a section of his bar for 'officers only'. Dave Marsh was furious when he was asked to leave his favourite bar in Bedford's Bridge Hotel.

> I do not recall ever using that bar again and there is some sat-
> isfaction at seeing that the hotel has fallen on hard times since.

The Bridge was gutted by fire and demolished in 1977.

Barbara Emerson was another early recruit. She joined the Women's Auxiliary Air Force (WAAF) as a driver in May 1939 though she was not called up until September.

> I realised what I had done when I found that our pay was 1s 4d
> per day – spent on 20 cigarettes (11½d) mid-morning coffee
> (2d), chocolate biscuit (2d).
>
> Within a few days, many of the R.A.F. drivers were posted
> and three vehicles were to be driven from Doncaster and
> delivered to White Waltham in Buckinghamshire. Nobody
> would give permission for WAAF to drive and it was not until
> our WAAF officer took responsibility for safe delivery that we
> were allowed to take what was called the first WAAF 'Convoy'
> of the war.
>
> So having no uniforms, three of us donned navy dungarees,
> berets with RAF wing badges and set off.
>
> The three vehicles were a light van, a 3-ton ambulance, and,
> best of all, a fire engine! This had a single seat perched up in
> the open – with right-hand gear change – outside the body
> and a perfectly gorgeous engine.
>
> I am afraid I was rather greedy with this and as I was the
> one who knew the route down the A1 and across to White

Waltham backwards, my companions let me lead most of the way as the fire engine seemed to clear the way – most kind of them.

Two of us were soon given the rank of Acting Corporal. Unpaid, of course!

Later I was allowed to drive any vehicle, which included towing a petrol bowser by tractor, an articulator, staff car and lorries – all very great fun.

As a Territorial, John Frost was told to report to his regimental headquarters, a couple of miles away.

It was chaos. There was no accommodation and so we were sent home and told to report next day. Even then, most of us slept in the vehicle sheds or in classrooms of a local school. A week later we moved off to the ack-ack [anti-aircraft] training camp at Stiffkey, Norfolk. Our first job was to paint the tents with reddish brown ochre. A few days later when it poured with rain, the ochre came through the leaky tents. We all looked like 'Red Indians'.

Among the privileged minority who could expect to be awarded a commission and a softer lifestyle was the politician and journalist Woodrow Wyatt. But he had to start at the bottom with a period of basic training at Colchester.

The barracks were bleak. They were built in early Victorian times with the manifest intention of indicating to private soldiers that they would not be cosseted. Even public school boys accustomed to rough living were shattered. The iron frames under the palliasses were not made for easy slumber.

There was no hot water for washing or shaving. There were no baths. There was no heating. The lavatories were in outdoor rows exposed to wind and snow.

It was exceptionally cold that winter on the Essex coast. The water in the lavatory-bowls froze; not that it mattered, it was impossible to pull the chain because the water in the cistern was frozen, too. The food was so horrible that many skipped breakfast and bought bottles of frozen milk from the milk-cart eccentrically allowed in at 6.30 a.m. on the barrack square. We huddled under the bedclothes and broke the milk into swallowable pieces with a penknife.[8]

If Colchester had its lighter side it was the fun that could be had baiting the obtuse officers who were in charge of training, presumably to keep them away from any activity where they could do real damage.

There was the martinet Colonel, who believed fervently that unthinking discipline alone could win wars. He told a story from the 1914 war. A German machine-gun post was overrun. All the gunners were found dead, chained to their posts so that they could not run away. 'If they had had better discipline – of the kind I am giving you – that wouldn't have been necessary.' He assumed instant obedience to his orders. One day he shouted to his driver 'Stop'. He opened the door and got out, without noticing that the car was still going at 15 mph. He broke his leg and we got a new CO.[9]

For those who expected the emergency to equate with instant action, the ways of the military were strange indeed. Ralph Arnold was a rookie publisher and writer when he was commissioned 2nd Lieutenant in a Scots regiment. Three days after he and other young officers had settled in, they were summoned to a special parade in the dining room.

> When we assembled we observed that one place, and one place only, had been laid on the long mahogany dining-table ... There was a lavish display of knives, forks, spoons and wine-glasses. Had we, the Adjutant inquired brought our notebooks? Some of us had; others, imagining perhaps that we were to receive encouragement in the shape of a buck-shee [i.e. free] and supplementary meal, had not. While the ill-equipped retired to make good their deficiencies, the rest of us regarded the dining-room table with puzzled concern. When we were all in a state of readiness the object of the exercise was explained.
>
> The Colonel, the Adjutant told us, had been concerned and shocked on the previous evening – a guest night – to observe that some of the newly joined officers had been in doubt about the correct implements and glasses to employ for the successive courses. If we would be kind enough to pay attention and take notes, he would give us a practical demon-stration. Without batting an eyelid this impeccable young man then sat down at the table and an equally solemn mess waiter served him first with token soup, then with token fish, then with token meat, then with a token pudding and finally with a token savoury. The wine waiter went through the motions of pouring out sherry, burgundy, port and brandy. Somewhere I still possess the valuable notes I made.[10]

Whether the notes ever came in useful, Arnold does not relate.

Being in the right place at the right time was a rarity for the military. At the outbreak of war, A.J. Noble, a 21-year-old subaltern with the Queen's Own Cameron Highlanders, found himself in Aldershot. Along with a company of semi-trained recruits, he had been sent down from Inverness to make space for an intake of new recruits. On September 7th they were on the move again, this time to Finchampstead, a village in Berkshire. With a piper in the lead they set off on a twelve-mile march to their new billet which turned out to be a modern dance hall set in an acre of garden. As they arrived, the piper bravely playing 'The March of the Cameron Men' found he was in opposition to a dance band playing at full throttle.

Negotiations with the manager who knew nothing of our impending arrival were surprisingly civil and we were left to our own devices. Bedrolls and blankets were laid out on the dance floor and I racked my brains for something to do when the rifles were cleaned for I had been told that they were not to leave the place. So we did nothing for an hour or two.

Then with the dinner arrived the C.O. Having quickly looked around and asked one or two men how they were, he called me outside – didn't I know that there was a war on, where were the slit trenches, what had I done with ammunition, why were the men outside not wearing their steel helmets (they hadn't any), what was my Alarm Scheme (I hadn't one) and so on and so forth. Luckily the ammu-nitionless guard on the main entrance which I had deemed expedient to protect had been ceremoniously mounted only half an hour before.

A telephone call to the Quartermaster produced a dozen picks and shovels, some .303 [ammunition] and 'some' steel helmets within the hour. And so our night was spent digging slit trenches in the garden where roses and chrysanthemums were ruthlessly cast aside. Of course my C.O. was quite right as I gradually began to understand; we all needed that spur to overcome the apathy of peacetime conditions. ... It was only later that I learned that slit trenches should be sited more than two yards apart.

We stayed in our dance hall for a day before we were ordered to march to Farnborough Station to entrain for Inverness, unexpectedly. I ensured that we marched in very open order! I have always regretted the damage done to that garden.

David Franklin, a professional singer who was later to be part of ENSA, spent the second day of the war leading a convoy of anti-aircraft vehicles from south London through the Blackwall Tunnel, on its way to defend the east coast.

Right in the middle of the tunnel, we met a similar convoy coming from north London to defend the south coast – a novel if rather eccentric piece of planning. It was just as well we had started early. It took a long time to sort out that traffic jam, and get on the road again towards the lonely lives we were to lead in Suffolk, with just a handful of men living in a tent, cooking for themselves, and sleeping beside a gun or searchlight.[11]

As a recruit to the WAAF, Joan Rice recorded in her diary her first day of military life:

It began with rain and nearly missing the train at Claygate; more rain, heavy bags and misery in the Strand; more rain, going the wrong way and arriving late at Hendon.[12]

Nonetheless, she decided there and then that there would be no going back to shorthand typing.

At the start of 1940, the BEF was still a long way short of readiness for war. Only ten divisions were reckoned to be fit for purpose. Trained or untrained, British troops had to make do with freezing billets, with the only warm relaxation to be found in the cafes of northern France. Chilblains, venereal disease and drunkenness accounted for more casualties than the enemy.

Well aware of the lack of enthusiasm for war in Britain and France, Hitler renewed his efforts to engender a mood of reconciliation building to a sense of false security. On October 6th, 1939, his 'peace offensive' was set in motion in the German press.

> My chief endeavour has been to rid our relations with France of all trace of ill-will and render them tolerable for both nations. ... Germany has no further claims against France, and no such claim shall ever be put forward. I have always expressed my desire to bury forever our ancient enmity and bring together these two nations, both of which have such glorious pasts. ... I have devoted no less effort to the achievement of an Anglo-German understanding, nay, more than that, of an Anglo-German friendship. ... I believe even today that there can only be real peace in Europe and throughout the world if Germany and England come to an understanding.

Led up the garden path by the Fuehrer once too often, he was given a dusty answer. Said the French prime minister, Edouard Daladier, possibly with more confidence than he genuinely felt:

> Herr Hitler's speech to the Reichstag means, in effect: 'I have vanquished Poland. I am satisfied. Let us stop the war. Let us hold a conference to consolidate my conquests.' We have taken up arms against aggression; we will not lay them down

until we have received guarantees of security, a security which will not be called in question every six months.

Chamberlain agreed. On October 12th, he told the House of Commons:

Either the German government must give convincing proof of the sincerity of their desire for peace by definite acts or by the provision of effective guarantees of their intentions to fulfil their undertakings, or we must persevere in our duty to the end. It is for Germany to make her choice.

Distrust of German intentions was well founded. Even while he was delivering his message of peace, Hitler was working on a timetable for an attack in the west. On October 9th, he outlined his objectives to the military high command.

The German war aim is a final military settlement with the West, that is, the destruction of the power and ability of the Western powers ever again to oppose state consolidation and further development of the German people in Europe. As far as the outside world is concerned, this aim will have to undergo various propaganda adjustments, necessary from a psychological point of view. This does not alter the war aim. That is and remains the destruction of our Western enemies.

The assault was ordered for November 12th. That it did not happen was thanks to the winter weather precluding a quick victory. Hitler had to contain his impatience until the spring.

From the vantage point at the Foreign Office, Halifax held to the daydream of Hitler's overthrow by conspirators friendly to the Allied cause. Reports from neutral Holland of intelligence contacts with a subversive in the Nazi elite were received with unwarranted enthusiasm. The source was Sigismund Payne Best, an MI6 officer who had served in the Great War before setting up in The Hague to oversee a clearing house for processing information filtering out of Germany.

Best's cover as a businessman in pharmaceuticals was transparent. From his monocle to his spats, Captain Best was the very model of a gentleman spy. Working alongside, though technically not with Best was Major Richard Henry Stevens, late of the Indian Army, whose knowledge of intelligence was based on his experiences on the North West Frontier. Best was at least fluent in German but Stevens was very out of his depth, a romanticist who thought spying was all about disguise and physical deception. Late in the day he came to recognise that he was the wrong man in the wrong place.

Since there was not much secrecy attached to Best's true role in life, he was open to approaches by opponents of Hitler while at the same time offering himself as a prime target for German intelligence. When he was given to understand that a certain German general was keen to meet him, he concluded, with almost touching innocence, that 'I might be on to quite a big thing'.[13]

By then, the Allies and Germany had been at war for nearly two months but Halifax was still hopeful that reason and goodwill would prevail. Given the go-ahead from London, Best set up a meeting for October 21st in Zutphen, close to the German frontier. Along with Best came Major Stevens and a young Dutch officer, Lieutenant Klop. But there was no German general. Instead, two German army officers arrived. Unbeknown to Best, one of them was Walter Schellenberg, a rising star of German intelligence, destined to become the right hand to SS chief Heinrich Himmler.

According to Best, the Germans were in a highly nervous state but Schellenberg, posing as an anti-fascist rebel, recorded merely that Best and Stevens 'offered us all the aid and support within their power'.[14] Further meetings followed, all without substance.

By now, the word from Berlin was to abort the operation. Any suggestion of peace feelers was an unnecessary distraction for Hitler in his determination to attack in the west. A failed attempt on his life on November 8th – when, leaving a meeting early, he escaped a time bomb – made him doubly sensitive to any indication, even fictitious, that he might be overthrown by force.

The climax came the following day when Best, Stevens and Klop drove to a customs post at Venlo where they confidently expected a meeting that could change the course of European history.

Noting that a road barrier, normally closed, had been lifted, Best, who was driving, slowed the car.

> The scene was peaceful enough. No one was in sight except a German customs officer in uniform lounging along the road towards us and a little girl who was playing at ball with a big black dog in the middle of the road before the café.

Having reversed into a car park by the side of the café, the three agents took stock of their surroundings. It was all clear but not for long.

> There was a sudden noise of shouting and shooting. I looked up, and through the windscreen saw a large open car drive up round the corner till our bumpers were touching. It seemed to be packed to overflowing with rough-looking men. Two were perched on top of the hood and were firing over our heads from sub-machine guns, others were standing up in the car and on the running boards; all shouting and waving pistols.

Four men jumped off almost before their car had stopped and rushed towards us shouting: 'Hands up!'

I don't remember actually getting out of the car, but by the time the men reached us, I was certainly standing next to Stevens, on his left. I heard him say: 'Our number is up, Best.' The last words we were to exchange for over five years. Then we were seized. Two men pointed their guns at our heads, the other two quickly handcuffed us.

Klop was not so fortunate. Using the open door of the car as cover, he made a run for it. Best and Stevens watched the young Dutchman,

Running sideways in big bounds, firing at our captors as he ran. He looked graceful, with both arms outstretched – almost like a ballet dancer. I saw the windscreen of the German car splinter into a star, and then the four men standing in front of us started shooting and after a few more steps Klop just seemed to crumple and collapse into a dark heap of clothes on the grass.[15]

Best and Stevens were hurried away along the road to the frontier. 'The black and white barrier closed behind us. We were in Nazi Germany.'

It is still unclear how much the two captives gave away in their interrogation. Schellenberg's claims that their kidnapping led to the breakup of the British intelligence network in Holland and beyond must be tempered by his later admission that he drew on other operations to spice up his report.

Even so, the Venlo Incident was a huge embarrassment to the British government. Churchill spoke out in Cabinet against the incompetence of the intelligence services and the pursuit of false hopes. Once installed in Downing Street, he was quick to set up his own spy and sabotage agency known as the Special Operations Executive (SOE).

Best and Stevens were held in Germany as 'high profile' prisoners until they were liberated by the US Army on May 4th, 1945.

CHAPTER 10

Almost at War

In the first action of the war, on September 4th, the RAF raided warships anchored at Wilhelmshaven, Germany's deep-water naval base, and at Brunsbuettel at the western end of the Kiel Canal. As written up for public consumption, it was a dramatic encounter full of incidents that told of a bold adventure.

> We could see a German warship taking on stores. ... We could even see some washing hanging on the line. Flying at 100 feet above mast height all three aircraft in the flight converged on her. I flew straight ahead. The pilot of the second aircraft came across from one side, and the third crossed from the other side. When we flew on the top of the battleship we could see the crews running fast to their stations. We dropped our bombs. The second pilot, flying behind, saw two hit. We came round, and the ship's pom-poms began to fire as we headed for home. My navigator saw shells bursting almost on the tail of the aircraft.

The truth was more prosaic. With strict orders to avoid civilian casualties, fifteen Blenheims and fourteen Wellingtons, the most advanced planes in Bomber Command, set off over the North Sea. Of the sixteen that found the target, seven were lost to German fighters or anti-aircraft fire. Little was accomplished. The *Emden*, a training ship, suffered repairable damage when a Blenheim, hit by flak, crashed on to the deck. Nine sailors and the Blenheim crew of four were killed.

Two bombs landing on the *Admiral Scheer* bounced off the deck and failed to explode.[1] The single most effective strike was not against the enemy. Lost in a rain storm, one aircraft dropped its bombs on the Danish city of Esbjerg, 150 miles off target. Two civilians died. In all, 24 RAF men gave their lives and two survived to be taken prisoner. Two DFCs were awarded. The information was given to the press in what was to become a typically convoluted and equivocating release.

> Whilst no official confirmation that the R.A.F. awards mentioned tonight are connected with the raids on Kiel, if any paper assumes that they are they will not be incorrect in doing so. If any paper assumes that Flt.-Lt. Doran was the leader of the Kiel raid and the officer with whom the interview was published on September 14, they will again not be incorrect.

The next day, an RAF Anson reconnaissance aircraft attacked two British submarines by mistake. Depth-charges scored a direct hit on the conning tower of the *Snapper*. Less than a week on, the Royal Navy planted another tick on the German scorecard when one of its submarines rammed and sank an unidentified submarine only to find that it was a British vessel. Two days later, after a false warning of a German attack, the RAF managed to shoot down three of its own aircraft.

By the end of the year, Bomber Command had sacrificed 63 aircraft and 171 men in operations over Germany. In addition, 69 aircraft had been lost in training exercises at the cost of 80 crew.[2]

By the standards of the second half of the war, the aircraft deployed by the RAF were hopelessly inadequate. With the intense cold of the winter of 1939–40, icing on the wings could be anything up to six inches thick. Instrument glasses had constantly to be wiped clear and it was not unusual for rudders to be frozen solid. On a night flight over Germany on October 27th, the pilot reported that his crew were numbed by the cold which seeped through the metal, gloves and heavy clothing.

> In an effort to keep warm, you slapped yourself and then slapped someone else. But that was no good. It only exhausted you more. Time and again the moon seemed to glimmer through a break in the clouds, but it might have been a mirage, for when you tried to find a break it always eluded you. There was no way out of the icy clouds.

Crews were denied the most basic comforts. The Hampden, in which men might be confined for up to ten hours, lacked even the simplest toilet. The crew had to take with them empty beer bottles or fix up their own primitive drainage with lengths of hosepipe.

With the instruments available, precision attacks were all but impossible and if the largest targets were hit, it was more by luck than judgement. Photographic reconnaissance had a slow start. Even when modified Spitfires with photographic equipment came on stream, images were of poor quality or too diverse to form a usable pattern. It was not until July 1940 that the Air Ministry set up an interpretation branch of the Photographic Development Unit.

Bombs were too lightweight to do much damage, this on the

unsafe assumption that they exploded on impact. A high proportion, though no one was prepared to put a figure on it, failed to detonate.

So it was that while the Air Ministry ruminated over plans for air attacks on German industry, the RAF had neither the planes nor the crews to fulfil their missions. After a successful maiden flight in October 1939, the four-engined Halifax bomber did not become operational until October the following year.

A few more isolated raids in late November and early December brought little reward. An attempted attack on the pocket battleship *Deutschland* off the coast of Norway had to be called off when it proved impossible to find the ship. The returning planes almost by-passed the British Isles, eventually landing in the far north of Scotland, courtesy of the crew of a British trawler who literally pointed the way to a safe landing.[3] A German minesweeper was sunk off Heligoland on December 3rd.

Three substantial raids, aimed at the German fleet, led to more losses with nothing to show in the way of diminishing German strength. Of the 22 aircraft that reached the target area, only ten returned. Yet the RAF's record, with the losses of men and machines, was somehow allowed to sidestep critical judgement. 'Reputations survived, even when aircrews did not.'[4]

Propaganda on both sides tried to make the best of a bad job. In what was described as the 'biggest air battle of the war' over Heligoland on December 18th, Germany claimed 34 RAF planes shot down; the RAF admitted only to seven, a more convincing figure since the German estimate was in excess of the total number of aircraft sent on the mission. The lesson from experience was that a day-time raid could only be attempted with any chance of success if there was a fighter escort.

That was about it for the rest of the year and for the early part of 1940 when snow and frost, followed by floods, made flying or even getting off the ground an impossible dream. The famous Baldwin claim that the bomber would always get through gave way to speculation as to whether any bomber would ever get through.

THE SEPTEMBER ASSAULT on Kiel, at best a heroic failure, must be measured against the string of successes scored by the German U-boats against British shipping. The first merchantman to be sunk was the *Bosnia*, caught off the Spanish coast on September 5th. The crew was picked up by a Norwegian ship. Later the same day, *U-48* sank the *Royal Sceptre*, an armed merchantman.

Patrolling off the Hebrides, the *Ark Royal*, Britain's most modern aircraft carrier, had a narrow escape when three torpedoes from *U-39* exploded prematurely. The *Courageous*, a First World War cruiser rebuilt as an aircraft carrier in the 1920s, was less fortunate. Three days after the attack on the *Ark Royal*, *U-29* came so close to *Courageous* it could hardly miss. With two torpedoes finding their mark, it took only fifteen minutes for the ship to capsize with a loss of 519 lives and 48 aircraft. Survivors were rescued by a Dutch ocean liner and a British freighter. Captain Makeig-Jones remained alone on the bridge of his ship, saluting the flag, as she went down. The *Courageous* was the first British warship to be sunk by German forces.

That the Royal Navy, supposedly the world's finest sea-fighting force, did not give a better account of itself can be attributed largely to poor intelligence and a failure of communication. Having made a start at breaking into the Royal Navy ciphers at the end of 1938, German Intelligence was soon able to read up to 30 per cent of the traffic intercepted in the North Sea. By contrast, knowledge on the British side was sparse.

German Intelligence put its faith in an electro-mechanical cipher machine known as the Enigma. Nearly 200 keys were eventually identified, with the settings of each key changed regularly to allow for millions of permutations. Hopes of breaking the system were raised when a leak from the cipher branch of the Germany army allowed two instructional manuals and lists of daily settings for the army key to fall into the hands of the French secret service who shared the information with their Polish colleagues.

With more than a touch of mathematical genius, the Poles were able to track all the changes made to the machine up to 1938. But further modifications put the Enigma beyond the resources of the Polish cryptanalysts. It was not until 1941 that the British government's Code and Cipher School (GC&CS) at Bletchley Park deployed early computers known as bombes to interpret a huge number of Enigma settings. Up to then, intelligence was based largely on captured documents and information from prisoners.

In his classic study of British Intelligence in the Second World War, Sir Harry Hinsley, referring to the loss of the aircraft carrier *Glorious* in 1940, the first news of which came to the Admiralty from a German radio broadcast, comments that 'no testimony could be more eloquent' to the 'poverty of naval intelligence' and to 'the failure of the entire intelligence system'.

The Royal Navy had other shortcomings, notably its failure to appreciate the destructive power of the modern U-boat. The first mistake was to assume that the development of Asdic, a sonic echo revealing the bearing and range of a detected object, had made submarines virtually obsolete. Putting its faith in Asdic, in 1937 the Admiralty declared that 'the U-boat will never again be capable of confronting us with the problem we faced in 1917'.

But Asdic was an imperfect device. What was thought to be a U-boat on the offensive was just as likely to be a school of fish or a wreck. Then again, Asdic could not identify a submarine on the surface or even underwater at close range. The deficiencies were all the more serious given that the submarine, despite its name, was still essentially a surface craft which submerged only to avoid danger or, a rarity, to make a daylight attack.

It was the submarine's efficiency as a surface craft that had been raised to a point where the machines were virtually unrecognisable to veterans of the First World War. Torpedoes no longer left a tell-tale swell when launched or an easily observed wake on course to their target. Magnetic firing devices allowed for detonation under a ship's keel where the torpedo could do maximum damage. With more efficient batteries, the U-boat was able to stay under water longer and operate noiselessly. Long-range radio allowed tactical planners to coordinate activities at sea from their land-based headquarters.

Fortunately for Britain, the German navy was far short of the number of U-boats needed for a decisive victory at sea. A commander of U-boats, Admiral Karl Doenitz, set a target of destroying Allied shipping to the tune of 600,000 tons monthly. But this assumed 300 U-boats on active service. Doenitz had 57, and of those only 49 were fit for operational duties and fewer than 30 suitable for long periods at sea. Moreover, the introduction of the convoy system on the Atlantic route in 1940 reduced the easy pickings of defenceless lone merchantmen.

A breakthrough for British sea defences came with the recovery of a German magnetic mine. With a delayed-action fuse, this 'secret weapon' was immune to conventional mine-sweeping. Resting on the sea floor, it remained undetected until a ship happened to pass over it. This was the fate of the destroyer *Blanche*, lost to a magnetic mine in the Thames estuary on November 10th, 1939. In the same month, 27 merchant ships were sunk by mines and many more were damaged, including the cruiser *Belfast*. Access to the Port of London was at risk.

Then on the night of the 22nd, a German plane was spotted dropping a parachute with a large object attached into the sea off Shoeburyness in Essex. At low tide the next day, a party from HMS *Vernon* went out onto the mudflats. It was led by Commander John Ouvry.

> We decided that Chief Petty Officer Baldwin and I should endeavour to remove the vital fittings; Lieutenant-Commander Lewis and Able Seaman Vearncombe to watch from what was considered to be a safe distance and make detailed notes of our actions and progress – for reference in case of accidents. There was a possibility that the mine had devices other than the magnetic one, which added to the hazard. If we were unlucky the notes which the two watchers had taken would be available for those who would have to deal with the next available specimen.
>
> I first tackled the aluminium fitting sealed with tallow. In order to use one of the special spanners which had been rushed through (by Commander Maton) in the local workshops for us, it was necessary to bend clear a small strip of copper. That done, we were able to extract this first fitting. Screwed into its base when we drew it clear we found a small cylinder – obviously a detonator, for in the recess from which the fitting had been withdrawn were disks of explosive. These I removed. This mysterious fitting proved to be a delay-action bomb fuse; it was necessary for the airman to tear off the copper strip referred to (before releasing his load) if bomb, not mine, was the requirement.[5]

An effective countermeasure was to have small boats sweeping long cables stretched out behind them to set off the mines and to fit larger vessels with loops of electric cable round their hulls to neutralise the magnetic field. Praise for the Admiralty in taking prompt action after the secrets of the magnetic mine were revealed by a conspicuous act of bravery, was tempered by the revelation that a faster response might have come had the Admiralty realised that it already had the essential knowledge in its possession. The Royal Navy had used its own prototype for a magnetic mine as early as 1918 and by 1939 a new design was ready for production.

It must be assumed that Churchill was unaware of this when he declared the losses caused by magnetic mines to be the result of the 'lowest form of warfare that can be imagined'. The *Daily Express* took up the cry:

> Of course, the German [mine warfare] is murder. Bloody murder. It is not war at all. Not even the new type of war.

When, in mid-November, the Dutch liner *Simon Bolivar* fell victim to a magnetic mine with a heavy loss of life, the press demanded action. Said the *Sunday Graphic*: 'Let us get on with the job of beating up the enemy that is doing his best to destroy us as well as peace and liberty.' Even the usually restrained BBC joined in the chorus of condemnation of the 'murderous' German mine warfare.

The sense that Britain was failing to get its war act together was given further momentum on November 23rd with the sinking of the merchant cruiser *Rawalpindi*. As part of the northern patrol between the Faeroes and Iceland, the *Rawalpindi* was outmanoeuvred and out-gunned by the battleships *Scharnhorst* (thought at first to be the *Deutschland* and reported as such in an Admiralty release) and *Gneisenau*. Ed Murrow reported the encounter for CBC:

> Smoke-floats were lit and thrown into the water to enable the *Rawalpindi* to escape. A second enemy ship was seen coming up to starboard. A shot bounced across the bows of the

Rawalpindi but she continued on her course. Captain Kennedy of the British ship ordered his crew to action stations. Course was altered to bring the enemy on the starboard quarter, then the German ship opened with the first salvo of her eleven-inch guns. The range was 10,000 yards – nearly six miles. The *Rawalpindi* replied with her four starboard six-inch guns. A third salvo extinguished the lights and smashed the electric winches of the *Rawalpindi*'s ammunition carriers. The fourth salvo carried away the bridge and the wireless room. By this time the second German ship was hammering the British merchant cruiser from the port side. The fight lasted about half an hour. By that time every gun on the *Rawalpindi* was out of action and the ship was ablaze. The British ship continued to burn until eight o'clock when she turned turtle and founded with all hands who had not escaped in the two undamaged lifeboats.[6]

Of 48 survivors, *Gneisenau* picked up 21; *Scharnhorst* six. The next day the British cruiser *Chitral* rescued eleven more survivors; a further ten were picked by German ships. Two hundred and thirty-eight died.

The Kriegsmarine did not have it all its own way. A self-inflicted setback in the early part of the war was a tragedy that, paradoxically, gave comfort to the Allies. The *Athenia*, an unarmed liner on its way to Montreal with 1,103 passengers, including 311 US citizens, was thought to be safe from attack. Germany had taken a pledge against unrestricted submarine warfare and Hitler had no wish to alienate neutrals, the US in particular. But identification of unprotected vessels was an inexact science. When the *Athenia* came within range of *U-30* patrolling off the coast of north-west Ireland, Captain Fritz-Julius Lemp assumed the blacked-out ship to be an armed merchant cruiser and thus fair game.

At around 19.40 hours on September 3rd, 1939, Lemp gave the order to attack. Two of his torpedoes were off target, a third hit the *Athenia* on the port side, exploding against the engine-room bulkhead. Most of the 117 who died were trapped between the lower and main decks after the stairways collapsed. Among them were 98 civilians, 28 of them Americans.

The unfolding drama, with eye-witness accounts, made news across the world.

Mrs Reginald Bacon groped for the two pairs of shoes she had put under her bunk, but failed to find them. She rushed into the passageway in her stockinged feet, on her way to find her son Keith, who, unknown to her, had been within feet of the explosion.

Eight-year-old Ruby Mitchell was awakened by the explosion, and thought the ship was going to turn over. Then water began to flow into her cabin, and she cried out in terror, for she was alone.

The table at which she was sitting collapsed in front of Mrs John Mitchell who was aged sixty-seven. She found herself on the floor, trembling, a pain shooting through her leg.

Seated at table Barbara Bailey listened to the dishes go crashing all around her. The ship lurched, first to starboard and then in a great swing to port. People were too stunned to say or do anything immediately. Then women and children began screaming; a rush towards the main stairs followed but Barbara sat quite still. As the two women beside her began to rise, she gripped them by the arms. 'For God's sake, sit still,' she shouted. 'We're probably doomed, but don't let's get crushed to death.'[7]

Of the ships that picked up distress signals, the Norwegian freighter *Knute Nelson* carried 430 survivors to Galway. But one lifeboat capsized in the heavy sea, killing ten, and another was crushed by the *Knute Nelson* propeller with a loss of 50 lives.

The American press gave the disaster full coverage. At Galway:

> Ten seriously injured stretcher cases were removed from the ship; among them were several elderly people, two *Athenia* crewmen who had been badly hurt in the explosion, and three children. Then the walking survivors made their way down the stairway, many only partially clad or wrapped in blankets, and some wearing makeshift footgear made of gunny sacks and bits of cloth. A number of survivors suffered from broken bones, burns and bruises. Many people seemed still in a state of shock, particularly the children, who were crying or calling for their parents. Even so, when asked how she was doing, one young woman called down blithely from the *Knute Nelson* to a reporter on the tender, 'I have lost everything except my sense of humour'.[8]

In a pattern that was to be repeated, the Admiralty sat on the news of the sinking for several hours. By contrast, the German propaganda machine moved quickly to deny responsibility with an emphatic statement from the War Ministry protesting: 'It is out of the question that a German warship torpedoed the steamer. All have the strictest orders to capture, not sink, merchantmen.'

The German Foreign Office weighed in with an attack on 'An infamous, shameless lie, a criminal attempt to influence U.S. opinion'.

A senior American diplomat was given a solemn assurance: 'The story cannot be true, because an order has been issued to the German

Navy to adhere to the International Rules covering warfare. No unit of the German Navy was in the vicinity.'

To which was soon added the repetitive claim that: 'The *Athenia* must have been sunk by a British warship or else have struck a floating mine of English origin.'

It was not until September 27th when *U-30* reached its home port of Wilhelmshaven that Lemp admitted to having seen the *Athenia* steering a zigzag course without lights and torpedoed her in the belief that she was a warship. The crew were sworn to secrecy and the ship's log expurgated. Though not on the scale of the 1915 sinking of the *Lusitania*, when 128 Americans were drowned, the loss of the *Athenia* undoubtedly helped to swing American opinion.

Towards the end of September, Churchill told the House of Commons that nearly 100,000 tons of merchant shipping had been lost in the first three weeks of the war, most of it to U-boats. Further losses could be expected. In the event, the total by May 1940 was close to 800,000 tons. By 1942, German U-boats were sinking Allied vessels faster than they could be built.

As navy minister it fell to Churchill to give a positive slant to the war at sea. He did so with characteristic gusto, serving up false optimism based on little more than doubling the figure he first thought of. In mid-November 1939 he was confidently declaring that it was 'pretty certain that half the U-boats with which Germany began the war have been sunk [the true figure was 8 per cent] and that their new building had fallen far behind what we expected'. The view from the bridge told a different story.

THE EARLY SUCCESSES of German U-boats reached a peak in mid-October 1939 with a strike on the British fleet at its main anchorage at Scapa Flow in the Orkney Islands. In what has been described as 'one of the most audacious naval missions in history', U-47, captained by Guenther Prien, set out from Wilhelmshaven on October 8th to make a surface crossing of the North Sea en route to the Orkneys. There were seven entrances to the Flow, all heavily defended, but air reconnaissance had shown a gap 50 feet wide at Kirk Sound between the island of Mainland and the islet of Lamb Holm. Cables obstructed half the entrance but there was just enough space for a submarine to squeeze through, a lapse on the part of the Royal Navy which could only be explained by wilful ignorance of U-boat capability.

U-47 entered Scapa Flow at around midnight on October 13th/14th. Since the Home Fleet was out at sea in a fruitless search for the Germany navy, there were fewer targets than Prien had been led to expect. But the *Royal Oak*, a semi-retired battleship which lacked the speed for front-line duty, was at anchor, her crew blithely unaware that they were in easy range of U-47. Four torpedoes struck home. The *Royal Oak* exploded, turned turtle and sank, taking with it over 800 seamen. With a ten-mile-an-hour current running against U-47, Prien had more trouble getting out of Scapa Flow than getting in.

Prien was well on his way home when the Admiralty acknowledged belatedly that the *Royal Oak* had met its end not by accident, as first assumed, but by design. Churchill recognised 'a remarkable exploit of professional skill and daring'. Awarded the Knight's Cross of the Iron Cross, Germany's highest military honour, Prien became the first German war hero, a gift to Goebbels' propaganda.

The loss of the *Royal Oak* brought a predictable response from a public short of good news. On the afternoon of the day of the sinking, a Mass-Observation reporter was in central London.

The large Saturday crowd was quite definitely *Royal Oak* conscious. More people than usual bought the mid-day and evening papers, and there were several little groups on the corners, busily discussing the tragedy. Of twenty-six overheard scraps of conversation, picked up while wandering round the market, nineteen concerned the *Royal Oak*. Here are some of the comments, mostly made by working-class women:

'… terrible, when you come to think of it. That's when you begin to realise what a war means. Nearly a thousand dead. …'

'… three captured U-boats are nothing, compared to the loss of a boat like that.'

'First there was that aircraft-carrier, and now this: we don't seem to be having a very easy time of it.'

'… a shame. All those men dying for nothing, like that. We might as well make peace and be done with it.'

'… so I said, and I say it again now, once they admit one defeat, you don't know how many defeats they's hiding from us. Them papers only say what they're told.'

'… we frankly can't afford it. A boat like that costs more than ten German U-boats: we simply can't afford it.'

'Terrible thing. Terrible. We simply aren't giving them our best. If we wanted to, we could smash them to bits in two minutes. There's something wrong with the organisation at the top.'[9]

There was more to talk about the following week after the first bombs fell on Britain and a civilian entered the records as the earliest to be injured in an air-raid. When, on October 16th British fighters and German bombers clashed over the Firth of Forth, a housepainter in Leith received a bullet wound. The Royal Navy was not so lucky. Twenty-five sailors and officers were killed or wounded on board the warships anchored in the Firth.

Intercepted signals should have given Fighter Command adequate warning of the attack but in the absence of confirmation the intelligence was ignored, with the result that the raiders were able to make an uninterrupted approach to the target. Two of them were brought down by RAF fighters but only after they had dropped their bombs.

The next morning, German bombers raided British warships at Scapa Flow. Two bombs fell on the Orkney island of Hoy. Another raid followed on November 13th when four German bombers dropped twenty bombs on the Shetlands. It was said that a rabbit was the only casualty.

Though it would have been hard to think of a less significant example of enemy action, repeats of bombs falling on British soil raised expectations of the war hotting up.

'Heard of air-raids in Scotland when I got back to digs', wrote a Londoner. 'Gave me for some reason *a sense of satisfaction*. Was even more pleased when I later heard that no damage had been done. I suppose that I am glad to hear of something happening.'

But the mood of anticipation soon passed. After spending the night in a shelter, a city householder was quoted as saying: 'I don't expect anything will happen. Nothing ever does.'

The expectation was of real fighting starting on the western front. Instead, the border between Germany and France remained weirdly quiet. With no real news to report, war correspondents fell back on speculation. 'All the world is keyed up to some great happening', wrote Tom Darlow in *The People*. 'There is no doubt that the whole of Northern France expects vital and tremendous events in the next few days.' But the Fuehrer did not oblige. 'We are still waiting for Hitler to do something.'

Major General Bernard Montgomery, commanding the 3rd Infantry Division of the BEF, was on the visiting list of the prime minister when he was over in France for a pre-Christmas inspection of the troops.

[Chamberlain] took me aside after lunch and said in a low tone so that no one could hear: 'I don't think the Germans have any intention of attacking us. Do you?'

Montgomery remained silent, reserving his comments for his private notes.

My soul revolted at what was happening. France and Britain stood still while Germany swallowed Poland; we stood still while the German armies moved over to the West, obviously to attack us later on; we waited patiently to be attacked; and during all this time we occasionally bombed Germany with leaflets. If this was war, I did not understand it.[10]

ATTENTION SHIFTED TO northern Europe where Finland was under threat from Germany's new-found best friend. Having grabbed his share of Poland and in 1940 occupied the Baltic states – Estonia, Latvia and Lithuania – Stalin set about imposing his will on another weaker neighbour. He had his reasons. As Russia's second city, Leningrad was vulnerable to a land attack across the Finnish border, a mere twenty miles away, or a sea invasion from the Baltic. To protect against this and as insurance against Hitler ratting on the Nazi–Soviet pact, Stalin demanded an exchange of territory that required Finland to sacrifice areas regarded as critical to Russian defence and to concede a long-term lease on the port of Hanko, sited strategically at the entrance to the Gulf of Finland.

This neat arrangement from Stalin's point of view did not appeal to the Finnish government. What made sense in the Kremlin was at the expense of Finland surrendering its front-line defences against a Russian incursion. With Finnish resistance came the inevitable false accusations from Moscow of unprovoked attacks across its frontiers, a preliminary to Stalin taking what he wanted by force.

'All we had to do', recalled Nikita Khrushchev, 'was to raise our voice a little bit, and the Finns would obey. If that did not work, we would fire one shot and the Finns would put up their hands and surrender – or so we thought.'[11]

Sure enough, on November 29th, 1939, diplomatic relations were broken off and on the following day Russian aircraft bombed Helsinki. Units of the Red Army crossed the frontier. A Soviet puppet government composed of Finnish communists living in Russia was set up in a captured town just inside Finland.

A short war was expected by all except the Finns themselves. The Red Army, a million strong, was backed by a formidable array of military hardware. The Finnish army was small and ill-equipped. But it was highly trained and strongly motivated with an outstanding commander-in-chief. Having led the campaign against communist insurgents for three years after the Great War, Field Marshal Mannerheim was recalled to duty to hold off the Red Army. Though it was a war that Finland could not possibly hope to win, the aim was to inflict such damage on the enemy as to force a negotiated peace that preserved Finnish independence.

Radiating confidence, the Red Army failed to realise that a land of forests, marshes and lakes in mid-winter did not lend itself to the tactics of mass attack. Finnish troops, though thinly spread, were able to destroy whole columns of tanks simply by picking them off one by one as they milled around unfamiliar terrain. On narrow snowbound forest roads, Russian infantry was exposed to ambush and to hit-and-run tactics. Finnish casualties were one tenth of the

Russian. Sixteen hundred Russian tanks and over 700 aircraft were destroyed.

'In the intense cold, the dead were frozen where they fell, sprawling or lying like waxworks in a staged spectacle of warfare.'[12] As a *Daily Express* correspondent covering the Winter War, Geoffrey Cox was able to send back words and images that, as he put it, gave 'a powerful impression of a Russian defeat'. That a small nation had stood up bravely to the Soviet steamroller attracted public sympathy in Britain and France where there were calls for sending arms and troops to reinforce Finnish resistance.

An Anglo-French expeditionary force was not an entirely unlikely proposition. Though there was no realistic prospect of the Allies taking on Russia as well as Germany, sending troops across Norway and Sweden would serve to cut off the supplies of high-grade Swedish iron ore vital to German industry. As with the Spanish Civil War, volunteers were quick to come forward. In early 1940 the London Fire Service sent a fully-equipped firefighting team who ended up as full-time members of the Helsinki Fire Brigade. When Germany invaded Russia in June 1941, they made their way to a Swedish internment camp and returned home via Portugal.[13]

But involvement on a bigger scale was abandoned after Finland decided to make peace while its army was still undefeated. On March 12th, 1940 the Treaty of Moscow was signed, in which Finland conceded not only the original Soviet requests but extensive areas in addition, including the city of Vyborg. Moscow however abandoned its Finnish Peoples' Government. Finland had lost territory and industry but not its independence or its honour.

It was not for long that Stalin was able to celebrate his victory. When Hitler did attack in June 1941 he was aided by a vengeful Finnish army, which overran in a matter of days the territory so expensively won by the Red Army a year before.

THE FIRST SEA battle of the war – which led to the destruction of the *Graf Spee*, the most modern of Germany's three battleships – was a tonic for the Royal Navy. With an impressive record of sinking merchantmen on the Atlantic trade routes, *Graf Spee* was tracked down and engaged by British cruisers *Ajax*, *Exeter* and *Achilles* off the estuary of the River Plate close to the coast of Uruguay. At dawn on December 13th, 1939, the *Graf Spee* opened fire on *Exeter*. Lieutenant Commander Washbourn, a New Zealander with *Achilles*, gave his eyewitness account of the opening skirmish in which *Exeter* was badly damaged.

From the personal point of view it was a tremendous moment when we suddenly realised that we had bumped up against her, and that *this* time it was the real thing. [...] The captain was on the Bridge, and we turned to each other and said simultaneously, 'My God, it's a pocket battleship!' I legged it as hard as I could go for my box of tricks, and just had time to wonder if there was anything in this gunnery business after all, and where I should be in half an hour's time, before all my lamps lit up and I was able to say 'SHOOT' for the first time in anger. Four minutes only, though most of the sailors were enjoying their very necessary beauty sleep at the time and we were only at cruising stations. We were rather proud of that, even though *Exeter* did beat us to it.

After that my impressions are rather confused. There were a lot of splashes growing up around that target and it wasn't a bit easy picking out my own. I can remember feeling a quite illogical resentment every time he put his great eleven-inch cannon on us, when I saw those damn great pieces belching their unpleasantnesses at myself and I can remember feeling unspeakably grateful to poor old *Exeter* every time I saw them blazing in her direction.

The *Achilles* crew suffered death and injury.

The survivors behaved just as one expected and hoped. They took no notice of the shambles (and it looked more like a slaughter-house on a busy day than a Director Control Tower) and took over the jobs of those who had been put out as if nothing had happened. One youngster had to seat himself on the unpleasantness that very shortly before had been a very efficient [radio operator] and carry out his job. He was a little wide-eyed after we had disengaged but otherwise unmoved. A splinter had jammed the door and prevented the medical parties from reaching us. The wounded never murmured. Shirley quietly applied a tourniquet to himself and saved his life thereby. A sergeant of Marines who was sitting right alongside me never let on that he was wounded. I didn't discover it until the first lull, an hour later, when he nearly fainted from loss of blood.[14]

With *Exeter* shelled out of action but with *Achilles* still active, *Graf Spee* ran to the shelter of the River Plate, finding refuge in the neutral haven of Montevideo. Captain Hans Langsdorff was given 72 hours for essential repairs before coming under a ruling by the Uruguayan authorities to leave neutral waters or risk internment.

Instead of heading for the open sea, *Graf Spee* turned west. The belief then was that the ship was on its way to Buenos Aires where internment conditions were thought to be more favourable. But when a large part of the crew transferred to the *Tacoma*, a supply ship following in *Graf Spee*'s wake, the probability of action intensified.

Just after seven o'clock the *Graf Spee* turned upstream to Buenos Aires but then anchored, just short of the three-mile limit. ...

Then at 7.55 there was a deep, dull explosion which was heard all over Montevideo. A great cloud of grey smoke arose, followed by sheets of flame and further explosions. The entire ship's company had been taken off: the crew into waiting barges and launches and Captain Langsdorff and his officers into a separate launch from which, exactly as the sun went down over the horizon, Langsdorff had pressed an electric button which blew up a mine placed in the ship's magazine. The *Graf Spee* had been scuttled. Within three minutes she had settled on the river bottom and flames were soon roaring her entire length.[15]

Langsdorff and his crew were taken to Buenos Aires where he was faced with a muddle of orders from Berlin. Hoping for repatriation but faced with internment, the likeliest option, Langsdorff, an honourable patriot serving a regime he did not much like, wrapped himself in the old imperial German ensign before putting a gun to his head. He was buried with full military honours.[16]

On December 21st, the *Columbus*, the third-largest ship in Germany's merchant fleet, was scuttled some 300 miles off the coast of Virginia after being intercepted by a British destroyer.

After the destruction of *Graf Spee*, there was more to cheer with the news that nine German U-boats had been sunk (a further fifteen were eliminated between January and May 1940) and that up to a million tons of German shipping was holed up in overseas ports, unable to escape the economic blockade. But the British public was unimpressed. 'Cabined, cribbed and confined' by doubts and fears, the war seemed hardly to have started, while regulations and restrictions piled up to make everyday life a marathon obstacle course.

CHAPTER 11

Gearing Up on the Home Front

A nd still the bombs did not fall. No one wanted them to fall, of course, but the sense of relief at being spared came with mounting frustration. Were we or were we not at war? Overheard in a north London pub by a Mass-Observation reporter, a man at the bar voiced the common view.

> It's a funny business. Why don't they begin fighting? Is it a war or isn't it? They're holding something back or don't want to fight. They just let the Germans get all nice and ready without trying to stop them. The boys are fed up. They've got it into their heads that it isn't a war because there is no bash, bang and blow-up … just this hanging around. Everyone's losing heart, that's it.

A big talking point was the blackout and the disruption it caused to everyday life. The complaints, said an observer, would fill a 500-page volume. Apart from the inconvenience of not being able to move beyond short distances after lights out, the blackout was the curse of those who had night jobs. Bakers were particularly hard hit but drivers of buses and other essential vehicles suffered. Postal deliveries were delayed often for days on end. It was like trying to work in a pea-souper fog except that dense fogs, though common in those days, were sporadic. The blackout was every single night.

At the end of September 1939, lobbying from business and industry compelled the government to set up an investigation led by the home secretary and the secretaries for war and air, to review the restrictions and to consider ways for making them less onerous. It achieved nothing, the Air Staff insisting that any change would hamper air defence. With dubious logic, a rider was added to the effect that public opinion would be puzzled by a relaxation of what had been touted as an essential war measure.

This was the line taken by home secretary Sir John Anderson, who wanted the Cabinet to reinforce dire warnings of a forthcoming catastrophe. In December he told his colleagues:

Criticism of the black-out, the strength of Civil Defence personnel, the emergency hospital scheme, all reflect the same tendency to call in question the need for the precautions which have been taken; and in the present state of public opinion there is real danger that the re-adjustments that have been made to meet present circumstances may be interpreted as an admission that the scale of our Civil Defence measures was out of proportion to any risks to which we are likely to be exposed. At the present moment public opinion is only too ready to discount the risks of large scale air attack, merely because no such attack has yet been delivered; and unless active steps are taken to counter this spirit of false optimism we may well find that, by the time the blow falls, we shall have dissipated the resources and broken the morale which we have built up to resist it.

Despite strenuous objections, Anderson flatly refused to backtrack on his power to impose a curfew. It was, he argued, an essential defence against sectarian disturbances and a discouragement to looting after a bombardment. Left unsaid was the knowledge that once started, an elaborate civil defence could not be dismantled without calling into question the ability of the government to get anything right. With a better idea of the public mood than most of his Cabinet colleagues, Churchill argued unsuccessfully for a loosening of the rules.

But some flexibility came with the deliberations of yet another committee, this one to examine the problems of managing night shifts in industry. Chief constables were given leeway to grant exemptions to such as steel workers, munitions factories and military establishments. Lighting experts were recruited to advise ports and shipyards on how to cope in adverse conditions.

With experience of what the blackout really involved came modest concessions to help make life bearable. Summer Time, due to end in early October, was extended to mid-November and the hours of shop closing were put forward. Also in November, the period of blackout was reduced by an hour, by starting a half-hour after sunset and ending a half-hour before sunrise. Suitably dimmed hand torches were now permitted in the streets, while civilian drivers could adopt a simple headlamp mask. On buses, a headlamp mask on the near side showed drivers where there were people waiting to board.

In the new year an improved headlamp hood was made compulsory on all civilian vehicles. Richard Brown, an engineer in Ipswich, noted in his diary:

> In a slight mist it looks like a large fan spread before the car, yet there is no glare and no light at all above 4ft. The trams have them. They seem a little ghostly rushing about with two dim sidelights, hooded headlamp and dim blue lights inside.[1]

But this was only a partial answer to what had become a serious hazard to life and limb. In the first four months of the war 2,657 pedestrians died as a result of road accidents, double the number for the same period of 1938. Of the 1,200 who were killed in December, no fewer than 900 gave their lives to the blackout. In the same month there were 30,000 injuries on the roads.[2] In other words, there was a greater risk of being killed or injured on the roads than from an encounter with the enemy.

The response from the government was to impose a 20mph speed limit after dark in built-up areas. But, said Anderson, the military aim of the blackout must remain 'the dominant consideration'. Though still lacking evidence of any sort that Germany had either the capacity or will to launch a bombing war on Britain, the blackout was said to deprive the enemy of 'the means of launching an attack unexpectedly on this country the consequences of which would be little short of disastrous'.

Well, yes, but this, like the government's entire strategy, was to hope for the best while waiting for the worst to happen. It was hardly an inspiring call to action. Further concessions such as another extension of Summer Time (in 1940 it was stretched to the last day of the year and henceforth and for the rest of the war to the entire year) and introducing 'diffused' or 'pin-prick' street lighting did little to mollify public opinion.

As the enforcement officers for the blackout, air-raid wardens were the chief target of public vilification. After Munich, the ARP had attracted over half a million volunteers. By September 8th, 1939, the number had increased to 1.5 million. They were a motley force. Mostly middle-aged or over, they were not necessarily able-bodied. Though technically part of a national force, many refused to stray far from their homes. Among those who were reluctant to take orders were a number only too happy to order others about.

When, with the first air-raid warnings, came the summons to duty, an instinctive desire to abide by the conventions of the daily routine took precedence over speed and efficiency. Having waved off her husband at the garden gate, a housewife in the Hertfordshire village of Redbourn saw him returning, cycling furiously. He had forgotten his cycle clips. Another eager defender of civilisation was held up because he couldn't find his tie.

The blackout was a gift to busybodies who took pleasure in making life unpleasant. Even the wardens who tried to do a half-decent job were pilloried for landing what was seen as a cushy number. Paid £3 a week (over £100 in today's money), they were better off than recruits to the army who earned little over £1.

Arbitrary rulings by the police were a common cause of frustration and discontent. At South Mimms, a garage owner was fined five shillings for causing a neon sign to be illuminated at 12.30pm. Albert Batchelor was motoring near Great Missenden when his radiator burst and washed the black paint off his lamps: he was fined fifteen shillings. Mrs Ann Fleming of Renfrew was fined £3 when her child aged six months was taken with a fit in the middle of the night, and she rushed to its screams, leaving an exposed light for a minute – this fine was eventually revoked when it got up to the Lord Advocate of Scotland. One chief constable announced that it might be an offence to show a lighted cigarette in the streets, if it glowed much. A girl was sent to prison for a month for shining a torch into the face of a policeman. Age was no defence. On Armistice Day, police inspector Wright told the Worthing police court that when he called on 90-year-old Fanny Smith to upbraid her for showing a light, 'I thought it was all over', she said, 'I thought the Germans had something better to do'. She was fined ten shillings.[3]

How to interpret the multitude of regulations was a constant worry for high street shops. Discreet lighting, up to 25 watts, for window displays and an illuminated 'open' sign on the door, were generally permitted but not always. Reported in the *Daily Telegraph* on November 23rd:

> The premises of several large firms in Regent Street were visited by the police, who said that window-lighting was not allowed in the black-out. The Regent Street Association had the impression from a recent statement by the Home Secretary, Sir John Anderson, that shop-lighting would be allowed.

The police knew better.

There was much to be said to the credit of the ARP. The hours of duty by day or night were long and often uncomfortable. Arrangements for sleeping, feeding and sanitation were rarely adequate.

Proud of being among the first to volunteer and eager to serve, many were soon discouraged by the lack of support and of getting bogged down in the administrative quagmire. Interviewees for Mass-Observation were quick to voice complaints.

> It rather puts a damper on it when you don't hear for six months. (Man, artisan, age 26.)

> We've finished our course and now it seems we're at a standstill. (Man, artisan, age 31.)

> When we have passed out we seem to be finished with. (Man, artisan, age 31.)

We finished the gas course and never heard any more. I sort of lost heart when they didn't ask me to continue with the first aid. (Man, artisan, age 33.)

Since I attended lectures I've not heard anything of 'em. It seems as though it's a wash-out – all that time hearing nothing from them at all. I don't trouble to wear me badge or anything. (Man, artisan, age 67.)[4]

Looking back after 30 years, Jessie Lobjoit-Collins recalled her days as a senior warden close by a Hawker aircraft factory. She was among the few women in her ARP sector. One of the bizarre instructions she was given on signing up had to do with the landing of German parachutists: 'I was told to walk up to the Germans and unbrace their trousers.'

Other weird experiences came her way.

Our ARP post in those days was a back room of a local public house, which was only manned in the event of an alert. Soon after the outbreak of war I was standing by, as it was my turn to man the post in case of an alert. Actually I was lying on my bed, complete in an outsize suit of dungarees, when the alert was sounded. I seized my helmet and gas mask, jumped on my bicycle and dashed along to the post, it was the first real show, flak, searchlights and everything. I dashed into the post, picked up the 'phone to report to Divisional H.Q. that the post was manned, whilst doing so the door opened and in came a young man in a black and white dressing gown and on his head he wore a real Victorian night cap, the type that ended in a tassel. I was completely amazed and thought perhaps that after all, the search lights, flak, etc, were just a bad dream, when in came another warden, complete in kit and said to this young man, 'What Gilbert, is your head cold?' Then I realised it *was* all real.

Much of Jessie's time was taken up by civil defence exercises to test ARP efficiency. The results were not always what the authorities had hoped for.

> 150 Etonians had been taken to a partially built factory, as casualties. I sent a message for help and started to deal with the injuries, writing on the tabs, which described their injuries, what treatment I had given, when I found there were far too many for me to cope with in this way and just told them the state of their injuries. The most 'serious' of these were two boys with 'abdominal wounds', I told them they must stand by as they would be the first to go when the ambulance arrived. After a long wait in which time I thought I might have some real casualties on my hands, as the boys became restive and started throwing building materials at each other, the ambulance arrived. I saw one of the 'abdominal injuries' and instructed the crew to take him, but could not find the other boy, and said, 'Where is the other boy who has to go on the ambulance?' A boy beside me saw him some distance away, the other side of the factory and called out, 'I say Somerset you're the chap with the guts hanging out, come over here you're wanted.' I must add that this was said in a very superior voice.

Another young lady with grit was Iris Davies, who joined the ARP shortly before the war, hoping to be allowed to drive an ambulance, 'even have a big bell blaring'. At a casualty centre:

We took over the local open air swimming baths in the lower part of a north London suburb. The first night or two I slept on the floor of the laundry. Very cold and draughty. Our ambulances for the first few weeks were commandeered local coal carts and greengrocers' vans. We swept them out and slid in the stretchers.

Essential equipment was in short supply. There were ARP units unable to provide volunteers with helmets. Refusing to allow her husband to report for duty without protective headgear, a housewife recalls fitting him with a large saucepan. There was some discussion as to whether the handle should be to the rear or to the side. Rooting through the attic, another family discovered a German helmet, a souvenir of the Great War. Mercilessly teased when he turned up at his unit, the wearer chose to go bare-headed until proper helmets were available. The general shortage of helmets was not solved until large-scale manufacture from manganese came on stream after 1940.

Complaints of civil defence over-staffing continued until well into the new year of 1940. Under pressure from employers whose work schedules were disrupted, local councils, trade unions and MPs having to cope with angry constituents, a scale-back was authorised. The responsibility for deciding priorities fell to the regional commissioners or 'gauleiters' as they were unkindly nicknamed. In daily struggles with local authorities who were innately averse to cooperation, one frustrated commissioner likened his job to that of a 'head of a breakdown gang'. Economies were achieved but often at the cost of letting go some of the best people.

THE WEAKEST SECTOR on the home front was the fire service – or rather the fire services. One thousand six hundred fire brigades, each attached to a local authority, ranged in size from the London Fire Brigade, by far the largest, to a village horse-drawn cart with a pump and hose attached. Each was fiercely independent. Coordination was unknown and any sort of cooperation extremely rare.

The first attempt to bring a semblance of order to a chaotic system came in 1937 with a Home Office order to local authorities to spell out their air-raid precautions and fire-protection plans. Progress was tardy. Councils were reluctant to embark on expenditure when there remained a good chance that central government could be persuaded to bear the financial burden. This is what happened less than a year later when money was allocated to cover up to 75 per cent of the cost of raising standards. Included in the grant was an allocation for the recruitment and training of a volunteer force to be called the Auxiliary Fire Service.

In June 1938 the BBC put out an appeal for recruits, while on hoardings across London appeared an adaptation of the first line of Ivor Novello's famous song from the Great War. This time the message was 'Keep the home fires *from* burning'. A recruitment slogan trailed behind two planes circling London.

Later in 1938, the Fire Brigade Act took up a recommendation of a committee under Lord Riverdale set up three years earlier, requiring local authorities to maintain '*efficient* fire brigades'. That it had taken all this time to arrive at a statement of the obvious (did anyone on or off the committee favour *inefficient* fire brigades?) is more than enough to show how far there was to go to put the fire service onto a war footing. Even now, much time was wasted in arguments between fire services as to which equipment should be adopted to achieve standardisation. In the London region alone there were six types of fire hydrant. Only half the services were equipped with the 2½-inch round thread screw favoured by the London Fire Brigade.

Signing on as an auxiliary, the writer and illustrator Nicolas

Bentley could hardly bring himself to believe the degree of culpable inefficiency.

> Among the various local authorities who were responsible in peacetime for running local fire services – in the county of Kent alone, for example, there were fifty-seven such author-ities – many had views of their own about organisation and training and equipment, and although these views sometimes differed considerably from those of neighbouring authorities whom they might have to help, and on whose help they them-selves sometimes had to rely, they stuck to their different views with the blindness and tenacity of leeches. Not until the blitz eventually beat it into their parochial brains that the Luftwaffe was no respecter of administrative boundaries were they forced to recognise the need for a standardised fire-fighting system throughout the whole country. But by that time, there had already been an appalling loss of life and property.[5]

Nicolas Bentley put the blame squarely on Sir John Anderson and the Ministry of Home Security.

> Nothing can excuse the timidity of the Ministry of Home Security towards those local authorities who stuck out for the right to run their fire services in the way they thought best, irrespective of the national interest. The attitude adopted towards them made about as much sense as if the War Office had deputed the training, equipment and battle control of the county regiments to their own county councils.[6]

The auxiliaries were the chief sufferers of official incompetence. Mac Young was posted to Winsland Street sub-station near the railway delivery stables at Paddington. He and 24 colleagues had to spend their first nights 'bedded down on straw along with 200 restless horses and 10,000 flies'. There was no food and no washing facilities. Auxiliary firewoman Owtram was called up to a sub-station in a public garage with a large loft.

> We had been told to bring blankets and a supply of food. But one or two girls had brought neither. Of some fifteen women, only three wore uniform. The rest had joined the service within the last two days. We gathered in the mews, amiably smiling and, as regards most of us, utterly lost. The men had not yet arrived. By the wall of the garage was heaped a small pile of sandbags. They were symbolic only. They could be used to no purpose in the loft. The rain fell lightly. The darkness gathered. 'This simply can't be true,' said, I suppose, the inner voice of each one of us, while we exchanged cigarettes and feeble jokes.
>
> The men arrived. They were forceful and efficient. The company officer ran up the ladder, smashed with his axe the broken balustrade of a gallery, unlocked the door, called us all to come up and, a little after, called the roll in the garage below.[7]

Water for fire service pumps was fed from the mains buried under the streets. When, belatedly, it was realised that brittle, cast-iron piping would fracture under heavy explosions, the London County Council began laying down steel mains on the road surface close to the kerb. After it was found that connecting up the pipes was a heavy job taking too much time, rubber-lined hose was substituted.

AT THE START of the war, 1.5 million Anderson shelters had been delivered free to those on minimum incomes. The production rate was then up to 50,000 a week. But many shelters, more than the authorities cared to admit, had yet to be installed or had been installed so badly as to be almost worthless. Later, they were collected as scrap metal to support the arms industry. This raised the question of whether the entire exercise was a misuse of scarce resources. How many tanks could have been produced from the steel allocated to Anderson shelters?

Experts who were not of the Ministry of Home Security were scornful of the Anderson. Two months after the war started, an ARP coordinating committee composed of architects, surveyors, engineers, doctors and scientists gave it the thumbs down. 'The first big raid will reveal the terrible inadequacies ... of the whole official shelter scheme.'

Anderson himself was given a rough ride when he addressed a National Service rally in Glasgow's St Andrew's Hall. Some one thousand demonstrators demanded 'real protection' to compensate for the inefficacy of gas-masks and Anderson shelters.

The provision of public shelters varied over the country. By November 1939 London had accommodation ready for 520,000 citizens with work in progress for another 300,000. Birmingham, however, could offer protection to only 5 per cent of its population while Cambridge still had no plans at all for public shelters. Where there was local authority backsliding, the blame was put on the shortage of bricks, timber and concrete, though apathy and worries about an extra burden on the rates were the more obvious culprits.

What were known as 'Munich trenches' were dug across London's parks. Lined with timber or concrete, they offered limited protection from blast and splinters but were favoured by many who felt safest in shelters that were both underground and in the open. Throughout the country, by early 1940, there were 'permanent' trenches for up to 1.5 million people. The Munich trenches were strengthened and many were equipped with ramps or stairs and some form of lighting, seating and sanitation.

Some communities were lucky enough to have shelters tailor-made by nature. At Ramsgate and Dover, the chalk caves that had given shelter in the First World War were re-utilised. Chislehurst in Kent had the advantage of a 22-mile network of tunnels, 100 feet underground, dug originally for chalk mining. At first occupied unofficially, the tunnels were soon acknowledged as a safe refuge. When came the blitz in September 1940, electric lights, running water and ventilation had been installed. Five thousand east Londoners made the tunnels their nightly home. The charge was six pence a week for adults, three pence for children. By 1941 facilities included a cinema, three canteens, a first-aid unit and a visiting barber.[8]

Among other easy conversions were church crypts, railway arches and the disused tunnels under the streets of Luton. Progress was made in the early part of 1940 but it is doubtful that more than half the intended number of public shelters was ready by the spring.

A ban was put on using London's tube stations as a public refuge. The official explanation was that they had to be kept clear for troop movements and the evacuation of casualties. With this in mind, flood-gates were installed on stations close by the Thames and where there was most risk of overflow from fractured water mains and sewers. It was not long, however, before the authorities were defied by people simply buying platform tickets and staying put. Eventually, some 80 stations doubled as shelters.

With home shelters, there was a recurring problem of damp. One housewife reported toadstools growing in her Anderson. Nellie Carver wrote in her diary: 'Mum doesn't want us to have an Anderson in the garden. She says it would be better to be bombed in the warm than to get pneumonia.'[9] With a cold winter coming on, one of the toughest in living memory, this was a refrain often repeated.

My own family rejected an Anderson. A practical man who would have had no trouble in erecting the metal hut, my father thought it a waste of time and effort, not to mention the unnecessary destruction of his vegetable patch. Instead, he bought a heavy oak table. When there was an air-raid, mother and I, a babe in arms, slept under the table while father made do with an easy chair in the cupboard under the stairs. Fortunately, his faith in the security of a solid wood topping was never put to the test.

Living close to Tower Bridge, an obvious target for the Luftwaffe, Wanda Handscombe's father was quick to erect their Anderson.

He also helped our next-door neighbours to install theirs as the man was suffering from asthma and couldn't do much heavy digging. Unfortunately, as our houses were built on a slope and theirs was lower down than ours, their shelter always had a layer of water, so it was common practice afterwards to abandon their shelter and use ours. This became dreadfully crowded at times, four of them, four of us, two cats, two dogs, a tortoise (which finally disappeared) and a rabbit. (Later it was to become more crowded, when my brother and the two boys next door were home on leave with their friends, and after my father became an organiser for strayed, frightened and bombed animals – it was really chaotic.)

After the first air-raid warning there was panic activity in the Handscombe neighbourhood.

All around us there was the sound of frantic digging and frenzied shovelling as all the people who 'knew that there would not be a war', knew that now there was, and they only had a matter of hours to get their shelters in before nightfall and what it might bring.

Early the following morning with the second air-raid warning, the Handscombes were back in their shelter. This time the siren was followed by a whistle blast.

It had been announced on the wireless and in the newspapers that there could be attacks of gas, and the signal was 'one peep on the whistle – gas, two peeps – gas attack over'. So we all donned gas-masks, including our poor neighbour with his asthma. We sat in the shelter, breathing horribly through these gas masks until daylight, when my brother decided to go outside to find out what was happening. It was with great relief that we learnt that the blown whistle had been a mistake and that the all-clear had gone some three hours beforehand, although we were making such a noise breathing in and out we had not heard it.

Householders with a talent for DIY were reported having transformed their Anderson shelters almost into a home from home.

They had some sort of rough furniture inside, home-made forms made from packing cases and boards, wooden boxes to sit on, stools or chairs. The favourite form of lighting was a candle, but a few people had fixed up electric light either by carrying a flex through from the house or by installing a battery inside the shelter. A few had made no arrangements for lighting. A board served for a rough door in most shelters, and nearly all had a blanket or a piece of woollen cloth hanging over the entrance. One or two people had an oilstove for heat-ing, and some had first-aid boxes.

A variety of plants were being grown on the mounds over the shelters – marigolds, cornflowers, nasturtiums, anti-rrhinums, cabbages and onions.[10]

But the best of intentions could easily be misinterpreted. A father and son seen digging in their garden late at night were reported to the police. The suspected grave turned out to be an Anderson shelter.

MEMORIES ARE STRONGEST of the oddities of war on the home front. On the technical staff of the company supplying electricity to Exeter, W.N. Lavis spent a day taking light bulbs out of street lights, presum-ably to protect against the wafer-slim possibility that they might be accidentally switched on during a blackout. Railway travellers who might be caught in an air-raid were instructed to draw the blinds on carriage windows as a protection against flying glass and to lie on the floor until the danger had passed. Bus interiors were equipped with tiny blue discs of light which were said to be insufficient to read by and were barely adequate for preventing passengers from banging into each other.

For Charles Ritchie, the barrage balloons made an indelible impression, 'floating airily high in the evening sky. These captive monsters may be seen between their ascents pinned to the ground in the parks or public places – lying exhausted, breathing faintly with the passing puffs of wind.' Joan Gilbert rang Kensington Town Hall: 'Do you need help, I have no qualifications but plenty of common-sense.' She was put in charge of a distribution centre for gas-masks where, in a damp and sultry September, she advised on controlled breathing.

A rush to buy what were regarded as essential products caused scarcities and higher prices. Torches and batteries were much in demand, also canned food including potatoes. Having a long life, tins were a protection against damp, mice and gas. Jars of butter substitute and lemon and apricot curd along with bottled grapefruit soon disappeared from grocery shelves. The supply of black paper as a window cover outpaced demand. Asthma sufferers were told that 'your best and safest air-raid precaution is always to have a Do-Do tablet ready'.

And from the BBC came an ever-rushing stream of bulletins with information on licences that had to be applied for and general advice on how to cope with the regime of restrictions, shortages and other myriad irritations.

Into October 1939, the BBC gave more time to practical sugges-tions – for example, on how best to conserve energy. 'Don't open the door to your fridge more than absolutely necessary', urged W.H. Barrington Dalby, adding: 'Cut down on ice consumption.' To encourage economical eating habits, a doctor gave guidance that would hold good in peace as in war. What he called the 'Oslo breakfast' – milk, wholemeal bread, half an apple and a raw carrot – was 'much healthier for children than the traditional English fried breakfast'. It was one reason, he said, why Norwegian children were generally taller and with better complexions than their English coun-terparts. Every morning there was a radio invitation to keep fit with exercises for men on one day, for women on the next.

Heard in pubs and clubs and over the garden wall, ill-informed gossip fed fear and comfort in equal measure. 'London and Paris will be roaring furnaces within the week'; 'our air force is twice the admit-ted size'; 'we have bought Rumania's oil output for two years'; 'half the German tanks are cardboard'; 'we have something up our sleeve that the Germans don't know about'. Contrariwise, there was always somewhere in the country where German parachutists were said to have landed. Parents were told to watch out for toy balloons containing poison gas. It was reported, unreliably, that lakes and large ponds were to be drained to prevent the landing of German seaplanes.

CHAPTER 12

Anything But the Truth

The impression given by Whitehall at the start of the war was of having no idea of the mood of the people it was supposed to serve. The manifest failure to inspire civilian morale speaks volumes for the bureaucratic mentality that was at once secretive and deceptive, holding back on knowledge that might be thought to cause panic in the streets while putting out false or distorted stories that led only to disillusionment and anger when the real facts could no longer be camouflaged.

Censorship as such was not the issue. The British people were used to restrictions, often heavy-handed, on what they could read or see on stage or screen. A puritan code, rigorously enforced, was extended in the Chamberlain years to cover political subjects, in particular those that might offend the dictators. Close attention was given to treating Hitler with the respect due to a world leader of impeccable credentials. In 1938, in the build-up to Munich, the young Terence Rattigan, riding on the success of his comedy *French Without Tears*, co-wrote *Follow My Leader*, a farce set in an imaginary European country which poked fun at Nazi pretensions. There was a dig too at submissive Britain. When, at a high point of the play, the British embassy is blown up, it is the British ambassador who apologises.

In his role as Lord Chamberlain, responsible for ensuring that the theatre kept within the bounds of propriety, Lord Clarendon consulted the Foreign Office. Predictably, back came the judgement that 'the production of this play would not be in the best interests of the country'. Rattigan's producer waited until July 1939 when it might reasonably have been assumed that appeasement was a lost cause, before submitting a revised script. The play had support within the Lord Chamberlain's office, where one reader concluded that any objections would only come from a country 'suffering a very far-fetched imagination and a guilty conscience'. Even so, Clarendon covered his tracks by deciding to seek the view of the German embassy, where a cultural attaché told him that *Follow My Leader* would 'not be helpful in improving Anglo-German relations'. The ban stayed in place. A month later Britain and Germany were at war. This farce over a farce was symptomatic of the lengths that the Chamberlain government was prepared to go in its increasingly desperate attempts to keep Germany sweet.

One who did get away with dramatic comment on current affairs was George Bernard Shaw. At 82, the grand old man of the theatre wrote *Geneva*, a mild satire on dictatorship with a thinly disguised Hitler, Mussolini and Franco summoned to a Committee of Intellectual Cooperation to answer for their transgressions. As he said in a note on *Geneva*: 'Instead of making the worst of all dictators ... I have made the best of them.' The only touch of controversy is a scene in which the foreign secretary, a parody of Halifax, threatens war if Germany invades another country. After a first outing in Warsaw, *Geneva* was premiered in English at the Malvern Festival in August 1938. The play was a resounding flop.

Songs and jokes about Hitler were rigorously excised. Herbert

Farjeon's lyric, 'Even Hitler had a Mother', was banned in 1936 and again in 1938. It was only when the war was a month old that the song had its first public airing.

As with the theatre, so with the cinema. Film censorship dated back to 1912 when the British Board of Film Censors, overseen by the Home Office, was set up with a president appointed by the home secretary. By the 1920s, a BBFC certificate was an essential precondition for a film to be exhibited in front of a paying audience. Moral and religious considerations were paramount but political suitability had also to be taken into account. The twice-weekly newsreels shown in cinemas had to obtain police permits to film in any public place and it was accepted by producers that sensitive topics, such as the coverage of Nazi rallies, had to be given the nod by the Foreign Office, Home Office and even, occasionally, Conservative Central Office.

Scripts were farmed out for assessment to regulars of the old brigade such as Major Harding de Fontblanque Cox, known to his friends as Cockie, aged 81, an authority on dogs and hunting who made it known that he would 'judge film stories as I would horse flesh or a dog. I shall look for clean lines.' Apparently it was no matter that Cox suffered a form of lethargy which caused him to fall asleep when he read anything.

As noted by film critic and historian George Perry, the movie industry

produced little that could be interpreted as comment on the world situation. No films about the Nazi menace were made before the war; British films kept a silence as close-lipped as any of the appeasers, and spared the German government from the embarrassment of criticism. Even documentaries did not look at the menace threatening the entire world; it was left to the American series *The March of Time* to produce a journalistic account of the events inside Germany, which was banned outright by the British Board of Film Censors. Similarly, the British cinema had nothing to say about the Spanish Civil War, which raged from 1936 onwards.[1]

As president of the BBFC from 1935, Lord Tyrrell, formerly head of the news department of the Foreign Office and ambassador in Paris, objected to the 'creeping of politics into films' and put the black spot on any film 'dealing with current burning political questions'. Even *The Relief of Lucknow* failed to get a certificate 'for fear of reviving memories of the days of conflict in India which it has been the earnest desire of both countries to obliterate'.

But it was in newspapers and journals that establishment intervention was most blatant. Chamberlain made no secret of his aim to shape the news to suit his ends. Criticism was unwelcome.

With the press barons, Lord Beaverbrook, Lord Rothermere, Lord Astor, Lord Kemsley and Lord Camrose, the prime minister was pushing at an open door. Each was keen on a settlement with Germany and each was convinced that Chamberlain was the man to bring it about. The facts were a secondary consideration.

A notorious example was a climb-down at *The Times* when the German embassy complained about an accurate report that the Luftwaffe had been involved in the bombing of Guernica in Spain in April 1937. In response to a temporary German ban on *The Times*, editor Geoffrey Dawson, one of Halifax's closest friends and a fellow Old Etonian, wrote to his correspondent in Switzerland pleading that he could not understand what 'precisely' had produced the antagonism in Germany, as he did his utmost 'night after night to keep out of the paper anything that might hurt their susceptibility'. Moreover, though convinced that the Guernica article was no less than the truth, there had been no attempts by *The Times* 'to rub it in or to harp upon it'.

When, in February 1938, Ribbentrop took over as German foreign minister, Beaverbrook sent gushing congratulations, pledging the 'loyal support of my newspapers' for Ribbentrop's efforts in pursuit of 'peace and tranquillity'. On March 10th, the *Express* ran the first of an often repeated prediction: 'There will be no European war.'

At the beginning of September 1938, Beaverbrook himself signed off on an article for the *Express* in which he tried to justify his optimism. 'There will be no European war. Why? Because the decision of peace and war depends on one man, the German Fuehrer and he will not be responsible for making war at present.' Ironically, given that Beaverbrook was later to join Churchill's war coalition as minister for aircraft production (and very effective he was too), he sacked his future boss from the *Evening Standard* when Churchill used his column to speak out on behalf of the beleaguered Czechs.

However, Beaverbrook did retain the brilliant cartoonist David Low, a New Zealander whose barbs against appeasement gave as much offence in Downing Street as they did in the Reichstag. Low was too popular to let go, though Beaverbrook tried to persuade him to tone down the volume of his wake-up call.

The strongest media opponents to appeasement were to be found on the *Manchester Guardian* and the *Yorkshire Post*, quality newspapers albeit with relatively small circulations. But even here, the editors came under pressure from their proprietors to temper their rhetoric.[2] Arthur Mann, editor of the *Yorkshire Post*, was not one to be intimidated. Describing Chamberlain as a 'commonplace politician' unequal to the challenges of statesmanship and leadership, Mann faced demands from the Yorkshire Conservative Newspaper Association for his resignation. Much to the surprise of the ministers who worked behind the scenes to bring about his downfall, he survived a vote of censure.

Of the national press, the *News Chronicle*, a traditionally Liberal newspaper, did not hold back on criticising Chamberlain. In November 1938, it gave prominence to an opinion poll showing that 37 per cent of the population was not satisfied with the prime minister and that 72 per cent wanted more to be spent on armaments. But the truly revelatory finding of the poll, that 86 per cent of the British people did not believe Hitler when he disavowed any further territorial claims, was held from readers on the orders of the *News Chronicle* chairman, Sir Walter Layton. Writing to Chamberlain, he explained that he had not 'withheld those figures from publication ... because I have any doubt that they faithfully reflect British opinion ... but because I fear that so blunt an advertisement of the state of British opinion ... would exacerbate feelings in Germany'.[3]

Most of the opinion leaders of the press were no more than agents for Chamberlain's foreign policy, encouraging him to pursue his dreams with no risk of being told that he and his compliant ministerial colleagues were living in a fantasy of their own making.

In March 1939, Chamberlain urged his home secretary, Sir Samuel Hoare, to use the opportunity of a speech to his Chelsea constituents to put a thick gloss on the international picture. Hoare duly obliged with a mind-blowing prediction of the forthcoming 'golden age' of peace and prosperity in which 'fine men in Europe, the three dictators and the prime ministers of England and France ... might in an incredibly short time transform the whole history of the world'.[4]

Chamberlain endorsed claims of his omnipotence with a briefing to lobby correspondents on the near certainty, once the Spanish 'affair' was over, of a resumption of negotiations for general disarmament. Press coverage was laudatory. For Lord Halifax, pacifier though he was, this was a step too far. Resenting Chamberlain's tendency to dictate foreign policy without reference to the Foreign Office, he made his feelings known. The response from Downing Street was apologetic, with Chamberlain professing 'to be horrified at the result of my talk with the press which was intended only as a general background but was transcribed by them verbatim'.

Did he really believe this? It seems unlikely. What does stand out is Chamberlain's conviction that he could manipulate public opinion while ignoring evidence that public opinion was drifting away from him. The clearest indication, if he had cared to note it, was the rising circulation of the *Daily Mirror* and its Sunday stablemate, the *Sunday Pictorial*, both papers having chosen to buck the trend by giving Chamberlain a hard time, not least by energetically touting Churchill as a leader who would stand up to Hitler.

With the declaration of war, the *Mirror* pulled out all the stops. On September 4th, the columnist William Neil Connor, better known as Cassandra, headed his page:

WANTED! FOR MURDER … FOR KIDNAPPING …
FOR THEFT AND FOR ARSON …
ADOLF HITLER
ALIAS ADOLF SCHICKELGRUBER

As editor of the *Sunday Pictorial*, Hugh Cudlipp encapsulated the editorial policy of the Mirror Group:

We are in the war. Let us fight it. No truck with the Nazis. Throw out the muddlers. Get on with the job … with no sinister truce leaving Hitlerism better equipped to turn all his savagery upon France and Britain …[5]

It made a welcome change from the mealy-mouthed sanctities found in most other papers.

A TIGHTENING OF the screws on the dissemination of news came when the Ministry of Information (also known widely as the Ministry of Disinformation) opened for business on the second day of the war. Based in Senate House in Bloomsbury, the Art Deco tower block designed to be the centre point of London University, its responsibilities included the management of news thought by the government to be fit to print, the censorship of newspapers, movies and the BBC to exclude information and opinion that might detract from the war effort, the dissemination of propaganda abroad, and the encouragement of morale-boosting initiatives at home. The latter function sprang from the Home Intelligence Division which, in a haphazard way, kept a check on rumours and gossip.

From the start, the MOI was bedevilled by the absence of clear guidelines as to what and what was not permitted to be in the public domain. Trying to tie down the government to a firm set of rules was a frequent parliamentary diversion, starting with attempts to clarify regulation 39b of the Emergency Powers Act which made it an offence 'to influence public opinion ... in a manner likely to be prejudicial to the defence of the realm or the efficient prosecution of the war'. Did this include idle chatter overheard in the pub or over a cup of tea? No one could tell. And what of written material, a letter, say, to a friend sounding off at a grievance against obtuse officialdom? Were critics of the government to be prohibited from expressing their views orally or in writing?

After taking over as home secretary, Sir John Anderson failed to give reassurance with his dry, didactic answers to questions in the House of Commons. While, for example, he could see no objection to 'leaflets couched in dignified language seeking to make an appeal to reason', he was strongly averse to material that appealed 'not to reason, but to passion and prejudice'. This left a lot of leeway for the definition of good taste.

But the biggest problem for the MOI was in finding the man-power capable of carrying out its allotted tasks. Given the job of planning a centralised news service that embraced all the ministries including those for the armed forces, Sir Samuel Hoare in his time as home secretary came up against the innate suspicion of the civil service of any attempt to intrude on what it saw as an exclusive pre-serve and the reluctance of Whitehall to share news that was not guaranteed against misinterpretation unless it was convoluted beyond comprehension.

Hoare had been struggling with the contradictions since 1936 when the setting up of an MOI was first mooted. Knowing nothing of public relations beyond a narrow political experience, he made the sensible decision to enlist as director designate Sir Stephen Tallents, whose background included the creation of the GPO film unit in 1933 and serving as controller of public relations and deputy director at the BBC under Lord Reith.

What amounted to an experimental outing for the MOI took place after the Munich crisis when a skeleton staff oversaw the coord-ination of foreign policy press releases and briefings. Such was the muddle and confusion caused by internecine warfare between gov-ernment departments as to discredit the whole idea of a general ministry to handle news and propaganda. Frustrated at every turn, Tallents threw up his hands in January 1939. That the MOI survived was less a tribute to the brilliance of the idea than to the inability of anyone in high office to come up with an alternative for keeping the public abreast with the 'right' news.

In a misguided attempt to play safe, a retired judge was chosen to succeed Tallents. Lord Macmillan was said by Hoare to be 'universally respected for his ability and imperturbability'.[6] If this was true of his time on the bench, it did not extend to the rough, tough life of front-line journalism. Macmillan's failure to understand how newspapers operated extended to his professional colleagues, mostly from the university cloisters, who knew nothing of daily news except what they read at their breakfast tables.

No better example of the disconnect from real life was recorded than on the day Germany invaded Poland. With the expectation of the war spreading to take in Britain, a committee of the Home Publicity Division met to suggest ways of ameliorating the suffering of an air attack on London.

> Lady Grigg said that the most comforting thing – at least where women were concerned – was to have a cup of tea and get together to talk things over.
>
> This was agreed to be a most valuable suggestion. Ways for carrying it into effect … were considered. It was decided that some … widely spread method was required and that an appeal should be made to householders to supply tea to anyone in their neighbourhood who needed it during or after an air-raid.
>
> Professor Hilton … referred to the value of sugar for steadying the nerves.
>
> Lady Grigg suggested that sensational newspaper placards should be prohibited, as was done in the last war.[7]

It got worse. On September 13th, 1939, the Ministry sent the Home Office a paper on boosting civilian morale. 'Expert advice' propagated deceit based on half- or quarter-truths.

> The people must feel that they are being told the truth. Distrust breeds fear much more than knowledge of reverses. The all-important thing for publicity to achieve is the conviction that the worst is known. This can be achieved by the

adoption, publication and prosecution of a policy. The people should be told that this is a civilians' war, or a People's War, and therefore they are to be taken into the Government's confidence as never before ... But what is truth? We must adopt a pragmatic definition. It is what is believed to be the truth. A lie that is put across becomes the truth and may, therefore, be justified. The difficulty is to keep up lying. ... It is simpler to tell the truth and, if a sufficient emergency arises, to tell one big, thumping lie that will then be believed.

While the bombs were falling:

People should be encouraged to keep themselves busy by knitting, doing crossword puzzles, playing games, etc ... The importance of laughter, which acts as a strong release, is not to be forgotten. After a raid people should be given as much to do as possible ...

Scared people sheltering during a raid should be made to sit quietly, be told their fear is only natural and given a cup of coffee after which they should be all right ...

Prayer or the psychological equivalent of prayer is important, i.e. relying on something bigger than yourself.[8]

At least one senior officer at the Home Office was sufficiently aware to give a dusty answer.

A lot of the material seems to me extremely elementary and condescending; some of it is misleading, some contradictory. Generally I think it greatly undervalues the spirit of our people ... The people of this country do *not* distrust the radio and the Press ... The suggestion that the propaganda value of a speaker is increased if he attacks the Government on other than war points seems to me entirely mischievous and wrong-headed. Trust in leadership is an enormous factor in maintaining confidence.[9]

One can almost feel sorry for Macmillan who, lost in the bedlam of competing egos, lasted only four months. However, it was in his time that the logical decision was taken to allocate news censorship to a Press and Censorship Bureau; also to set up a separate department to disseminate propaganda calculated to disaffect and demoralise the enemy. But it was not so much the administrative structure that was at fault as the limitations of the staff who stayed to the end of the Chamberlain government. When Duff Cooper took over the Ministry in May 1940, he found too many 'brilliant amateurs'.

Ex-ambassadors and retired Indian Civil Servants abounded, the brightest ornaments of the Bar were employed on minor duties, distinguished men of letters held their pens at the monster's service, and all were prepared to work at any hour and without holiday in their enthusiasm for the cause. It was tragic to see so much ability, so much goodwill so nearly wasted.[10]

Among the fiercest critics of the MOI was the dramatist, author and popular broadcaster, J.B. Priestley, who, getting out and about, was able to report on the views of ordinary citizens. He lost count of the number of favourable references to Hitler and his achievements in putting Germany back on its feet. His conclusion: 'We have a magnificent case but we are handling it very badly.' As to the MOI, 'What is wanted … is a little less Lincoln's Inn Fields and a bit more Gracie Fields.'

For all the talk of a 'people's war', no effort was made to raise the offensive spirit or to produce a convincing rallying call to action. H.V. Morton noted:

> There was no flag-wagging, no bands, no appeals to patriotism, no pictures of the King and Queen; no one knew the names of any generals or admirals, and the attempt on the part of the Press to give 'Tiger' Gort heroic status fell completely flat. The cold, objective attitude of the Government, and that of the Prime Minister, who rattled his umbrella ominously once or twice, did not exactly help the country to get excited about the War. There was nothing full-blooded about it. And, indeed, how could there be when the mental attitude for a quarter of a century in Parliament, the Press and on platforms had been one of disarmament and pacificism? ...
>
> The tepid attitude of the Government was such that it almost seemed to be apologising for the War. While calling upon the country to plunge into the war effort, it at the same time deplored the necessity for doing so, which was extremely confusing.[11]

Solemn declarations served only to antagonise those on the receiving end. As *The Times* commented:

> [T]he insipid and patronising invocations to which the passer-by is now being treated have a power of exasperation which is all their own. There may be no intrinsic harm in their faint, academic piety, but the implication that the public morale needs this kind of support, or, if it did, that this is the kind of support it would need, is calculated to provoke a response which is neither academic nor pious.

It was significant that David Low refused to work for a ministry that was known only for its 'ineptness and futility'.

THE MYTHICAL ATTACKS that prompted the first three air-raid warnings were assumed to be real for hours or even days after the All Clear. Either Whitehall did not know or, if it did know, was slow to reveal the truth on radio or in the press. In the case of the dawn alarm on September 6th, it was late afternoon before there was any official reaction.

With the multitude of corrections, contradictions and denials, news management became something of a joke. Eager for a positive take on how the war was progressing, imaginary or feeble successes were blown up out of all proportion only to be quickly deflated. On September 24th, wide coverage was given to a supposedly success-ful bombing of the Zeppelin factory at Friedrichshafen. Three days later the story was denied. The mantle of secrecy, though largely ineffective, grew heavier with every blunder. As London regional commissioner, Harold Scott took it all in good part:

I was asked to take a party of journalists round our HQ in the Geological Museum so that they could let the public know what was being done. Elaborate precautions were taken to conceal the identity of the building: the pressmen were col-lected from a rendezvous at night, and were driven in a coach with drawn blinds to Exhibition Road. Their inspection lasted for over two hours, and as they were leaving one journal-ist said to me drily: 'You're quite right, of course, to keep your location secret, but I think you ought to take that notice down.' He pointed to a printed notice about fire precau-tions on the wall inside the main door: it was clearly headed

'Geological Survey'. Before the next conducted tour, I made an even more careful search for tell-tale evidence, determined not to be caught out a second time, but once again I failed. Another observant visitor pointed out that the name of the original occupier was still conspicuous – on the towels in the cloakroom.[12]

A columnist on the *Express* happened to mention that he had spent the previous Sunday in Bognor when the weather was perfect. He was told by the censor that no indication of weather conditions could be given until after ten days. The offending sentence was changed from 'last Sunday' to 'a couple of Sundays ago' and was passed.

The heads of the armed forces and their ministers made the task of the MOI no easier. They thought as they had always thought, that no news was good news. Their treatment of war correspondents was lamentable. Their military minders were old-school warriors, 'relics of a vanished England'.[13] Their leading light was Captain Charles Tremayne, an Old Etonian ex-cavalry officer and landowner, who was rarely sober. He drank neat gin for breakfast and could get through six bottles in two days. His job, as he saw it, was to keep journalists permanently sozzled.

It would have helped if the government had published a clear statement of war aims. Instead, there were no answers forthcoming to perfectly sensible questions asked whenever the war was discussed. If Britain was unable to go to war for Czechoslovakia, why was it suddenly possible to act on behalf of Poland? If Germany was to be punished for invading Poland, why not Russia?

In his brief tenure at the MOI Lord Macmillan was impotent. The ministry's propaganda, he opined, was based on the restoration of: 'The sanctity of absolute values; the sanctity of the individual and of the family [and] the comity of nations.' That Chamberlain was not prepared to come straight out with determination to engage with the enemy was a sure sign that a negotiated peace was still on the agenda.

A fresh start was promised for the MOI in January 1940 when Macmillan made way for John Reith. Having moulded the BBC in his image, Reith had gone on to head Imperial Airways, a job he found to be unfulfilling. He was eager for a new challenge. It proved to be beyond him.

Reith started with a brave attempt to explain to the government where it was going wrong.

> Among the less informed classes a passive, negative feeling of apathy and boredom is apparent. Associated with this is a reaction to grievances and discomforts. There is a general feeling that individuals do not count in the conduct of the war and that the only thing to do is to live as normal a life as possible.

He followed up with a proposed set of war aims, spelling out that 'a compromise peace with an unbeaten Germany would be a defeat in the long run'. This was too much for Chamberlain. The Cabinet ruled that such a bold assertion was 'liable to misinterpretation'. Instead it was agreed that 'no peace could be justified' without a guarantee of basic freedoms in a new world with values 'Christian and not Satanic, spiritual and not material'. Hardly able to believe what he was hearing, Reith was told to lay off the German people who were not to blame for the sins of their leaders. It was not until Churchill came to power that the tone changed with stark warnings of what would happen if Germany invaded. As a Ministry of Information handout proclaimed, contrary to common opinion that everyday life would carry on much as usual,

If Hitler won you couldn't make a joke in the pub without being afraid that a spy may not get you run in or beaten up; you could not talk freely in front of your children for fear that they might give you away (in Germany they are encouraged to); if you were a worker you would be at the mercy of your employer about hours and wages for you would have no trade union.

Meanwhile, with no headline news to release, the MOI found itself to be a popular target for press attacks. As Sir Samuel Hoare later recalled:

The American correspondents were restive under any restrictions. The British Press complained that broadcasting was given a favoured position. Still more serious, the Service Departments, although they had agreed to pool their news, showed that in practice they were determined to keep control of their communiqués and censorship. Lastly, the public was convinced that the absence of news did not mean that nothing was happening, but that information was being withheld by the Government for sinister reasons.[14]

Inevitably, families were confused as to what best to do in an emergency. In a Leeds household, the youngest member was asleep during an air-raid warning. He was woken up by his mother.

'Austin, what do you make of this noise?' He told his mother it was an air-raid siren, so they went downstairs and sat on the couch in the drawing-room. He asked what had happened to his father, and his mother said he was fast asleep, so she had thought it a pity to wake him.

They stayed for a while, and then his mother said she could smell mustard gas; he sniffed and decided he could. So they went upstairs to wake the father.

Austin went back to bed; his parents decided to go into the next-door shelter. When they were there they heard whistles and wondered what they were for. Their neighbour said they were the warden's whistles, and were to supplement the sirens. When he said this he suddenly realised that he was a warden himself, so he dashed out of the shelter in his pyjamas and without his false teeth into his car. It was so dark he could not see to drive very well, and when he arrived at his destination, the all-clear signals were going.[15]

Posters delivering limpid messages festooned buses and trams, telephone boxes and shop windows, libraries and post offices. 'Freedom is in Peril – Defend it with all your Might'; 'We're Going to see it Through'; 'Our Fighting Men Depend on You'; 'Careless Talk May Give Away Vital Secrets'. Insofar as these exhortations registered, they were greeted with apathy or derision. The image of an ogre-like, finger-pointing Goering that appeared on poster sites with the legend 'I need your help, neglect your work' was withdrawn for fear that some might take it literally. One poster in particular gave offence. The message, under a crown logo, appeared in vivid red on hoardings, in shop fronts and on public transport.

FREEDOM IS IN PERIL
DEFEND IT WITH ALL YOUR MIGHT.
YOUR COURAGE
YOUR CHEERFULNESS
YOUR RESOLUTION
WILL BRING US VICTORY.

That no one in charge foresaw the likely misinterpretation of the transition from 'your' to 'us' underscores propagandists' myopia. Who else could 'us' be but the ruling class? Then again, to suggest that 'freedom is in peril' begged the question as to what is freedom? With the plethora of rules and regulations appearing by the day and the closing of most entertainments, there did not seem to be much freedom worth fighting for – unless, of course, you happened to be part of the elite.

The uproar prompted a reworking of an old story of the Great War when a young Oxford woman presented a youngish-looking don with a white feather, asking him why he was not defending his vaunted culture. He said: 'Dear lady, I am the culture which is being defended.'

Malcolm Muggeridge made the same point, rather more seriously, in his book *The Thirties*:

> What freedom was to be fought for? they may have wondered. We are all free to sleep under the arches of the Seine, Anatole France had said; we were all free to read what Lord Beaverbrook decreed should be printed in the *Daily Express*, to earn money, to buy and to sell, to vote for … Mr Chamberlain who had brought us peace with honour from Munich. How varied was our freedom – stockbrokers freely buying and selling shares, lawyers freely obtaining briefs and clergymen freely obtaining benefices, each individual freely struggling to feed and clothe and house himself as best he might. This so varied freedom was in peril, and needed to be defended.[16]

Or, as the crime writer Donald Henderson observed, 'There are a thousand forms of slavery under the title Freedom'.[17]

It took some time for Tory politicians to realise that an over-emphasis on restoring Britain to what she was in the good old days was counterproductive. As Churchill was to discover in the 1945 general election, most people had no great affection for the static and complacent Britain of the earlier part of the century.

For those who had to deal directly with the MOI, indignation boiled over when Sir Edward Grigg, parliamentary secretary to the ministry, confessed to the House of Commons that of a staff of 999, only 43 were journalists. Among the barely qualified were a professor of Christian world relations from Boston University, a retired major of Marines, a headmaster and a titled lady whose previous occupation was marked with a blank.

Even after a shakeout of the hangers-on, the quality of those remaining in Senate House never rose above sub-standard. 'Instead of a large badly run Ministry of Information', said one critic, 'we now had a small badly run Ministry of Information'. As the ministry's parliamentary secretary, Harold Nicolson, wrote in 1941, it was 'the most unpopular department in the whole British Commonwealth'.

THOUGH A SEPARATE entity, the BBC was forced into an uneasy relationship with the MOI. In his history of British broadcasting, Asa Briggs describes the BBC as the 'elephant in the room'. Its charter gave it independence from government interference but in the current emergency there was a case to be made for using the airwaves to support the national effort. Radio, with over 9 million licence holders by 1939, was the easiest and most effective means of reaching out to the public.

Then again, the BBC was a recent creation with most of its potential still to be realised. At the start of the war, those who were responsible for its creative output were excited by the prospects but were unsure of the Corporation's status as a vehicle for news and comment. The BBC's tendency was to play safe. Throughout the 1930s every effort was made to avoid subject matter that was liable to upset the establishment or threaten the entrenched order. Interviews were closely scripted to ensure that predictable answers were given to predictable questions. High marks went to broadcasters with 'safe' views. Churchill was among those thought to be too controversial to be counted among the regular contributors.

Consultation with the Foreign Office was a matter of routine, with the BBC happy to go along with the advice of Whitehall on sensitive issues. All BBC employees were vetted by MI5, a process that continued well into the 1990s. Yet ministers were outspoken in their criticism of the BBC in not being sufficiently 'positive' in putting across government policy; an accusation that was occasionally deflected by the BBC. In his time as foreign secretary, Sir Samuel Hoare had to be reined in for assuming that it was up to him to 'allow' broadcasts on such topics as the Italian claims on Abyssinia.

Even so, the BBC submitted to pressure from the Foreign Office to be more pro-Franco in the Spanish Civil War and to drop the term 'insurgents' when describing the generals who had rebelled against their elected government.[18] The BBC's compliance to 'keep off Communism and Nazi-ism and Fascism' led to radio silence on the major political topics of the period. A chief news editor was later to conclude 'that in the past we have not played the part which our duty to the people of this country called upon us to play. We have in fact taken part in a conspiracy of silence.'[19]

This is in contrast to the spurious claim made in 1939 when the BBC news department was all for 'telling the truth and nothing but the truth, even if the truth is horrible'.[20]

But the chief complaint against the government was its slow recognition of broadcasting as a social unifier and a force for gearing up the nation for the supreme effort to defeat fascism. At one stage, Chamberlain had in mind to save the state some money by closing down the BBC.

Pre-war, broadcasting had been organised on a regional basis with a high proportion of programmes serving chiefly a local interest. The national station was responsible for general news bulletins and for programmes of countrywide interests. Come the war, government prompting led to a merging of all the regional outposts into a single national or Home Service. The ostensible justification was to permit greater technical efficiency. The largely unspoken but more pressing reason was to allow for central (i.e. government) control over the network.

News bulletins, the daily church service and *Children's Hour* were the only fixed points in a schedule that gave unlimited time to 'What to Do in an Emergency' programmes and to the endless round of official announcements. As for reports from overseas, the BBC had no foreign correspondents on its staff and had no plans to employ any. The European Service was starved of funds and there was even talk of cutting programmes that were not within the narrow remit of the Home Office.

Likewise radio propaganda aimed at the German public, most of which was facile to the point of imbecility. What schoolboy, one wonders, was responsible for the ribald verses put out by the anti-Nazi 'Freedom station'?

I'm Hermann the German,
The lad with a girth!
My bluster should fluster
All nations on earth!
The Führer securer
Becomes when I bawl;

I'm Hermann the German,
The fattest of all!

And the follow up:

I'm Göring now spurring
A peaceful career;
As huntsman and stuntsman
I'm quite without peer!
Just trust me and, bust me!
You'll come to no harm —
I'm Göring the purring
Exponent of charm!

A succession of 'commandments' were delivered to a long-suffering
German public.

If you are a soldier, do not fight.
If you are a workman, work slowly.
Wherever you are, broadcast the truth about Hitler's
    abominable deeds.
Do not believe Hitler's lies.
Do not believe any Nazi newspaper.
Do not allow the Nazis to rob you of your money, do not
    give it to a bank.
Make no difference between yourself and your neighbour
    on racial or religious grounds.
Help all victims of the Nazis.
Help to organise systematically the fight against Hitler.
Beware of false friends.
Fight against Hitler with all your might, because he

has expelled the best German thinkers, murdered the workers' leaders, slaughtered the Jews.

Down with Hitler.

As with much else at this stage of the war, the Germans were ahead of the game. Quite properly feared as a ruthless manipulator, propaganda minister Joseph Goebbels made no secret of his ambition to transform Germany by initiating a 'mental revolution', suppressing all that impaired the strength of the Reich at home or abroad, along with anything that was deemed 'offensive to the honour and dignity of a German'. Anyone voicing doubts as to the justice of the German cause was liable to be arrested. Britain and France carried the blame for the war.

But if Goebbels was cavalier with the truth, he was effective, not least in targeting opinion in neutral countries. In early 1940, Germany launched an English-language radio network, purporting to be based in Britain. The most effective output was from the Christian Peace Movement, a supposedly pacifist station with its signature hymn, 'Oh God, Our Help in Ages Past'. A recurring theme was the peaceful intent of the Nazi–Soviet pact, claims also made by the Workers' Challenge, said to be run by socialist revolutionaries. But the best known of the German propaganda outlets was the New British Broadcasting Station (NBBS), also called the New BBC, the mouthpiece for William Joyce, immortalised as Lord Haw-Haw.

The line taken by Joyce and by other Oxbridge-accented broadcasters of NBBS (who sounded just like the real BBC announcers) was of the need for the British public to prepare for the inevitability of invasion and conquest. Not that there was any cause for concern. In 'Guidance for Britain if Invaded', a regular feature, listeners were fed the soothing message that civilians were in no danger and that everyday life would proceed as normal.

Lord Haw-Haw was a nickname invented by journalist and broad-caster Jonah Barrington. The aim was to use ridicule to bring Joyce into disrepute. Barrington gave Lord Haw-Haw a wife called Winnie of Warsaw or Winnie the Whopper and other relatives such as Auntie Gush and Uncle Smarmy. But familiarity does not necessarily breed contempt and it is arguable that Barrington's attempt at satire actually helped to promote Joyce. Trading on the popular discontent with the way the war was being conducted and with those who were conduct-ing it, Lord Haw-Haw attracted a following that gave more credence to his social and political comment than to the official pronounce-ments from the MOI.

And with some justification. It was not unusual for Joyce to be a step ahead of the MOI in reporting events, each in itself not particu-larly significant but collectively suggesting that he had an equal claim to be trusted. His attacks on the 'hyenas of international finance' and the 'decadent upper classes' were rewarded with nods of approval from left-wing campaigners and by worried shakes of the head from those who saw themselves in the firing line. By 1940 almost 30 per cent of the British people (one in three adults) listened in to German broadcasts from Hamburg.

The heavy hand of the censor reached out to all letters arriving from and sent to overseas. Hot in their search for information, delib-erately or accidentally planted in mountains of correspondence, the staff of Postal Censorship were housed in the former headquarters of Littlewoods, the Liverpool-based football pool promoters. H.V. Morton recorded:

One of the censors took me first to the place where all out-ward and inward foreign mails are stacked before inspection. Mail-bags of many colours, and from every country, were sus-pended in wooden racks.

The outward mails are of two kinds: letters and parcels from Great Britain to addresses in neutral countries, and mail-bags consigned to Germany, but seized on the way by the Contraband Control.

Inward mails are the usual foreign mails to this country from all parts of the world. This means that every communication to and from a neutral country must pass through the filter of postal censorship before it finds its way to the address on the envelope.

Upstairs, under one gigantic girdered roof, sit the one thousand, three hundred censors. The male censors occupy one section of the room, and the women the other. They sit at long tables and look like students in an oversized public library.

At the end of each table, printed on a card, is the list of languages spoken at that table. People who speak the ordinary European languages are as common as blackberries in September. Persian, Urdu, Hindustani, Yiddish, Hebrew are also ordinary accomplishments.

But there are rarer specialists. Some tables can produce men who have made Chinese dialects a life study, and others there have written learned works, known only perhaps to the Foreign Office, on the language spoken by tribes on the Afghanistan frontier.[21]

As the war progressed the number of postal censors increased to over 10,000. Allowing for letters being the chief means of communication for ordinary citizens, the number of censors might be thought not unreasonable, but this is on the assumption that strict censorship was essential to the war effort. Since there is no way of telling what was cut from letters, the value of the system is impossible to assess, though common sense suggests that 90 per cent, or even 99 per cent of the work was wasted effort.

In the early days of the war, postal censorship was made more laborious for the Post Office having no clear indication of official sanction. Many letters were caught in circular motion, being censored two or three times before they reached their destinations.

CHAPTER 13

Keep Smiling

After Chamberlain's broadcast and the air-raid scare on September 3rd, the BBC resumed its delivery of the new rules of engagement. These included the duty of every citizen 'to observe the black-out from dusk till dawn; to listen regularly to news bulletins; to carry a gas-mask everywhere; to make sure that his name and address were carried on his own and his children's persons; and, when he heard the air raid warning, to go immediately to shelter and stay there until the "All Clear" sounded.' London's tube stations were needed for traffic and would not be available as air-raid shelters.

None of this came as a surprise but there was one monumental shock. The Ministry of Information announced:

> All cinemas, theatres and other places of entertainment are immediately to be closed, and [...] football matches and similar gatherings involving large crowds are henceforth forbidden.

This 'masterstroke of unimaginative stupidity' as Bernard Shaw called it, was not the first and certainly not the last demonstration of administrative myopia. Crowds were vulnerable to massacre, therefore crowds had to be prevented. It seems not to have occurred to anyone in Whitehall, least of all Anderson, that the typical citizen under threat of death and destruction was in need of diversions stronger than sitting at home listening to the radio or reading a good book. Of all the official documents on civil defence published up to the outbreak of war, only one mentioned the importance of maintaining 'the sense of humour, balance and confidence of the people'.

It did not pass notice that the upper level of politics was dominated by men of puritanical disposition. Chamberlain was a Unitarian, Sir John Anderson a Presbyterian, and Sir Samuel Hoare a Quaker. The chancellor, Sir John Simon, air minister, Sir Kingsley Wood and Lord Macmillan, head of the Ministry of Information, were all sons of parsons. Ernest Brown, as labour minister, was a Baptist preacher. Not for them the escapist joys of the cinema, theatre or music hall, or the anticipation of a win on the football pools or at the races. They were soon brought into touch with reality. Grievances were heard at all levels of entertainment. As one of the many thrown out of work, Pamela Collier, appearing under her stage name Terry Randal, had been touring in *Little Ladyship*, a comedy by Ian Hay.

> We opened in Bridlington on the 24th July, 1939, and were playing at the Pleasure Gardens Theatre, Folkestone the week war was declared. My really big disappointment was that we ceased touring for the next two weeks, and I missed the two towns I really wanted to play! Cardiff, my home town, and Dublin, where I had never been.

Out of work and out of money, Terry Randal was rescued by her mother.

She was sure Hitler would be across the Channel in five minutes, and of course making straight for the theatre. She sent
my brother post haste by car from South Wales to drive me
to safety!

Opposition from the showbusiness lobby and from its customers soon
turned to direct action. It started in Aberystwyth where, on the second day of the war, the Pier Cinema opened for two performances.
The decision to be flexible in enforcing the new rules was taken by
the local chief constable who felt justified in balancing the pleasure
of the community against the improbability of Aberystwyth being
a prime target for the Luftwaffe. The Home Office was unmoved.
The chief constable was told that neither he nor anyone else had the
power to act independently. The chief constable begged to differ. On
Wednesday, another of the town's cinemas was allowed to open. By
now it was beginning to dawn on Whitehall that, maybe, discretion
was the better part of stubbornness.

On September 9th, it was announced that in evacuation reception (i.e. safe) areas theatres, cinemas, football grounds and other
places of entertainment could reopen. Those living in danger zones
were urged not to use their cars to seek amusement in safe areas.
On the same day, a letter in *The Times* from the Poet Laureate, John
Masefield, advised householders to lay in a plentiful supply of books
against the long autumn and winter nights.

A series of executive orders allowed chief constables to act within
broad limits. By September 14th, all theatres and cinemas outside
London and other high-risk areas were allowed to stay open until
10.00pm. But within the capital a 6.00pm closing was enforced until
December, when all places of entertainment had open doors until
11.00pm or 11.15pm. A notice flashed on the screen told cinema audiences that 'A qualified fireman is present during every performance

to give warning of any air raid alarm'. Should the worst happen, 'you will be asked to leave quietly and in an orderly manner by the nearest exit'.

Sporting fixtures were severely hit, particularly in areas thought to be most at risk from enemy bombing and particularly those sports played chiefly after dark and by floodlights – greyhound racing, speed-way, ice-hockey, snooker and all-in wrestling. It was ruled that all evening sports had to be shifted to Saturday afternoons, a slicing back on time and attraction that produced a catastrophic fall in takings. Since entertainers, whether on stage or on the playing fields, were not among the reserved occupations, many of the rising generation of star performers were lost to conscription or to the ARP.

Of all the inanities inflicted on the public, the shutdown of the postal service for football pool coupons ranks highest. Leading pool-promoters such as Littlewoods and Vernons were forced to close, though later they were allowed to get together to create Unity Pools. Forms were printed in newspapers with the injunction to write clearly and not to leave ink blots that might confuse the checkers. Winnings were modest by pre-war standards. Part of the profits went to war charities.

Museums and art galleries reopened but without their treasures, which had been moved away to secure hideouts. To avoid the prob-lems of the blackout, churches held their evensongs in the afternoon, a reversion to the Victorian practice in rural areas where the farmers in the congregation with livestock to care for wanted to get home before dusk.

WITH THE RELAXATION of opening hours for dance halls, young people took to dancing their cares away. By late December, bandleader Joe Loss was celebrating the 'biggest dance boom' of his career. In the

West End, the Dorchester, Quaglinos and the Café de Paris reported 'tremendous business'. New nightclubs were often attached to hotels where there were few limits on hours of opening.

The first wartime dance was the 'Blackout Stroll', the perfect answer to the 'Air Raid Blues'. As the publicity handout put it, none too gallantly:

> You ladies called 'wallflowers', fated to sit out all the dances, because perhaps your face isn't your fortune, or you aren't too good a dancer, or your figure isn't the cuddly kind ... HERE'S YOUR CHANCE TO DANCE THE 'BLACKOUT STROLL', LONDON'S LATEST STEP IS YOUR GODSEND ...
>
> You start dancing with a partner, doing forward walking steps, a break-away (much toned-down jitterbug step), and 1, 2, 3, hop (the Romp), then more walking steps. The lights go out, and when they go on again you are dancing with somebody else.
>
> How's that help you, wallflowers?
>
> Dash it, you aren't dumb, are you?[1]

Borrowing a Cockney folk tune, the prolific music hall composers Harris Weston and Bert Lee made a song and dance of 'Knees Up, Mother Brown'. Despite much tut-tutting from the ranks of respectability, it was not long before every dance night had to have 'Mother Brown' in its programme.

> Joe brought his concertina, and Nobby brought the beer,
> And all the little nippers swung upon the chandelier!
> A black-out warden passin' yelled, 'Ma, pull down that blind;
> Just look at what you're showin',' and we shouted, 'Never mind.'

OOH!

KNEES UP, MOTHER BROWN! Well, KNEES UP,
MOTHER BROWN,

Come along, dearie, let it go; ee-i, ee-i, ee-i, oh!

It's yer bloomin' birthday; let's wake up all the town!

So knees up, knees up! Don't get the breeze up.

KNEES UP, MOTHER BROWN.

Having a 'knees up' became synonymous with having a party.

In competition with 'Mother Brown' was the 'The Lambeth Walk', the hit song and dance from *Me and My Girl* which opened in 1937 at the Victoria Palace. It starred Lupino Lane as a Lambeth boy who, inheriting an earldom, converts his new wealthy friends to the simple pleasures of the working class by singing 'The Lambeth Walk'. The catchy tune was composed by Noel Gay.

Any time you're Lambeth way

Any evening, any day,

You'll find us all doin' the Lambeth Walk.

Ev'ry little Lambeth gal

With her little Lambeth pal,

You'll find 'em all doin' the Lambeth Walk.

Ev'rything free and easy,

Do as you darn well pleasey,

Why don't you make your way there,

Go there, stay there,

Once you get down Lambeth way,

Ev'ry evening, ev'ry day,

You'll find yourself doin' the Lambeth Walk.

While he sang, Lupino Lane walked up and down the stage with a swagger and roll of the shoulders, concluding each verse with a spirited 'Hi' as he cocked his thumb. A BBC excerpt from the show introduced millions of listeners to 'The Lambeth Walk'. Their response was overwhelming. When Locarno Dance Halls developed Lupino's walk into a dance it was soon taken up in Europe and America. On September 6th, 1938, the *Daily Express* reported:

> Czechoslovakia's Little Man is keeping his head ... Over the weekend his thoughts turned to ... a strange new English dance, the 'Lambeth Walk', which has just hit the dance-halls of Prague.

Twelve days later the same paper ran a story on the French reaction to the Cockney craze:

> Paris was herself last night, the restaurants were filled, and they were all doing the 'Lambeth Walk', and when a Frenchman does it, it looks like drill in a gymnasium. They love the song, and think it is a sort of national anthem.

Eddie Cantor made his own record of the song and added some words of his own:

> What a happy old world this could be
> If the leaders of the nations would just agree
> To make their people forget about war
> And teach them the Lambeth walk.

Another top West End show was Ivor Novello's *The Dancing Years*, an operetta with a background theme of Vienna 'under the heel of tyranny'. It opened on March 29th, 1939 at Drury Lane. After the closing and reopening of the theatres, the show went on tour before returning to the West End at the Adelphi where it ran for 969 performances until July 1944. A string of hummable tunes included 'Waltz of My Heart', 'I Can Give You the Starlight' and 'My Dearest Dear'. Throughout the Phoney War, light relief was the predominant theme for West End productions. Of the nineteen plays recommended by *Theatre World* in February 1940, fourteen were comedies or revues.

High on the list of patriotic songs were 'Rose of England', written by Ivor Novello in 1937 for his musical *Crest of the Wave*.

Rose of England thou shall fade not here
Proud and bright from growing year to year
Red shall thy petals be as rich wine untold
Shared by thy warriors who served thee of old
Rose of England breathing England's air
Flower of chivalry beyond compare
While hand and heart endure to cherish thy prime
Thou shall blossom to the end of time.

Another staple of family sing-songs around the living-room piano was 'There'll Always Be an England'. The sheet music sold over 200,000 copies. Other popular songs, often heard as voices were raised in pubs just before closing time, included 'South of the Border', 'Roll Out the Barrel', 'The Last Time I Saw Paris' and 'Hang out the Washing on the Siegfried Line'. What is striking about the Siegfried song is the note of belligerence that was conspicuously absent in government propaganda. With the addition of 'We're gonna' as the first words of the first line, there was an underlying message to Chamberlain and his friends to get on with the job instead of sitting around waiting for something to happen.

We're gonna hang out the washing on the Siegfried Line.
Have you any dirty washing, mother dear?
We're gonna hang out the washing on the Siegfried Line
If the Siegfried Line's still there.

Predictably, the song did not go well in Germany. The official response appeared in the *Daily Telegraph* of October 6th.

This is not a soldiers' song, because soldiers do not brag. It was not written in the soldiers' camps, but by the Jewish scribes of the B.B.C. The Englishman's washing will be very dirty before they come anywhere near the Siegfried Line.

THOSE WITH MONEY to spend could always find ways to lighten the mood. A contribution to *Country Life* observed the *cocktail dansant* with the young women often in uniform.

Dancing is spirited and an air of pleasure replaces the indifference of a few weeks ago. This may be largely due to the fact that there is now plenty of room on the dancing floors. The men's uniforms are very mixed, privates no longer avoiding the leisure haunts of officers …

Smart hotels converted their cellars into dining rooms.

The foremost hotels and restaurants have now made their blackout and air-raid shelter provisions. It is odd to find rows of gilt chairs in the underground apartments of places like the Dorchester. … Only a small minority of diners in public places have been in evening dress, but there is a growing feeling that if one goes out to such places at all it is better to dress formally, especially if one's escort wears an imposing uniform. The fluffy and crinolined dresses have been killed by their unsuitability for these queer times, but at the Hartnell and other shows there were many evening dresses of an appropriate sort – decorative without being frivolous, enveloping in cut but bright in colour.

With an eye to popularity and profit, commercial companies did their best to jolly things up. The *Christian Herald* ran a children's feature called 'Brighten up the Black-out', which was meant to raise their intelligence and general knowledge. The Gramophone Company reported that they were producing 30 per cent more records than the same time last year, their St John's Wood studios doing a seven-day week.

Chewing gum was promoted as 'first aid to the nerves' while the vitamin A in Crooks Halibut Liver Oil 'will help you see in the blackout'. Less cheerfully, the national body representing opticians launched a campaign to show that the blackout caused eye strain.

Whether you wear glasses or not, you should have your eyes examined at regular intervals by a Qualified Practitioner. … The obvious eye-strain from which many are now suffering is due to a definite physiological reaction in the eyes, produced by changing conditions.

Cigarettes were said to provide relaxation and even illumination. The American broadcaster Ed Murrow, reporting on a night in London, found

It prevents collisions; makes it unnecessary to heave to until you locate the exact position of those vague voices in the darkness. One night several years ago I walked bang into a cow, and since then I've had a desire for man and beast to carry running lights on dark nights. They can't do that in London these nights; but the cigarettes are a good substitute. For a moment to-night I thought I was back in the London of Mr Pickwick's time. I heard a voice booming through the stark London streets. It said, '28 Portland Place, all's well'. It was an air-raid warden; he had shouted to someone an order to cover their window; they had done so; and he was telling them that no more light came through.[2]

The men's outfitter, Hector Powe, advertised in the *Evening Standard*: 'The tonic of new clothes will be greater now than at any other time within recent memory.'

While places of entertainment thrived, for most people the safest and simplest option for coping with the blackout was to stay at home. Listening to the radio and reading became the chief leisure activity, with board games and cards running a close third. The occasional visit to a pub (almost every street had its local) helped to break the routine. As a popular song had it:

There's no place like home,
But we see too much of it now.

There was no getting away from the low spirits of having not much to do in the precious hours away from the workplace.

Nothing, no amount of experience, makes you really used to the black-out. And however little it may change your hab-its, the consciousness of it, waiting for you out there, behind the black material on the window, is a threat to any of the pre-war happy-go-lucky. Each evening expedition is now an event, maybe a dangerous adventure. No one in New York or Buenos Aires can successfully imagine what it's like. For when the bright lights of a city are turned off, bright life is turned off too.[3]

As one of the closest observers of the scene, Ed Murrow saw central London in October 1939, starting in St James's Park:

Practically no private cars about. Green canvas deck-chairs, empty and wet, were scattered through the park. Piles of sand waiting to be shovelled into bags. A few new signs in Harley Street, the home of London's medical aristocracy. Signs reading, HOUSE TO LET or LEASE TO BE DISPOSED OF. Those expensive shops in Bond Street, all of them sandbagged; the windows boarded up; others criss-crossed with strips of brown paper to prevent shattering. Tailors' shop windows full of uniforms. They used to display well-cut dinner jackets and tweed sports jackets. Windows of the women's shops filled with heavy-wool evening dresses and sturdy shoes. Some of those shops show a new kind of women's wear – a sort of cover-all arrangement with zippers and a hood – one-piece affairs, easy to put on. They are to be worn when the sirens sound. So they are called, appropriately enough, siren suits. There are big black and red arrows pointing the way to air-raid shelters. A discreet little sign in the window of the most expensive automobile showrooms in London saying BUSINESS AS USUAL.

Murrow noted that policemen had lost 'all the dignified solemnity of peace time' wearing their tin hats instead of helmets. And he was sad to find that Eros was no longer at the centre of Piccadilly Circus, having been removed to a place of safety.

> The streets are clean and orderly. The sandbags seem to have softened the contour of some of London's harsh-looking buildings.[4]

This consolation was little noticed. By the end of the year, morale was dangerously low. Said one interviewee for Mass-Observation:

> Well, what are we doing? You tell me. As far as I can see, so far we've rationed petrol, put all the food prices up, commandeered all cars, lorries and taxis we can lay hands on, had a beautiful black-out which is killing more people than an air raid would, and now we're going to number everybody, and tell them how many ounces of food the kind Government is going to allow them to eat. Fine; if we go on like that we're sure to win the war. That is, when Hitler dies of old age, and the German people take pity on us.[5]

With the disruption of theatre business in London, many of the popular shows departed on provincial tours. Left vacant by the withdrawal of *The Dancing Years*, Drury Lane was dark. But not for long. It was taken over by film producer Basil Dean as the headquarters for the newly created Entertainments National Service Association (ENSA). A pioneer of troop entertainment in the Great War, Dean was an autocrat who made enemies. But no one doubted his energy and determination. He needed every ounce to give ENSA a leading part in the war effort. With the derisory rate of pay, the talent attracted by ENSA in the early days was second-rate or worse. A manager for a show produced by Archie de Bear witnessed an audition at Drury Lane.

I sat between Archie and Lilian Braithwaite with Basil Dean on the other side. This poor soul, who was well over fifty, came out wearing a blue dress, her hair heavily tramlined, iron-waved, especially for the occasion. She only had one leg and a crutch which she put down in the wings. She then hopped to the centre of the stage and started to sing, very off-key, 'Abide With Me'. Archie turned to me and said, 'God, I should hate to!' The auditions went on and on. They were pathetic. He told me that for every two or three hundred they saw, they might find two or three they could use.[6]

Companies sent out on the road were confronted with challenges as forbidding as the toughest of peacetime venues. Dispatched to the army base at Catterick where young recruits were eager for relief from the tedium of military training, a touring variety show collected a sack full of unforgettable memories.

When we got there we had to go to the Hooge Lines, to a Naafi with a stage. There hadn't been a show on there for months and it was filthy, but we had been told about roughing it and assumed this was it. The girl in charge knew nothing about us but she found some pails and scrubbing brushes and scrubbed the stage, while we climbed up to the rafters and fixed our curtains. Two sergeants then said they would rustle up some lads. They arrived looking forward to seeing Jack Buchanan and Phyllis Robins; since we hadn't either, that was it as far as they were concerned. We ended up with about 150 men, started the show and were doing very nicely indeed when, halfway through, there was a banging on the door. A brigadier came in playing bloody hell about everything. I was on stage. 'Bloody well get him off!' he shouted. It turned out that we were in the wrong place – we should have been in the Aisne Lines where there had been 2,000 men waiting for us for an hour and a half! We stopped the show and went over. When we got there, they had been running an impromptu entertainment – chaps getting up, singing and so on – and an escapologist was on, tied up, trying to get loose. We bundled him off, still tied up, into the wings and got on with our show.[7]

It was with the early half-baked entertainments that ENSA earned itself the tag 'Every Night Something Awful'. However, in its first month ENSA put on 500 shows. By the end of the year that figure had more than trebled, while audiences totalled more than 600,000. Big names were still hard to get, but programmes covered a wide range from straight plays to concert parties.

The music halls had suffered a decline in the 1930s when many of the Empires, Hippodromes and Palaces converted to cinemas. With the start of the war, the ribald energy of live variety came back into vogue. There was a certain type of comedian who found radio and film uncongenial but for whom the stage was a natural habitat. As the reigning monarch of his craft, Max Miller topped the bill at the Holborn Empire and Kingston Empire.

The master of Cockney patter and the double entendre, appearing on stage in outrageously floral plus fours, he invited his audience to decide the jokes they wanted to hear – those from his white book or from his blue book. Having heard the inevitable choice, he would come forward, leaning over the footlights, while glancing into the wings as though looking to see if the manager was taking notes. Then, ''Ere, listen – 'ere's one'.

'As I always say, lady, some girls are like flowers – they grow wild in the woods. 'Ere, did I tell you the one about the chorus

girl who married a rich, old invalid? She took him for better
or worse. It turned out worse – he got better …'

By today's standards it was all very innocent. But when he spotted
servicemen in the audience he risked bringing a blush to the cheeks
of the Lord Chamberlain.

'This girl had a little dog, and it was very hairy. So she went
to the chemist and said, do you have anything for removing
superfluous hair? And he said yes, I've got my own prescrip-
tion, you just rub it on your legs and ten minutes later the hair
will be gone. Oh, she said, but it isn't for my legs, it's for my
little Chihuahua. He said, in that case don't ride your bike for
a fortnight …'

His best jokes, though linked to wartime, have stood the test of
repetition:

'My wife came in the other day and she said, "What's different
about me?" And I said, "I don't know – what is different about
you? Have you had your hair done?" She said, "No." I said,
"Have you got a new dress on?" She said, "No." I said, "Have
you got a new pair of shoes?" She said, "No." I said, "Well what
is it? What's different?" She said, "I'm wearing a gas mask."'

A comedian of another bracket was Rob Wilton who made his reputation playing a bumbling incompetent in charge, say, of a fire station
or the front desk of a police station. In the latter role he has to cope
with a woman who confessed to poisoning her husband. After throwing papers around and toying at making notes ('There was no system
here until I joined the force') he gives the woman a long reproachful

stare. 'So you've poisoned your husband.' 'Yes', she screams. 'So what do you want me to do about it, find you another one?'

Making fun of authoritarian figures carried over all too easily to wartime. But it was Rob Wilton's monologues of the hapless spouse having to 'do something' in the emergency that really kept audiences happy. His opening line delivered in a soft Lancashire drawl entered the currency of British folklore.

'The day war broke out, my Missus looked at me and she said, "What good are you?" I said, "Who?" She said, "You." I said, "How do you mean, what good am I?" She said, "Well, you are too old for the Army, you couldn't get into the Navy, and they wouldn't have you in the Air Force, so what good are you?" I said, "How do I know, I'll have to think." ... [So I joined the Home Guards.] The first day I got my uniform I went home and put it on – and the Missus looked at me and said, "What are you supposed to be?" I said, "Supposed to be? I'm one of the Home Guards." She said, "One of the Home Guards, what are the others like?" She said, "What are you supposed to do?" I said, "I'm supposed to stop Hitler's Army landing." She said, "What, YOU?" I said, "No, not me, there's Bob Edwards, Charlie Evans, Billy Brightside – there's seven or eight of us, we're in a group, we're on guard in a little hut behind 'The Dog and Pullet'."'

Standing alone centre stage, Rob Wilton's world-weary accounts of his war effort were the inspiration for the long-running television saga of *Dad's Army*.

WITH THE CANCELLATION of live concerts, classical music went into abeyance for several months, though the BBC helped to compensate by increasing its output of music for all tastes. Interestingly, on the classical side there was no attempt to cut back on German compos- ers. Beethoven and Bach (the Shakespeare of music) had been BBC favourites pre-war and remained so despite the conflict, a contrast to the chauvinistic bluster of the Great War when Teutonic composi- tions risked cat-calls or worse in the concert halls. Even Wagner got a look-in.

The undisputed star of the music scene was the pianist Myra Hess who commandeered the now denuded central hall of the National Gallery for her lunchtime recitals. The first concert, on October 10th, 1939, started a series, five days a week, that lasted until April 1946. The *Musical Times* acknowledged 'the most successful musical venture of the war period'. By the end of 1940, the attendance figures had reached 170,000. Myra Hess was made a Dame in 1941.

Much of the credit for the Council for the Encouragement of Music and the Arts (CEMA), the predecessor of the Arts Council, goes to the composer Ralph Vaughan Williams. Set up in December 1939 as the highbrow version of ENSA, the aim of CEMA was 'to maintain the highest possible standard in our national arts and music, drama and painting at a time when these things are threatened and when they also may mean more in the life of the country than ever before'. Orchestras were sent out on tours of industrial regions, along with 'music travellers carrying the live arts of playing and singing to remote places'.

Many book publishers closed their doors. 'We haven't the slight- est idea what is going to happen', wrote one literary front-runner. 'Our publishing plans change nearly every other day.' The strongest sale was for cheap reprints. But the bestseller list was by no means barren. With such as Graham Greene, George Orwell, Christopher Isherwood, T.S. Eliot, Raymond Chandler and Agatha Christie, not to mention Enid Blyton, with new titles on offer, the public could not be said to be short of reading material. For pure escapism, P.G. Wodehouse offered *Uncle Fred in the Springtime*, set in the idyllic Blandings Castle where domestic entanglements were the harmless source of amusement and war was inconceivable.

For juveniles of whatever age, Richmal Crompton brought out *William and ARP*, a topical adventure for her schoolboy hero William Brown, the forerunner of Dennis the Menace of *Beano* fame. Living in a south London suburb, home ground for the author, the Brown family in 1939 boasted a cook, a maid and a gardener, a style of living that was soon to be inconceivable for all but the richest. William is a stout-hearted patriot whose idea of helping the war effort is to give lessons in bandaging imaginary wounds and practising putting on gas-masks. His efforts are not appreciated. Adults, William complains, have all the fun.

'They have a jolly good time,' said William. 'Smellin' gases an' bandaging each other an' tryin' on their gas masks. I bet they bounce out at each other in their gas masks, givin' each other frights. I've thought of lots of games you could play with gas masks, but no one'll let me try. They keep mine locked up. Lot of good it'll be in a war locked up where I can't get at it. Huh!'[8]

In the newspapers, humour thrived on the inventive genius of Nathaniel Gubbins, whose column 'Sitting on the Fence' appeared in the *Sunday Express*. Its sister daily paper was graced by the immortal J.B. Morton ('Beachcomber') with his collection of surreal characters led by Mr Justice Cocklecarrot, a judge guaranteed to make an ass of the law, Captain Foulenough, a smooth con man and trickster (a familiar figure in wartime Britain), Dr Smart-Allick, head of a school specialising in turning out card sharps and, of course, Dr Strabismus ('whom God preserve') of Utrecht, the inspiration for countless use-less inventions such as a method for freezing meat skewers. The joy of Gubbins and Morton was their skill in getting their readers to laugh at the inanities of wartime bureaucracy, a talent shared by the cartoonists Osbert Lancaster, David Langdon and Nicolas Bentley. The harder edged political cartoonists were led by Vicky of the *Daily Mirror* and David Low of the *Evening Standard*.

Fighting shy of politics ('Civilization is on the operating table and we sit in the waiting room'), a literary journal, *Horizon*, made its debut in December 1939, edited by Cyril Connolly. More prosaically, Edward Hulton launched a new magazine for women. With its tips on making the best of scarcity, *Housewife* was an immediate hit.

Film production, soon to be the biggest morale-booster of the war, was in the doldrums in late 1939. With studios requisitioned, up to two-thirds of the industry's technicians conscripted into the military and a certain number hot-footing to Hollywood as soon as hostilities started, there was a fear that British-made feature films would disappear altogether from the high street cinemas. In the event, however, the war turned out to be a boost for the British cinema in that it provided a genre – the war movie – that was all its own.[9]

A turning point was *The Lion Has Wings*, a propaganda movie star-ring Ralph Richardson and Merle Oberon. Put together in less than a month, the story contrasts the supposedly easygoing, tolerant and essentially decent British society with the goose-stepping Nazi men-tality. The climax has the RAF seeing off a raid by Luftwaffe bombers. With extensive use of documentary material, the joins between fact and fiction are plain to see, while an over-long epilogue has Merle Oberon as the dedicated wife at home telling her wing commander husband how the women of Britain, having once given their sons to the land and sea, must now give them to the air to defend the British way of life. At the end of her speech, with a touch of self-deprecating humour, the camera shifts to Richardson who has dropped off to sleep. But whatever its limitations, *The Lion Has Wings* set the lie to the killjoys who believed that film production was an unnecessary luxury at a time of crisis.

Sadly, the logic did not extend to television. With its dismal failure to appreciate the reach and power of modern communications, the government gave up on Britain's pioneering lead in the medium. The world's first television programme in high definition, called *Here's Looking at You*, had been transmitted from Alexandra Palace on August 26th, 1936. The official opening of the television service followed on November 2nd. Live programmes, from 9.00 to 11.00 every evening, were interspersed with Disney cartoons and cinema newsreels. Outside broadcasts covered big events such as Chamberlain's return from Munich, test matches and the cup final. One hundred and forty-five plays were produced for TV in 1938.

Pre-war television ended on Friday, September 1st, 1939 between 11.00am and noon when a Mickey Mouse cartoon was showing, called *Mickey's Gala Premiere*. The cut-off was abrupt. 'I think I go home', said Mickey and that was it. No closing announcement was made.

Most of those engaged in sound broadcasting joined the evacuation. As head of radio drama, Val Gielgud and his team along with the BBC Repertory Company were shunted off to Evesham in Worcestershire. When he heard that the move was imminent, Gielgud was producing Somerset Maugham's play *The Circle* for television, the first full-length play on the small screen. It was scheduled to be transmitted on September 3rd. Gielgud feared the worst.

None the less the shock was considerable when just about noon I was called to the telephone; informed that Alexandra Palace was closing down; and instructed that the B.B.C. 'emergency period' had begun. I had just put down the receiver when an office messenger arrived with various 'properties' for the play, including two tennis racquets and a number of balls. I have occasionally wondered what happened to those racquets and balls, ... forgotten relics of a dead world.[10]

The move to Evesham did not go well. The local people were angry and resentful at having to accommodate a bunch of what were inevitably judged to be leftie intellectuals and poseurs, unacceptable in polite society.

They were quick to assume that the keeping of irregular hours was not the result of conditions of work, but of the irregular lives led by everyone connected with that home of original sin, the Theatre. They admitted us grudgingly to their homes. They made no attempt to admit us to their hearts.

Gielgud was turned away from his first billet on the ground that his Siamese cat was a dangerous wild animal. To prevent the cat from languishing behind bars at the local vet's, he rented a furnished house.

Most of my colleagues could not afford such an extravagant and drastic solution to the continuing problem of the discomforts of their quasi-domestic backgrounds.[11]

Working conditions were no better. A large country house, formerly the home of a Pretender to the French throne, had to be adapted to make studios, rehearsal rooms and offices. All this took six weeks and even then confusion was rampant.

Distinguished officials found difficulty in remembering how to ride their bicycles, and occasionally fell off them. Less distinguished officials found that beards or Inverness capes looked unimpressive when awheel. A good many stenographers missed mother. Scripts went easily and frequently astray. Actors found themselves playing leading parts in two plays on the same night. Plays went from first read-throughs to microphone in a single day.[12]

At the end of the year, BBC drama exchanged Evesham for Manchester where the daily round was more congenial.

By mid-October the drama department had managed sufficiently to get itself together to start transmitting original radio plays and drama documentaries. The biggest impact was made by *The Shadow of the Swastika*, a reconstruction of the rise of Nazi power. The challenge for Gielgud was to cast an actor to play Hitler.

Recordings were made of several likely candidates for what must hold the palm as the least 'sympathetic' of roles. And I remember a hideous afternoon when I spent two hours in a listening-room, my ears assailed alternatingly by Hitlers histrionic and Hitler real. At the close of that experience I felt that by far the best punishment for our arch-enemy, should he fall alive into our hands, would be to confine him in a small indifferently ventilated room, and play recordings of his own voice to him twenty-four hours a day. In the event Marius Goring played the part with marked ability, stamina and success.[13]

It helped that Marius Goring was fluent in German.

By far the most popular radio show of the war was *ITMA*, an acronym for *It's That Man Again*, a recurring headline adopted by the *Daily Express* to mark yet another of Hitler's territorial claims. The star of *ITMA* was Tommy Handley, a snap-and-crackle comedian from Liverpool who was already well established as a broadcaster. Come the dispersal of the BBC, Handley was among the variety artists posted to Bristol. It was there that he and his producer Francis Worsley and script writer Ted Kavanagh put their heads together to come up with a comedy idea that would appeal to a mass audience. Wrote Kavanagh:

> Suddenly there was the strange outbreak of initials on every car on the road – the labels presumably being intended to get priority of passage. Everyone remembers the sort of thing: A.R.P., R.A.F., M.O.F., R.N.V.R., VET., W.V.S., W.D. and so on. Half the initials were private ideas born of pomposity and self-importance, and I admired the girl who used to run around Bristol in an old two-seater with a large label on the wind-screen bearing the words: 'JUST ME'.
>
> There did, however, seem humorous possibilities in the epidemic of abbreviations. There was also the phenomenon of gigantic Ministries which, though planned secretly months before, seemed to the newspaper reader and listener to bloom overnight. After every evening news bulletin came a spate of orders issued by these Ministries ...
>
> On scraps of paper the new Tommy Handley emerged – as Minister of Aggravation and Mysteries, provided with accommodation by courtesy of the Office of Twerps.[14]

Those who were small children at the time remember the catchphrases spoken by such as Colonel Chinstrap who turned every question into an offer of a drink ('I don't mind if I do'), Mona Lott, a gloomy laundry woman ('It's being so cheerful as keeps me going') and Mrs Mopp ('Can I do you now, Sir?'). 'Ta Ta for now', or TTFN, was adopted as a nationwide adieu.

With topicality as the guiding principle, most of the content for *ITMA* is meaningless today but some of the inspiration for the jokes can still raise a laugh – as when an order from the Ministry of Agriculture instructed Welsh hill farmers to 'postpone' the lambing season by a month. *ITMA* had its first outing at 9.30 on the evening of September 19th, 1939. It ended a ten-year run with the death of Tommy Handley in 1949.

ITMA was not the only source of catchphrases. A favourite was from *Garrison Theatre*, a variety programme which made the name of Jack Warner, subsequently to be a considerable film actor and stalwart of the television police series, *Dixon of Dock Green*. Warner recalled:

Most comedians had their catchphrases then as now and I had several. There was, 'Veree good, sir', 'Blue pencil' and, of course, 'Mind my bike!' The last one, as with most, owed its existence to chance. I was constantly trying to think up new gags for my entrance to the show. One week, I was supposed to come up through the orchestra; another time down through the wings and once was supposed to be helping the electrician to put bulbs in the footlights. ... We spent a lot of time trying to discover how it would sound if light bulbs were dropped – as they were assumed to be – by me, the awkward soldier. ... Eventually we achieved the right effect by making popping noises with cardboard boxes but it took us ages to perfect the sound.

The week after the bulb incident, the producer asked me how I planned to make my entrance. ... I said that I wanted the listeners to imagine that I was riding down through the stalls on a bicycle and ringing the bell. Harry didn't bat an eyelid. He just said, 'Good! I've got a bell and hooter in the prop box.'

There can be few people who listened to those broadcasts who don't remember 'Mind my bike'. You can write
something you think will make people fall about in helpless
laughter and it expires on delivery, while a simple remark can
be inexpressibly funny.[15]

Catchphrases had a role to play in wartime. Though not funny in
themselves, when heard at work, in the street or in the pub, they were
a bond of mutual recognition, like a handshake, a mark of compan-
ionship in adversity.

WHILE THE NEWS division remained in London, the BBC's Emergency
Headquarters was established at Wood Norton in Worcestershire
where 600 bicycles were bought for staff use. The depopulated
Broadcasting House was a forlorn shell.

All inside-corridors have gas-proof doors at ten-yard intervals, and the front entrance is entirely bricked up except for
a narrow passage through which one squeezes, pass in hand,
into the gloomiest foyer ever imagined. The receptionists,
well-groomed rather officious young ladies known as 'the
canaries', have all gone, although their counter remains, dusty
and scattered with out-of-date reading matter and someone's
forgotten cap.[16]

But those left to hold the fort were busy enough. Initially, the plan was
for round-the-clock broadcasting in the hope that listeners would stay
tuned in for emergency announcements. But it was soon realised that
there was not enough material to justify overnight broadcasts. The
revised schedule began daily at 6.00am and continued uninterrupted

until midnight. In between news bulletins came a mixed bag of items to gladden the heart, mind and stomach. On January 9th, 1940, the day started, after the news, with the semi-religious *Lift Up Your Hearts* and a 'Thought for Today'. This was followed at 7.35 by *Up in the Morning Early*, physical exercises for women. After rousing music from the Manchester City Police Band and Folk Songs from Maryland, it was time for *Kitchen Economy*. *The Daily Service* took the listener up to the lunch break of what promised to be less than a fascinating day by the radio. But there was a treat in store for those into animal husbandry. Come the evening, *Rabbit Keeping in Wartime* would command the airwaves.

Live performances were a BBC rarity. The over-reliance on records shows up in the programme schedule for September and October. A popular cartoon had a dinner-jacketed announcer standing before a microphone to announce grandly, 'And now, live from the BBC, here is another gramophone record'. An exception was the ubiquitous Sandy Macpherson, who seemed to be on permanent duty at the BBC theatre organ. His popularity was matched by Radio's Wizard of the Piano, the American-born musician Charlie Kunz with his gentle, relaxed style of playing popular melodies. But there were voluble protests from musicians who were no longer in demand for live performances and from composers whose creativity was left on the shelf. If there was any consolation it was in knowing that the Ministry of Information was pressing the BBC, not altogether successfully, to favour the work of British composers by cutting down on 'enemy' music.

Sensitivity on timing was not a BBC forte. Concert performances were cut short if they overran their slot. One aggrieved listener protested in vain against a fade-out of Handel's 'Music for the Royal Fireworks' to permit a tea-time talk on 'Making the Most of Your Looks'.

My talk this afternoon is on deportment. First of all I want you to stand with your back to the wall – about half a yard distant – then step back against the wall. Now, girls, what part of you was the first to touch the wall? Tell the truth! It was your behind, of course, and it ought to have been your shoulders.

A BBC talk on 'How to Sleep Well' advised, 'Be careful how you spend the evening. It's what you do out of bed that affects you when you turn in.' Several listeners wrote to point out that the converse was equally true.

High on the list of listeners' complaints was the abandonment of radio weather forecasts, this on the assumption that the Germans, apparently incapable of producing their own forecasts, would otherwise rely on the BBC for guidance on flying conditions.

CHAPTER 14

Making the Best of It

A state of war prompted a rush into marriage, a reversal of the early 1930s when nuptials were postponed or abandoned because of economic hardship. August and September 1939 broke all records for the number of marriages. The total for the year, 495,000, was almost 100,000 up on 1938. The number went up again in 1940, to 534,000. The wedding announcement columns of *The Times* and *Daily Telegraph* ran to double or treble their usual length, with the declaration of war or cancellation of leave given as reasons for hurrying things along. But honeymoons had to wait for more peaceful times, while wedding ceremonies were soon to be images of austerity. A paper shortage made it illegal to manufacture confetti, and to throw rice at the newlyweds was frowned upon as a waste of food.

The celebration of life in marriage was at variance with the funeral march for domestic pets. One of the saddest things, Marion Rees noted in her diary,

> ... is the way thousands of panic-stricken people are having their pets put to sleep, so that animal clinics are frantic to know what to do with all the dead bodies, some of beautiful

creatures, and the newspapers are appealing for it to stop. They say there will be danger of the country's being infested with rats and mice if any more cats are put to sleep. As yet, it is all quite unnecessary, too.

By the early spring of 1940, the reorganisation of civil defence was on a more professional footing. The permitted hours put in by unpaid volunteers and by paid workers were clearly set out and for those who did night duty made more tolerable. Shifts of no more than four hours now became standard. More effort was put into providing sleeping accommodation in or near posts and depots. Only in the most vulnerable areas were posts to be continuously manned. The number of ambulances and decontamination squads on standby duty was reduced. A new training plan, intended to 'establish a uniform practice in training throughout the country', was published in April. Training officers were appointed in all regions.

But there was resistance, largely on economic grounds, to setting up a home defence force, more pro-active than the ARP. The idea originated with Percy Harris, MP who wrote to *The Times* on September 5th, 1939 to urge a force of part-time soldiers prepared to defend the country against invasion. 'There are a great number of men over military age and men who are prevented because they are scheduled in reserved occupations who would like to train in the use of a rifle.' Churchill was an enthusiast. In October he was pressing for a 'Home Guard of half a million men over forty'.

But until May 1940 when, as newly appointed secretary of state for war, Anthony Eden broadcast an appeal for local defence volunteers, the initiative was left to strong-willed community leaders. In Ross-on-Wye, Lady Helena Gleichen recruited her staff and tenants into the Much Marcle Watchers, demanding of the local battalion commander that he should provide 80 rifles and ammunition 'with a couple of machine guns if you have any'. In Essex, the self-styled Legion of Frontiersmen was said by the *Daily Mirror* to be the 'vanguard of Britain's part-time army'. After Eden's appeal to the nation, the Home Guard came into its own with 250,000 volunteers within 24 hours.

THE FIRST WARTIME budget was presented to the House of Commons by Sir John Simon on September 27th. The standard rate of income tax was raised to 35 per cent (soon to be 37.5 per cent), the highest direct taxation in the country's history. There were few exemptions. Any single person earning more than £120 a year (in today's money, roughly £6,300) was liable to the full rate. For high earners, a surtax of 82.5 per cent was imposed on income over £30,000 (around £1.5 million). Duties were increased on sugar, tobacco, beer, whisky and wines. In anticipation of public anger at those businesses which seemed to be doing very nicely from government contracts, a 60 per cent levy was imposed on profits above those of a pre-war standard. But why not 100 per cent? asked the critics. A War Savings Campaign to encourage the public to invest in War Bonds was to be launched in November.

But with the increasing and conflicting demands of military and civil agencies, money remained tight. As the chief Eeyore among ministers, Simon set the tone when launching the War Bonds. With his trademark manner of address which assumed an audience of slow-witted bovines, he urged a strict adherence to counting the pennies.

I should like everyone to understand that if at this time he spends unnecessarily on himself, he is making it more difficult to carry on the war. If he saves all he can and lends it to the

Government, he is not only making a useful provision for himself, but he is himself helping to fight the war and hastening the day of victory.

The emphasis on war production meant that the comforts of life would be curtailed. This, in turn, demanded a 'special need for restraint'.

For if supplies are restricted and at the same time the public, instead of saving, tries to buy as much as or more than in peace-time – why, all this helps to raise prices unnecessarily. It is literally true that if the citizen strictly limits his purchases he is helping to keep prices down. A general resolve all over the country to save what one can and to avoid all unnecessary spending will have a great effect.

With Christmas approaching, the decision, not so much to dampen the holiday as to drown it, did not go down well with shopkeepers and other traders who depended on the festive spirit for a large part of their income. Following the lead of the advertisers, the press urged their readers to have a good time while opportunity allowed. The conflicting advice tried the patience of the family breadwinner. As a popular refrain had it:

Simon says SAVE.
Missus says SPEND.
Tax collector says PAY.
Shopkeeper says BUY.
Everybody says GIVE.
My pocket's EMPTY.
What shall I do?

Pushed to make concessions, the government lifted some restrictions, notably on the sale of meat, while announcing that the long-mooted introduction of food rationing would be postponed until the new year.

There was an administrative virtue in this. The experience of petrol rationing, introduced in September, suggested that rather more careful planning was needed before the scheme was extended to other commodities. That car owners would not be able to move about freely had come as a nasty surprise. With no warning given under the Emergency Powers Act it was only days before war was declared that the motor trade stopped promoting the latest models under the banner, 'Better Motoring for 1940'.

As the first Viscount Nuffield, William Morris, founder of Morris Motors and soon to be one of the country's leading philanthropists, had held out to the last for civilian motoring. A clever idea, initiated when Lord Swinton was air minister, for 'shadow factories' whereby vehicle manufacturing could be quickly converted to aircraft engines, was abandoned under pressure from Nuffield who saw no reason to compromise on the joys of the open road.

Though generally accepted that petrol would soon have to be diverted from civilian to military use, the timing was ill-judged. Originally intended to be enforced after September 16th, upper limits on the buying of petrol were put off for a week while coupons were distributed. The result was a rush to the pumps. Screw-top cans were hot in demand, though for some eager hoarders, any handy receptacle was called into service. One woman turned up at a garage with a four-foot-high metal dustbin which she demanded to have filled.

Converted water tanks and washtubs, even bottles were utilised. The penalty for storing petrol without a licence was £20 a day and confiscation. But this proved to be no deterrent to many otherwise respectable citizens. A common offence was for black marketeers, equipped with lengths of rubber tubing, to siphon off petrol from parked cars. Warnings of the risks of keeping petrol at home went unheeded. Inevitably, when rationing did come in, garages reported a petrol shortage.

Applicants for coupons had to go to their post office where the quantity of 'motor spirit' allowed them depended on the rating of the vehicle registration book. Each coupon represented one gallon. The average family car qualified for one coupon a month, which had to be used in the month of issue. With such a small allocation and no rollovers (in 1942 petrol for private use was withdrawn completely), the volume of traffic was cut drastically. Given a special allocation to help him research a book on wartime Britain, the travel writer H.V. Morton was surprised by the emptiness of the roads.

> So accustomed have we become to chains of cars upon all the main roads that this sudden thinning of traffic seemed to me almost unbelievable: it was like going back to the year 1919, or even earlier. The roads looked strange, too, because on the eve of war, overnight, as it were, a broad white band was painted in the centre to guide night travellers.
>
> The only traffic I encountered in open country were lorries and military transport. Near the towns, however, a few private cars were to be seen. Upon that four-mile stretch of straight road between Ovington Down and Winchester there was not a single car, just the long road with its central strip of white stretching into the distance. For the first time for years it was possible to enjoy motoring as those who remember the first Morris Oxfords enjoyed it long ago.[1]

Many cars were simply locked away in garages. My family reminiscences reveal an uncle in the building trade who spotted the petrol shortage as an entrepreneurial opportunity. Anticipating a successful outcome to the war, he invested in unused and unwanted vehicles, covered their engines in protective grease, and put them into storage against the day when demand for cars would outstrip supply. After petrol for private use was available once more, my enterprising relative made a tidy profit.

Supplementary petrol coupons were issued to those for whom transport was essential to their work. Doctors came under this heading, as did undertakers. In another tale from the Turner archive, my father, who enjoyed nothing more than a day at the races, persuaded the town funeral director to take a party of friends to a local point-to-point. My mother waved them off as they departed in the back of a hearse.

The government dithered on food rationing. After a protracted debate on implementation, ration books were issued in September. Rationing was announced to begin in November, then denounced (particularly by the Beaverbrook press which called it 'a dreadful and terrible iniquity') and postponed, then announced again in the new year.

From January 8th, 1940, bacon and ham were limited to 4 ounces per person per week; also butter (4 ounces) and sugar (12 ounces). This represented a cutback by at least half for the average middle-class household, though poorer families would have counted themselves lucky to be able to afford the official ration. As a result of poverty, there were so many unused coupons that grocers found themselves with surplus butter and bacon. Waking up to this, the Ministry of Food doubled the ration, but not before the Daily Express had plastered the country with posters demanding 'Stop Rationing'. That the campaign had little effect was suggested by opinion polls showing that six people out of ten thought rationing to be necessary.

But that was not to say that people were content. Dissatisfaction with the government and its handling of the war intensified with the deterioration of the weather. The winter of 1939–40 was the coldest for 45 years, with January one of the coldest months on record. Frosts, biting winds and heavy snowfalls were the norm. The Thames was frozen for eight miles between Teddington and Sunbury, while stretches of the Mersey, Humber and Severn were iced over. The February thaw brought slush and floods.

With the elements giving more trouble than the Germans, civil defence regulations came a poor second in the routine of day-to-day living. Apart from civil servants and others in state employment who were under orders to set a good example, fewer pedestrians were seen to carry gas-masks. Tucked away into cupboards, it was not unusual for householders to forget where they had put them. As later justification for the distribution of gas-masks that were never used, it was argued that protection had been so thorough as to persuade Hitler against using gas as an offensive weapon. Insofar as Hitler was deterred, it is more likely that he was aware of Britain's lead in chemical warfare, an advantage that could lead to massive retaliation if he struck first. As it was, after four months of war that wasn't really a war in any way that had been expected, civil defence was often circumvented or ignored. In June 1940, it was found that in London, apart from the blackout, 38 per cent of families had taken no precautions against air-raids.

False alarms were a frequent cause of broken sleep.

We awake at three in the morning to sirens. I go for my overcoat, my gas-mask, my shoes and stumble through the French window into the garden where the other inhabitants of this boarding-house are already in the shelter. They are making jokes and meeting with sleepy or nervous responses from their neighbours. The cook says, 'We shall be used to this in ten years.' Then she goes off to the kitchen and comes back with a tray of tea. I get bored with the shelter and come up for air in the quiet garden. The old man we call 'Uncle' is looking at the stars. He has appointed himself an outside watcher. He often thinks he can hear sounds of enemy planes coming over. So far he has been mistaken. His wife 'Auntie' talks all the time in the shelter. She gave us quite a clear little description of different kinds of poisonous gases. I think she has a relish for horrors. Chris appears in the shelter with her hair tied up in a pink gauze scarf. She looks better like that than she does in the daytime with her blondined curls – a little better but not enough to matter. I came in and had a bath before the all-clear signal went. People will get less careful each time – especially if we have so many false alarms.[2]

Bizarre prosecutions for offences under the Emergency Powers Act became a staple of light relief in the newspapers. One of the oddest stories was the case of an elderly clergyman charged with impersonating an army officer by appearing in the uniform of a captain. In the dock at Bow Street he explained that in the reign of Henry II one of his ancestors, as a reward for service in Ireland, was granted permission to bear arms for the defence of the nation. Inclined to be merciful, the magistrate released the accused with the hope that a relation would take care of him.

Among common transgressions was the accidental setting of an alarm that could be mistaken for a warning to take cover. A Fareham pensioner, a victim of a snatch and grab, who blew a whistle to attract the police, got more than he bargained for when he himself was put on a charge.

As an increasing number of evacuees returned to the cities, preferring to risk the bombs rather than to live with strangers, there was resentment among those who had no choice in the matter. Foremost were the civil servants who had been dispatched to the shires. As minister of labour, Ernest Brown found himself under attack from his own department over muddles with billeting, ill-equipped and uncongenial canteens, and lack of recreation and medical care. That government staff were averse to evacuation there could be no doubt. In particular, married men demanded to know why, if their families could not join them, they were not allowed more visits home. There were even cases where husbands doing vital war work were living in rural seclusion while their wives and children were left in areas most liable to bombing.

The none-too-sensitive requisitioning of hotels prompted a press campaign against high-handed bureaucracy. Examples were given of hotels in spa towns where invalids and permanent residents were ordered to be out in a matter of hours or, in one case, one hour. In the House of Lords, where hotel requisitioning was described as 'incompetent Bumbledom' and 'common puerile stupidity', Lord Grenville told of a hotel manager who, remembering how his premises had been seized in the First World War, tried to find out from Whitehall whether this was likely to occur again, in order that he could give his guests fair warning. He heard nothing until an official drove up, told him to clear out everybody in 24 hours and began to stick labels on the furniture.

Compensation was paid, but only after a lengthy argument over the level of claim for lost income. At the turn of the year, there were reports of hotels still standing empty, being returned to their owners.

Though officialdom bore the brunt of attacks on incompetent meddling, when private enterprise was involved in the procurement and allocation of vital raw materials, suspicions of favouritism and profiteering were rife. It did not pass notice that while the Ministry of Supply and the Ministry of Food were technically in control of their brief, the day-to-day operation was in the hands of bodies set up and run by businessmen put in place by their trade associations. Thus, the chairman of the British Iron and Steel Federation was controller of iron and steel, while a director of the British Aluminium Company was responsible for allocating supplies of aluminium.

The government argued that the value of having people in charge who knew what they were talking about outweighed the risks of profits taking precedence over efficiency and fair trading. But the imbalance in the pecking order for the distribution of licences and the location of control centres was plain to see. As Richard Stokes, the Labour MP for Ipswich interjected in a Commons debate on the control of employment, 'Labour is now bound hand and foot but the manufacturer is still free to go off with the swag'.

In vain did the minister of supply assure the House 'with absolute sincerity' that 'I have not seen a single case in which a specific allegation has been made that a servant of the Crown has been bribed or offered an improper advantage in connection with a Government contract'. The suspicion remained that businessmen with friends in high places were able to manage affairs to their own advantage.

The government case might have been more convincing if backed by genuine evidence of equality of sacrifice. But despite Sir John Simon's declaration that there would be no war profits, in his second war budget, in April 1940, instead of increasing taxes on excess profits, concessions were made on death duties. A suggestion from Hugh Dalton, Labour MP for Bishop Auckland, for a capital levy on individual wealth, was dismissed out of hand.

MEAT RATIONING BEGAN on March 11th, 1940, with an allocation worth one shilling and ten pence to every person over the age of six. Excluded from the calculation was offal – liver, kidneys, heart and other delicacies. To take advantage of this concession, customers had to be on good terms with their butcher. There were shopkeepers who began to think less of giving service and more of exercising power.

Though the black market was never allowed to get out of hand, back-door dealing when producers and retailers 'obliged' their friends was widespread. Butchers, fishmongers and grocers invariably had 'something under the counter' for favoured customers.

But the complaints were not all one way. Shopkeepers felt aggrieved by the way they were bullied by their wealthier customers.

> One of them wolves came in here wanting six pounds of gran-ulated sugar. I said 'I'll let you have one pound.' She wasn't a customer of mine. She wouldn't have it, said it was no use; then she came back later, and said, 'Well, I'll have that pound of sugar', and I said, 'Oh no, you won't; it's sold now.' Another man came in wanting tins of cheese, biscuits – dozens of them – so I sent him up the road to young Blank, who keeps his father's grocery, and he didn't half let him have it. Wolves, that's what they are.[3]

Though fines could be imposed, hoarding was second nature to some families. As a post-war schoolboy in a small market town, I had a friend whose mother was housekeeper to a prosperous corn mer-chant. Allowed the run of the attic and the quarters once occupied by servants, we came across a treasure trove of chocolate, sweets and other goodies bought, presumably, before rationing came in and then forgotten until we made our discovery. Unfortunately, it was all too far beyond what we would not call its sell-by date to be edible.

The Ministry of Food had an injection of energy and talent in April 1940 when the lacklustre William Morrison, formerly an equally undistinguished agricultural minister, made way for Lord Woolton.

Morrison's tenure at the ministry was best remembered for a mis-conceived attempt to decentralise London's main fish market away from Billingsgate. The result was truckloads of rotting fish with nowhere to go.

The new man in charge had made his name and earned his peer-age as managing director of Lewis's, a chain of department stores with its headquarters in Liverpool. Having served on several govern-ment committees, Woolton appealed to Chamberlain as a non-party man, one who would not give him trouble at Westminster while out-performing the lamentable Morrison. Knowing something of nutrition, Woolton took advantage of food shortages to promote healthy eating.

Among his resolutions was the provision of one pint of milk daily to every nursing and expectant mother and every child under five, at no cost to those on tight budgets. Determined to stamp out diseases caused by malnutrition, Woolton also made concentrated orange juice and cod liver oil part of the daily diet for young children.

A cardinal rule was to make best use of whatever was available and not on ration. Hedgerows were scoured for dandelion leaves, nettles and rose hips to be transformed into nourishing soup or jam. When blackberries were in season, family outings soon stripped the hedges.

Among the exotic recipes that were put to the test one was for carrot jam:

Ingredients: 8oz carrots, 1lb cooking apples, 1lb sugar.
This delicious jam can be made when fruits are not avail-able. First peel and cook the carrots in a little water. Then slice the apples and cook in one-quarter of a pint of water until a smooth pulp. Mix the carrots and apples together, and for each one pint measure add 1lb of sugar. Return the mixture to the

saucepan and continue stirring until the sugar has dissolved. Boil the jam until it has stiffened.

And eggless cake:

Ingredients: 1lb flour, 3ozs sugar, 4ozs margarine, 4ozs of raisins, a little mixed spice or ginger, a teaspoonful of bicarbonate of soda, half a pint of milk, teaspoonful of vinegar.

Cream the margarine and sugar. Dissolve the bicarbonate of soda in the milk, and add this alternately with the flour and fruit to the creamed margarine, beating all the time. Leave the mixture for approximately one hour to rise. Then add the vinegar, and bake in a lined and covered tin for one and a half hours in a moderate oven.

Orthodoxy in the kitchen counted against ugly and strange-tasting fish such as snook, caught and tinned in South Africa. And housewives drew the line at adopting the French partiality for snails and frogs, even though the wild amphibians of Norfolk and Cambridgeshire were said by some to be delicious.

For much of what Woolton achieved as food minister, the way had been paved by an exceptional minister of agriculture. One of the few MPs sponsored by the National Farmers' Union, Reginald Dorman-Smith brought a practical knowledge of farming and of farmers (he was elected president of the NFU when he was only 32) to his ministerial duties. A natural communicator with a winning personality, Dorman-Smith set about persuading farmers, landowners and agricultural workers that after years of neglect, poor returns on investments and low wages, the industry was now at the centre of a campaign for national survival.

Efforts to boost home production started with a modest subsidy to encourage farmers to plough their grassland. Cereals and vegetables gave more nutritional value than meat and were more easily stored. The aim was to convert 2 million acres of pasture and otherwise 'idle' land. That there was no time to lose was demonstrated by the shortage of reserves. While the government had the entitlement to buy and stockpile key goods such as wheat and sugar, at the outbreak of war the country had only sixteen weeks of supplies in hand. In November 1939, some mills had to stop work because of a shortage of wheat.[4]

With the Emergency Powers Act, the Ministry of Agriculture was able to requisition farms thought to be inefficient. Decisions rested with the County War Agricultural Executive Committees (CWAEC) or 'War Ags', of which there were 48 in England and twelve in Wales. Composed of representatives of farmers and agricultural workers with at least one landowner, the War Ags dispensed information and advice, not all of it welcome to the sturdy, independent yeomen who worked on the land.

The War Ags were also responsible for administering grants and credit schemes, such as they were. Dorman-Smith found himself at the centre of a row between farmers and the banks reluctant to advance funding to what until recently had been regarded as dodgy investments. In the House of Commons, the minister had to face down the champions of farmers who felt 'sullen and resentful' at the 'missed opportunities of the past twenty years'. Chamberlain was no help with his vague references to a 'well balanced, solidly established agriculture' without ever explaining what that really meant.

Dorman-Smith had a better reception when he made his pitch to a nation of gardeners. On October 3rd, 1939, he spoke on the BBC to introduce what became known as the Dig for Victory campaign.

It is clearly our duty, just as it is a matter of elementary wisdom, to try to make doubly and trebly sure that we will fight and win this war on full stomachs. To do this we want not only the big man with the plough but also the little man with the spade to get busy this autumn. We are launching a nation-wide campaign to obtain recruits to the ranks of the food producers. Half a million more allotments properly worked will provide potatoes and vegetables that will feed another million adults and one and a half million children for eight months of the year. The matter is not one that can wait. So let's get going. Let 'Dig for Victory' be the motto of everyone with a garden and of every able-bodied man and woman capable of digging an allotment in their spare time.

In the same month, the first *Grow More Food* pamphlet, prepared by the Royal Horticultural Society, was distributed to households.

Vegetables for you and your family every week of the year. Never a week without food from your garden or allotment. Not only fresh peas and lettuce in June, new potatoes in July, but all the health-giving vegetables in Winter, when supplies are scarce ... Savoys, Sprouts, Kale, Sprouting Broccoli, Onions, Leeks, Carrots, Parsnips and Beet. Vegetables all the year round if you DIG WELL AND CROP WISELY.

A three-year rotation plan allowed for a vegetable garden to be divided between peas, beans and onions followed by potatoes and root crops followed by winter and spring green crops.

This made sense to serious gardeners but there were recipients of the leaflets who were less than impressed by exhortations to Dig for Victory. They included an octogenarian invalid and a nonagenarian grandmother – though it has to be said that a more carefully targeted mailout was probably more effort than it was worth.

Radio features such as *In the Garden*, delivered by W. Beach Thomas, gave the impetus to domestic gardeners to sacrifice their lawns and flower beds to growing vegetables. Though not without opposition from the keep fit lobby, parks and playing fields were turned over to agriculture. The grounds of Windsor Great Park were transformed into what was claimed to be the country's largest wheat field, rows of cabbages were planted in Kensington Gardens, while in Hyde Park, space was made for a piggery. In rural counties, grass verges were utilised, golf courses shrank from eighteen to nine holes, and at Aintree the boundaries to the racecourse sprouted vegetables.[5]

At his home in Chartwell, Winston Churchill took enthusiastically to growing, though it is unlikely that he did much of the digging.

Support from the National Allotment Society was deemed essential, though for a time relations with the ministry were strained by the niggardly grants available and by the tendency of the War Ags to commandeer the larger allotment areas for farming or market gardening. Once peaceful relations had been restored, allotments as well as back gardens became home to easily manageable livestock such as chickens, rabbits and goats. A Small Pig Keepers Council gave advice on setting up pig clubs. One that attracted publicity was run by the Hyde Park police.

Devoting heart and soul to helping farmers get their act together was the Women's Land Army. Mostly singles between the ages of 20 and 30 who might otherwise have been relegated to the typing pool or other dingy office work, recruits responded eagerly to the opportunity of a life in the fresh air where they could meet a wider range of young people. Preparation was a month-long course at an agricultural college. In his wanderings through Britain, H.V. Morton met a college principal who showed him round his domain.

As we were walking, a shapeless female figure in voluminous

garments passed across the weeping landscape. Her feet in gum-boots made great kisses as she withdrew them from the glutinous earth.

'She used to be a fashion artist,' said the Principal.

Another figure in corduroy breeches clumped past with a spade across her shoulder.

'She was a typist,' said the Principal. 'No, I'm wrong, a ladies' hairdresser.'

A herd of wet cows came slowly down the lane, presided over by a girl with fair fluffy hair. She hovered on the flanks, grasping a small hazel switch with which, now and again, she administered a timid tap.

'She,' commented the Principal, 'used to be a children's nurse.'

So I watched a fraction of the Women's Land Army pass on its duties. Forty-five women and girls from every kind of city job ... At the end of the month they would be fitted out by the Government with garments suitable for the Tropics, and then turned out into the wintry countryside.[6]

Many had a hard time persuading die-hard farmers that they could do a 'man's job'. But by 1944, the Women's Land Army was 80,000 strong.

CHAPTER 15

The Usual Suspects

One of the enduring myths of 1939 is that the Allies were motivated by a desire to save the Jews. There was some sympathy for the Jewish predicament in Germany – the anti-Semitic legislation had begun to bite almost as soon as Hitler came to power in 1933 – but outside Jewish organisations, direct action was limited to help given by such as the Quakers, of whom there were only 23,000 in Britain and 160,000 worldwide.

Papers recently released from the National Archives reveal that British prejudice towards Jews intensified during the war. Paradoxically, the rise of anti-Semitic feeling was blamed on those who suffered it. Traders were inclined to believe that somehow the Jewish community had access to supplies denied to the general run of business and that it was the Jews who operated the black market. There was no evidence for this, but shortages had to be blamed on someone.

As for the western governments, their policy was spelt out in mid-1938 at the US-sponsored Evian ('naive' spelt backwards, as someone said) conference which appealed to Germany to set fair conditions for emigration but otherwise imposed tight limits on entry for refugees and a blanket refusal to accept financial responsibility for resettlement.

On May 25th, 1939, Labour MP Colonel Josiah Wedgwood wrote to the home secretary to complain of Britain's modest role in helping the persecuted. 'Washing our hands like Pilate is bad for our consciences and traditions', said Wedgwood. Perhaps so, but there was barely an occupation that did not have a powerful lobby to campaign against immigration. No migrant doctors, dentists, nurses, lawyers or academics were allowed to practise. With high unemployment still the norm, trade unions were hard-headed. Their case was aptly summarised in the *Evening Standard* of January 17th, 1939:

> It is not possible to contemplate permanent increased Jewish settlement in this country. British traders and those employed in the professions cannot be expected to view a large influx of competitors with equanimity. British workers, particularly the 1,800,000 unemployed, cannot be deprived of the prospect of earning their livelihood by unchecked immigration from the dictator countries ...
>
> Another and equally important side of the problem is raised by the belief which seems to have grown in the dictator countries that the democracies are willing to aid their policies of expulsion by unlimited financial support for the refugees. ... We hope that illusion has been effectively dispelled ...
>
> It is not possible for the British Government to allow immigrants to pour into this country. We can only allow harbourage here so long as provision is being made at the same time for refugees to move on elsewhere.

Refugees 'stealing' jobs from Britons was a common theme of the right-wing press throughout 1938 and 1939. 'Elsewhere' was taken to mean the United States, though immigration controls there were just as tight if not tighter. The other favoured destination was Palestine, the home of Zionism, governed by Britain under a League of Nations mandate. But here too, there was no question of free access. Account had to be taken of the Arab population already in revolt against Jewish settlers. The Palestine quota for Jewish refugees was set at a maximum of 10,000 a year.

Chamberlain was not anti-Semitic but nor was he particularly pro-Semitic. Though horrified by *Kristallnacht* and other Nazi brutalities, he prevaricated. As president of the Board of Deputies of British Jews, Neville Laski claimed in 1938 that the prime minister had never 'expressed a word of sympathy for the Jews in Germany'. This was not quite true, but Chamberlain was wary of creating a 'Jewish problem' in Britain and was well aware that among his strongest supporters were rabid anti-Semites.

Leading the campaign for Jewish refugees was the Central British Fund set up in 1933 by Lionel de Rothschild and Simon Marks, head of Marks & Spencer. The aim was to bring together the various Jewish factions for a 'united effort in aid of their German brethren'. Adopting the policy of the already existing Jewish Refugees Committee, a promise was made that no Jewish refugee would become a charge on public funds, a commitment that got round the immigration law which gave officials the power to reject refugees who arrived 'without means'. But such was the rush of applications, it was not long before the money ran out. Some relief was offered by an appeal set up just before Christmas 1938 to which the former prime minister, Stanley, by then Earl, Baldwin gave his name. It raised over £350,000, collected largely from donations of £5 or less, to support the settlement of refugees and to give them a start in their new lives.

Leaflets handed out to adult newcomers – *Helpful Information and Guidance for Every Refugee* – stressed the need to learn English, to refrain from speaking or reading German and to accept, without criticism, the way things were done in Britain. Stress was put on the need to refrain from political activity and the need to get permission from the Alien's Department of the Home Office before starting any new business or accepting any employment. As a stern recommendation, 'Do not make yourself conspicuous by speaking loudly, nor by your manner of dress. The Englishman greatly dislikes ostentation.'

Finally, refugees were warned: 'Do not expect to be received into homes immediately because the Englishman takes some time before he opens up his home wide to strangers.'

Precise numbers of Jewish refugees entering Britain from 1933 to the outbreak of war are impossible to come by. But the best estimates are of around 40,000 admitted into Britain with some 95,000 going to America. The majority of those remaining in Germany and occupied territories died in Nazi camps and ghettos.

Even after resettlement the refugees' troubles were far from over. A foreign accent, a German accent in particular, was suspect and there was no scarcity of busybodies eager to share with the police or air-raid wardens their fantasies of night prowlers flashing signals to low-flying aircraft. From the first day of the war the security forces went in fear of the unseen enemy: agents and *agents provocateurs* smuggled into the country under the guise of fugitives from Nazi persecution.

Recalling the experience of the First World War when 30,000 foreigners were interned in miserable conditions and, in most cases, without just cause, Sir John Anderson, recently appointed home secretary, stood up to the military who wanted a clean sweep of all aliens living in Britain.

The compromise was for a nationwide network of 120 investigative tribunals headed by lawyers who were empowered to call before them all adult foreigners living within their jurisdiction. The plan was to categorise aliens under one of three headings. A small number were assessed as category A – Germans and Austrians with specialised military knowledge which could be used to hinder the British war effort. They were immediately interned. Category B covered those who had lived in Britain for some time and showed no obvious signs of hostility. They kept their basic freedom but were not allowed to own a car, a camera or any large-scale maps, and were forbidden to travel more than five miles from home. Those who could produce evidence of 'character, associations and loyalty' were placed in category C and were left to their own devices, at least for the time being. Home Office guidelines suggested that refugees from religious, racial or political persecution had the strongest case for a C registration.

The tribunals began their work in the first week of October 1939. Since they met behind closed doors and no provision was made for legal representation, decisions were heavily dependent on the sensitivity of individual chairmen. Not surprisingly, their deliberations revealed wild inconsistencies. In Leeds, aliens of whatever background were given a B label, whereas in Manchester they were designated grade C. Several tribunals put the unemployed into B category, telling them to apply for a transfer to C when they found jobs. One tribunal decided that all women qualified for a B rating on the entirely erroneous assumption that domestic servants were a prime source of disaffection. It was not until the Home Office called the tribunal chairmen together to clarify the guidelines that the ratio of Bs to Cs began to fall.

Some 300 Jewish teenagers, cared for by the Refugee Children's Movement, were stuck with a B rating. Protests were made on their behalf but, as Henry Toch discovered, self-help was the only effective recourse.

When the war broke out my brother and I went to a tribunal at King's Cross Police Station. My brother went one morning and I went the next. My brother was classed as 'B' (dangerous enemy alien). I thought this was unfair. I went on my own to the police with our registration books and told them they had got it wrong. They asked me what I wanted and I said: 'I'm the dangerous one and he's the friendly.' The police sergeant, seeing an unusually small boy of sixteen, laughed and said: 'I'll see what I can do.' He went to the judge, took both books in and he came back and said, 'You're both friendly now.'

By the end of November, the tribunals had considered 35,000 cases and ordered the internment of 348, just less than 1 per cent.[1] Most of those were sent to a former Warner's holiday camp at Seaton on the coast east of Sidmouth in Devon. On a low-lying meadow, the camp was often waterlogged in winter. In the early part of the new year, the number of internees increased to around 2,000. A ship loaded with German migrants on their way to a new life in Australia was stopped at Port Said. The passengers were taken off and interned. Distance was no defence.

Ramsey on the Isle of Man was among the list of internment camps drawn up by the War Office in 1939. It came as a complete surprise to the hoteliers of Ramsey when they were given notice to quit their premises within six days, leaving behind 'all furniture, bedding, linen, cutlery, crockery and utensils'. In Port Erin, where a women's camp was set up, landladies were asked if they would accept internees at three shillings a day. As the summer tourist trade was looking gloomy, the offer was taken up enthusiastically.

THE TINY MINORITY of Britons known to be Nazi sympathisers were not so much dangerous as pathetic. Typical was George Pitt-Rivers, a wealthy aristocrat and part-time academic whose leanings towards fascism were prompted by his belief that democracy or, as he said, rule by the lowest common denominator, was a system of government that must inevitably lead to racial and national decline.[2] A prominent figure in the international eugenics movement, he supported sterilisation of the unfit as the means to racial improvement and approved of Germany's Eugenic Sterilisation Law which came into force in 1933.

Pitt-Rivers was not alone in his views. *The Fight for Our National Intelligence* by Raymond B. Cattell was a bestseller when published in 1937, while intellectuals of the stature of W.B. Yeats were convinced that 'the principal European nations are all degenerating in body and mind, though the evidence of this has been hushed up by the newspapers lest it harm circulation'.[3]

Dotty though they may appear, the sentiments of Pitt-Rivers had their echo across the British establishment. It was the same with his anti-Semitism, which permeated society albeit in less virulent form. Look no further than the Shylock caricature of the Jew – that was a commonplace of popular fiction.

Any unfounded suggestion of Jewish extraction was strenuously denied. Sir John Simon found it necessary to issue a statement that, despite a biblical name, he was of Welsh extraction; Lord Camrose, proprietor of the *Daily Telegraph*, brought a successful libel action against the British Union of Fascists for having falsely implied that he was a Jew; in one of his articles, Dean Inge, priest and author, three times nominated for the Nobel Prize in literature, suggested that Jews were using 'their not inconsiderable influence in the Press and in Parliament to embroil us with Germany'.[4]

We may not take to Pitt-Rivers, but the question remains as to why he was put behind wire while others of like mind went free. The answer, of course, is that internment was almost entirely a hit or miss affair. This did not stop sections of the press playing up to blind prejudice.

'I have just visited one of the camps in which Germans are interned', wrote William Hickey of the *Daily Express*.

> The commandant – a quiet kindly colonel – is trying to instil sound British public school principles into these Teutonic bullet-heads. He has appointed lesser, so to speak dormitory leaders, one for each few bedrooms, with approximately the function of prefects. If I go back next summer, I shall expect to find them playing cricket and talking Wykehamist slang …[5]

The article elaborated on the comforts that inmates enjoyed.

> Again and again, walking round with the commandant, I thought, how unlike the concentration camps of Nazi Germany, how remarkably humane.

Well, that was true enough.

Foremost in the press campaign to toughen up on aliens was the *Sunday Dispatch*. In an article about the 'enemy alien menace' on March 31st, 1940, the newspaper parroted claims by 'Scotland Yard men' that the Home Office tribunals had adopted a 'kid-glove policy' and reported:

> Servant girls in country districts have supplied valuable information about German girls in their own job who seemed to spend a good deal of time near important military and Air Force Centres.

The following week, on April 7th, the *Dispatch* managed to link two of its *bêtes noires* in the same front-page headline: 'The Great Aliens Scandal – Our Money for Communist Propaganda'. The story complained that communists among the Czech refugees in Britain, who had been granted £2½ million by the British government, were living together and distributing leaflets. This permitted the *Dispatch* the further headline: 'Red Cells Formed by Subsidized Refugees'.

The Home Office warned of 'German parachutists landing disguised as British policemen [presumably with helmets] and air raid wardens'. An Air Ministry circular gave notice that parachutists landing with arms held aloft did so to lull defenders into assuming they were ready to surrender when in fact they would be holding a grenade in each hand.

A few Germans did arrive on British soil but rarely by intent. Lieutenant A.J. Noble encountered some early captives.

> A day or two after I got back to Inverness, one of the first German aircraft in the north of Scotland was shot down. The crew were being sent south by train and our Depot were ordered to guard them for the night. There were two Officers amongst them and there was heated discussion in the Mess as to whether we should not ask them to join us for dinner – there were no orders of course about such things. There were very quickly for we had them in and dined them – we in dinner jackets and very unmilitary and they in their flying uniform. One of the two was an arrogant type and reckoned that he would soon be in a privileged state as he claimed he was related to the then Secretary of State for War. The other was very subdued and said little. He seemed to have an idea of what was ahead of him.

As the prospects of an Allied victory dimmed, sympathy for internees, however unjustly incarcerated, was all but extinguished. With the fall of the Netherlands, Belgium and Luxembourg in May 1940, anti-alien feelings mounted to near paranoia. Addled by the speed of events which sent him scurrying from The Hague, the erstwhile British minister, Sir Nevile Bland, warned that:

> Every German or Austrian servant, however superficially charming and devoted, is a real and grave menace ... when the signal is given, as it will scarcely fail to be when Hitler so decides, there will be satellites of the monster *all over the country* who will at once embark on widespread sabotage and attacks on civilians and the military indiscriminately.

In fact, the Germans experienced limited success with their Fifth Column in Holland. They did install agents in The Hague with instructions to guide paratroopers to the Dutch seat of government. But they were unsuccessful (Queen Wilhelmina and the government escaped) and they were certainly not disguised as servant girls.

Anderson warned against a panic reaction to the Bland report, pointing out the enormous difference between the Netherlands and Britain, starting with the absence of a common frontier with Germany. Britain had exercised tight control over the entry of aliens for as long as anyone could remember. Moreover, the vast majority of the 73,000 Germans and Austrians in Britain were refugees from Nazi oppression. It was ludicrous to see them as a threat to security.

However, Bland's nightmare vision had a powerful effect on the government's thinking and on public opinion.

As Vice-Chief of the Imperial General Staff, Sir John Dill pushed hard for a round-up of all enemy aliens in areas vulnerable to invasion. This, even though he conceded that '90 per cent of such aliens are well disposed to this country'. Anderson put up a token resistance to what he regarded as a panic measure but gave way when faced by an otherwise united Cabinet.

The order to intern all male category B aliens was posted on May 16th. A week later the order was extended to women and their children. Then a start was made on rounding up the C grade, those who were known incongruously as 'friendly enemy aliens'. By July, more than 30,000 men and women were interned, among them some 1,000 refugee children from the *Kindertransporte*. Anyone with an accent was labelled a potential saboteur, including refugee children. As Dorothy Hardisty, general secretary of the Refugee Children's Movement recorded:

> One of our girls was reported for sketching a village green (an unlikely military target) and a boy who was overheard describing his home in Vienna was branded as a spy, though presumably not a very intelligent one.

A light-hearted tone was generally adopted. There was a war on; inconvenience could be expected. But as the war intensified, the jokes wore thin. It was still with a sense of amazement at the flights of inanity that Ruth Michaelis related the experience of her brother Martin, who found himself in serious trouble with his foster family:

> They discovered he had built himself a crystal set and he was listening in German in the night when he thought nobody was about – he wanted to hear his mother tongue. They accused him of being a spy (he was 11) and they called the police in. From that time both Martin and I were regularly interrogated by the police.

One of the first decisions of the Churchill government was to tighten security along the vulnerable south and east coasts. Starting on May 10th, all male category B and category C Germans and Austrians living in these areas were detained, among them boys just past the age of sixteen who were taken from foster parents or schools without explanation. Ruth Michaelis recalled:

> We found ourselves arriving at Seaton in South Devon and were taken to a holiday camp with chalets, dance-halls, swimming pools etc. But the atmosphere was not pleasant. The whole camp was surrounded with barbed wire, electric fences, armed guards, screened with canvas and dotted with look-out towers. We were herded in; the officers had their revolvers drawn. Whenever the sirens went – which seemed to happen frequently – they drove us, blowing their whistles, into the chalets.[6]

It was a brief stay at Seaton. The next stop was Bury in Lancashire, where home was a disused cotton mill.

> It was empty; long halls supported on cast-iron pillars; there was oil and dirt everywhere and there were our 'beds' – straw palliasses, meagre ones and blankets, laid out in rows along the pillars. When we arrived our suitcases were searched thoroughly – this had already happened in Seaton but here they were more thorough. Everything was emptied on to the floor; a few essentials were returned to us; the rest was heaped in two piles, one for the officers and one for the men, they seemed especially keen on toilet articles and stationery. This was a symptom of that time but was not legal: a year later the commandant of that camp was sentenced to a term of imprisonment for these thefts.

There were pockets of tolerance where human rights were defended.

In the small town where I was brought up, a long-time resident Italian greengrocer attracted hostile attention. Happily, his customers rallied to his cause. He was allowed to carry on his business uninterrupted throughout the war.

CHAPTER 16

The End of the Beginning

It is the supreme irony of Churchill's career that he was brought to power by a monumental cock-up of his own making. Frustrated by inactivity and dismissive of Chamberlain's disinclination to provoke Germany or upset the neutral powers, Churchill fastened on to a plan for disabling Germany's economy by cutting off supplies of Swedish high-grade iron ore.

In principle, this was a game plan that attracted Chamberlain, intent as he was on inflicting damage on the enemy that did not involve wholesale slaughter. He was less inspired when he realised precisely what Churchill had in mind.

For much of the year, iron ore shipments to Germany, essential to its armaments industry, were from the Swedish port of Luleå on the Gulf of Bothnia, the northernmost part of the Baltic. In the winter months when Luleå was ice-bound, the favoured route was via the Norwegian port of Narvik. Securing a total blockade demanded no less than an Allied incursion into neutral territory to take possession of the Swedish ore fields. A less risky modified strategy was to stop traffic the length of the Norwegian west coast. This would force ore-carrying ships from territorial waters into the open sea where they would face capture or destruction by Royal Navy destroyers. Lengthy deliberations by the War Cabinet led merely to a resolve to keep both options open. Churchill's anger at prevarication erupted in a letter to Halifax in which he asserted 'that victory will never be found by taking the line of least resistance'. On January 16th, 1940, almost in desperation, he wrote to Admiral of the Fleet Sir Dudley Paul:

> The squandering of our strength proceeds in every direction, everyone thinking he is serving the country by playing for safety locally. Our Army is puny as far as the fighting front is concerned; our Air Force is hopelessly inferior to the Germans; we are not allowed to do anything to stop them receiving their vital supplies of ore; we maintain an attitude of complete passivity dispersing our forces ever more widely. ...
> Do you realize that perhaps we are heading for *defeat*?

For public consumption, Churchill struck an upbeat note with exaggerated claims of naval supremacy ('Things have never gone so well in any naval war'); but there was no disguising the vacillation and confusion at the heart of government or the lack of urgency displayed by Chamberlain and his immediate colleagues. Content to let Germany make the first move and hoping against all the evidence that it would never come to a pitched battle on the western front, the War Cabinet gave every indication, as A.J.P. Taylor put it, of 'moving into war backwards'.

At weekends, when most of Whitehall closed down for 48 hours, Chamberlain was invariably to be found taking his ease at Chequers, the premier's country residence, where he doubtless reflected on Churchill's impetuosity.

In fairness to Chamberlain there were serious objections to a Nordic venture. To infringe on the rights of neutrality was to risk antagonising American opinion. That was bad enough, but there was also the question of how far a costly and potentially hazardous operation would actually damage the German war economy. The supply of high-grade ore to Ruhr industry was critical in the long run but German stocks of essential raw materials were said to be substantial, enough to support the war machine for some time.

Halifax was quick to point out a limited action with minimum risk, as favoured by some in the government, would be a fruitless exercise since it would not put a stop to ore exports. Rather, he suggested, a diplomatic effort should be made to bring Norway and Sweden on-side with the Allies. Then again, if a more ambitious strategy was approved with the troops having to be deployed, where were they to come from? The British army had not a single unit trained and equipped for an amphibious operation, let alone fighting in a northern mountainous region in one of the coldest winters on record.

Churchill would have none of this, arguing that 'every week the prize is melting'. He had no fear of bringing the Scandinavian countries into the conflict. Extending the war could only be an advantage to Britain. Halifax disagreed. As Chief of the Imperial General Staff (CIGS), General Ironside prevaricated. Accepting that 'our front line is in France', he recognised that public morale was in need of a boost. His colleagues in the French military felt the same way, though the motivation across the Channel was driven primarily by the desire to deter Hitler from striking in the west before the French military was brought up to strength.

AN EVENT, SMALL in itself but big on implications, excited opinion in mid-February 1940. On Churchill's orders, the *Altmark*, a German supply ship, was boarded by sailors from HMS *Cossack* while both were in Norwegian territorial waters. The *Altmark* had twice been intercepted by Norwegian torpedo boats. On the first occasion, it was merely to check that the necessary papers were in order. Allowed to go on its way, the *Altmark* then came up against another inspection vessel. After a categorical 'no' was given to the question, 'Are you carrying prisoners?', the German ship was again given the all-clear. It was harder to satisfy the Royal Navy. With reliable information that the *Altmark* was indeed carrying British merchant seamen from ships sunk by the *Graf Spee*, it was pursued by the *Cossack* and trapped in the Josing Fjord. After a brief fight in which four Germans were killed, 299 prisoners were released.

A Norwegian protest at a violation of neutrality was rejected. The Norwegian navy, it was argued, had neglected a clear duty to inspect the *Altmark*. If anyone had broken the rules of neutrality it was the captain of the Norwegian vessel who had assured *Cossack* that no prisoners were being held on the *Altmark*.

German propaganda made much of the enemy's 'inhuman behaviour' while the British press retaliated with fabricated stories of Prussian brutality and of prisoners holed up in barbaric conditions. The afterglow of lavish praise for the Royal Navy and for Churchill in the British press ('a story of a kind to delight the authors of *Treasure Island* and *Westward Ho'*, said *The Times*) strengthened the case for testing German resolve in the Baltic.

As commander-in-chief of the German navy, Grand Admiral Erich Raeder had already impressed on Hitler the advantage of having naval bases in Norway. The response had been lukewarm until word came of a 150,000-strong Anglo-French expeditionary force to support the Finns in their struggle against the Russian invasion. If this proposal was taken up, the troops would have to cross Norway and Sweden to reach their objective. Cutting off Swedish ore exports was bound to follow. The *Altmark* incident was all it needed to determine

Hitler to fly the swastika over Norway and, while he was at it, to take Denmark into the Reich.

German intentions were no secret. Troop ships with tanks on board were seen to be making ready in the Baltic and North Sea ports, signals picked up from a German spy ship in Norwegian waters suggested forthcoming hostilities, while German reservists fluent in Norwegian and Danish were served with their call-up papers.

The Joint Intelligence Committee made little of all this. Even a Luftwaffe attack on the Royal Naval Air Station at Hatston on Orkney, the British airbase closest to Norway, was not judged to be significant. That no attempt was made by the JIC to establish a pattern was excused on the basis that whatever happened 'will depend less on logical deduction than on the personal and unpredictable decisions of the Führer'. A warning from the American embassy in Copenhagen of an imminent invasion was thought to be 'of doubtful value', merely 'a further move in the war of nerves'.

With escalating signs of activity, including increased naval radio traffic in the Baltic, the War Cabinet was compelled to make up its mind. That there could be no more hedging was stressed in Paris where Daladier had been replaced as prime minister by the more bullish Paul Reynaud. He urged Chamberlain to 'seize the initiative'.

On March 30th, Churchill was given a stronger platform for his call to mine the Norwegian coast. Succeeding the ineffectual Lord Chatfield as chairman of the Military Coordination Committee, he was able to bring his formidable personality to bear on the other service ministers. In his own department, Churchill dominated his First Sea Lord, Sir Dudley Pound, who was in poor health and, in any case, no great strategist. Churchill now also had the support of General Ironside who spoke from his heights as CIGS when he gave it as his conviction that Hitler, not wanting to divert from the west, would keep clear of Scandinavia: 'I personally don't think very much will happen.' He agreed with Churchill that if there was an attempt to frustrate action to stop the Swedish ore exports, the Royal Navy could be relied upon to see off the opposition.

With the risk of the latest French administration collapsing if nothing was done and with public opinion at home pushing for action, Chamberlain was uncharacteristically assertive. On April 3rd, he declared: 'Matters have gone too far for us not to take action.' The following day, speaking in Birmingham, Chamberlain was upbeat on the progress of the war. Hitler, he said, 'had missed the bus' by failing to attack Britain and France when they were at their weakest.

On April 7th, eight British destroyers entered Norwegian waters south of the Lofoten Islands to mine the approaches to Narvik. A few hours later came the first naval encounter of the Norwegian campaign. A hundred miles west of Trondheim, the British destroyer *Glowworm* came up against the German cruiser *Hipper*. In heavy seas and poor visibility, the outmatched *Glowworm* got close enough to collide with the heavier ship, ripping off a chunk of the *Hipper*'s side armour plating. On fire and with her bow broken off, *Glowworm* dropped astern and sank. A posthumous VC, the first of the war, was awarded to *Glowworm*'s captain, Lieutenant Commander Gerard Roope.

On the morning that *Glowworm* met her end, villagers near the southern tip of Norway heard an explosion at sea. A few hours later, fishing boats brought in German soldiers from the transporter *Rio de Janeiro* who let it be known that they had been torpedoed on their way to Bergen where they were being sent to protect the Norwegians against the British.

By now, it should have been clear that Germany was engaged on a major operation. But despite the accidental encounter with the *Hipper* and the sinking of the *Rio de Janeiro*, the Royal Navy remained unaware of the arrival in strength of German troopships and destroyers in neutral waters. Many of them had been at sea, unobserved, for nearly a week.

Invaded by land and sea, Denmark surrendered early on April 9th. Norway made a fight of it.

Narvik, Trondheim, Bergen and Kristiansand soon capitulated but the heavy guns of the fort at Oscarsborg on the Oslofjord and direct hits from land-based torpedo batteries put paid to the Germany heavy cruiser *Blücher* and turned back the German seaborne invasion of Oslo. However, the city was taken that same afternoon by troops flown in by a squadron of Junkers 52s. Stavanger, with the main west coast airfield Sola, fell early on the 9th. By the evening, all the main cities, ports and airfields of Norway were in German hands.

London was in shock. As General Ismay was to recall:

In the very early hours of 9 April I was awakened out of a deep sleep by the telephone bell. It was the Duty Officer at the War Cabinet Office. I could not make head or tail of what he was saying, in spite of frequent requests for repetition; so, suspecting the trouble, I suggested that he should draw the black-out curtains, switch on the lights, find his false teeth and say it all over again. My diagnosis was evidently correct, because after a pause he started speaking again and was perfectly intelligible. His report was brutal in its simplicity. The Germans had seized Copenhagen, Oslo, and all the main ports of Norway. ... As I hurried into my clothes I realised for the first time in my life, the devastating and demoralising effect of surprise.[1]

Norway was not about to give up. Over the next week, home forces concentrated on bottling up the invaders in the cities. Then, on the 14th and 15th, German troops struck out to the south-east and west.

Meanwhile, the British fleet made for Narvik where five destroyers entered the fjord to attack ten larger German vessels, destroying two for the loss of two. In a follow-up attack on the 13th the other German ships were sunk, thus cutting off the German force in Narvik. The first Anglo-French troops landed at Harstad, 40 miles from Narvik, on the 14th. With the aim of recapturing Trondheim, more troops were landed at Namsos and at Andalsnes, a fishing port at the mouth of the River Ranma. But in a heavily mountainous region and lacking the airpower, the advantage was with the Germans who drove back the Allied and Norwegian forces. The decision was taken to withdraw from central Norway. The last Allied troops left Andalsnes on May 1st and from Namsos the next day. The remaining Norwegians surrendered on the 3rd.

A SILENT HOUSE of Commons listened to Chamberlain's statement on the evacuation. The shock of disappointment was all the greater for the strenuous efforts of the Ministry of Information to give the impression that success was a synonym of failure. The wildly inaccurate reports of victories that never happened and attempts to mask defeats that did happen, not least by Chamberlain – who claimed that German losses 'are far greater than ours', which was hardly the point – stoked up opposition to the government with calls for Chamberlain to go and to take his discredited crew of yes-men with him.

But who, then, was to take the helm in restoring the country's fortunes? With hindsight the only possible successor was Churchill. But what is obvious now was far from obvious then. Though a leading, if not the leading parliamentarian, his record was smirched. He had changed parties twice and his policies more often than anyone could count. Distrusted by many on the Tory side, the left denounced him as a diehard imperialist who believed in white rule and as an antediluvian renegade on social reform. Fancying himself as a strategist, he had courted disaster with his Dardanelles adventure in the Great War – only to repeat the error with the Norwegian campaign. But for all that Churchill had the ability to inspire, the essential quality of leadership in a crisis. Moreover, as the principal anti-appeaser, he was the antithesis of Chamberlain.

The gathering movement for a change at the top culminated on May 7th and 8th with a Commons debate on the failure of the Norwegian expedition. Chamberlain opened the debate with a matter-of-fact defence of the conduct of the operations and the character of the War Cabinet. He was interrupted with taunts about 'missing the bus'. 'Everywhere the story is "Too late"', declared Labour leader Clement Attlee, who said of the entire Cabinet that it consisted of men who had 'an almost uninterrupted career of failure'. His words were endorsed by younger Conservatives, already in uniform, who told of untrained soldiers, poor equipment or no equipment at all, and of the failure of military intelligence to uncover German plans.

A slightly bizarre note was introduced into the proceedings when the 68-year-old Admiral Sir Roger Keyes, Conservative MP for Portsmouth North and a fierce anti-appeaser, entered the House in full uniform to denounce the government for not ordering a full-scale naval attack on Trondheim. 'Beachcomber' of the *Daily Express* had fun parodying Keyes as a one-track exponent of British dominance at sea.

The most effective speech was given from the government benches by Leo Amery, another Churchill supporter. Calling for change at the centre – 'We cannot go on as we are' – he quoted Cromwell's words to the Long Parliament:

You have sat too long here for any good you have been doing. Depart, I say, and let us have done with you. In the name of God, go.

Next day, May 8th, Labour decided to move a note of censure. It was a risky strategy, one that allowed government whips to appeal to party loyalty as the first consideration. But then Chamberlain himself came to the aid of the opposition with an ill-judged plea to keep the faith.

> No government can prosecute a war efficiently unless it has public and Parliamentary support. I accept the challenge. I welcome it indeed. At least we shall see who is with us and who is against us, and I call upon my friends to support us in the Lobby tonight.

To try to turn a momentous debate on the future of the country into a personal issue was all it needed to persuade a sizeable minority to put principles before party. Of the 615 members entitled to vote, only 486 entered the lobbies. Deliberate abstentions on the government side were thought to be about 60. More critically, 41 Tories went into the Labour lobby. When the votes were counted, an expected Tory majority of 200 had fallen to 81. The government had survived but in circumstances that were humiliating for Chamberlain. 'He walked out', wrote parliamentary correspondent Alexander Mackintosh, 'with the pathetic look of a surprised and sorely stricken man'.[2]

May 10th started early for Churchill. At 6.00am he was closeted with the service ministers. Two hours later he was at a meeting of full Cabinet at No. 10. The news was uniformly bad. Holland and Belgium had been invaded and bombs had fallen in northern France. Clinging on, Chamberlain told Churchill that 'the great battle which has broken upon us' made it necessary for him to remain at his post. By late afternoon, when the War Cabinet was again in session, he had changed his mind.

He knew that the Labour party would not join a coalition

government under his leadership. He was also aware that his preferred successor had decided not to put his name forward. As a peer, Halifax felt, rightly, that he was disqualified from the premiership. His decision made, Chamberlain went to Buckingham Palace to submit his resignation. The King assumed that Halifax would take over. 'No', said Chamberlain, 'Winston is the man to send for'.

Having secured Labour and Liberal agreement to serve in a war coalition, Churchill made his appearance in the House of Commons. Sitting alongside was Clement Attlee as his deputy in all but name. They did not get a rapturous reception. That was reserved for Chamberlain, a consolation prize for abject failure.

Churchill's call to battle stations was short and very much to the point.

> I would say to the House, as I said to those who have joined this government, that I have nothing to offer but blood, toil, tears and sweat. We have before us an ordeal of the most grievous kind. ... You ask, what is our policy? I will say: it is to wage war, by sea, land and air, with all our might and with all the strength that God can give us: to wage war against a monstrous tyranny, never surpassed in the dark, lamentable catalogue of human crime. That is our policy. You ask, what is our aim? I can answer in one word: It is victory at all costs, victory in spite of all terror, victory, however long and hard the road may be; for without victory, there is no survival.

On the list of new ministerial appointments Chamberlain appeared as Lord President of the Council, a grand-sounding job that could be anything the prime minister wanted to make of it. Chamberlain was not long in office. Weakened by cancer he resigned on September 30th, 1940, and died six weeks later.

THE NORWEGIAN CAMPAIGN ended ingloriously. Heavy snow brought a lull in the fighting around Narvik, which was not recaptured until May 28th by a mixed force of British, French, Norwegian and Polish forces. By then, the disaster in France compelled Churchill to order a withdrawal. The last convoys left Harstad on June 8th when the remaining Norwegian fighters capitulated. On the same day, the German battle cruisers *Gneisenau* and *Scharnhorst* sank the aircraft carrier *Glorious* and two escorting destroyers off Harstad with heavy loss of life. Damage inflicted on the German vessels which forced them to return to Trondheim saved the troop convoys.

The British-led Nordic adventure was a classic example of how not to fight a war. In his exhaustive study, John Kiszely gives Britain zero marks for planning and execution. The Germans 'achieved complete strategic and tactical surprise' while the British military was 'outclassed in every way'.[3] Almost as damning was the verdict of Field Marshal Lord Alanbrooke, CIGS from December 1941. His diary for February 2nd, 1940 deplores 'history repeating itself in an astonishing way'.

The same string-pulling as in the last war, the same differences between statesmen and soldiers, the same faults as regards changing key posts at the opening of hostilities, and now the same tendency to start subsidiary theatres of war, and to contemplate wild projects!! We shall apparently never apply the lessons of one war to the next.[4]

It was small comfort that the German fleet had suffered a loss of three cruisers and ten destroyers which possibly, just possibly, might have deterred Hitler from mounting a direct assault on Britain.

Churchill was saved from the ignominy of Norway by the diversion of public attention to France, where it was becoming increasingly apparent that the German advance could not be stemmed.

A British businessman in Peronne in northern France, George Dace saw the debacle at first hand.

Peronne was suddenly teeming with thousands of refugees who had fled the German forces. My premises became a casualty clearing station. I was able to help many who had been wounded by machine gun fire from German aircraft. As the situation became more tense and the population of the town began to evacuate, I witnessed the panic retreating of French troops. A cannon and motor machine guns were abandoned in the square in front of my premises. French soldiers were looting and changing into civilian clothes, throwing away their uniforms.

On the 27th May at 11 a.m. the evacuation of Peronne was ordered by the Prefecture. I had lent my car to a farmer friend who wanted to ensure the safety of his elderly parents who lived just outside the town. He never returned. Soon after leaving me, Peronne was heavily bombed, the five storey building in front of my place received a direct hit and was down. All the glass in my place was shattered. I waited and waited for my car, as the time passed the town emptied of its inhabitants. I waited until 4 o'clock in the afternoon, when with my wife, I left on foot. We only had our winter coats and a few odds and ends in a rucksack.

The resourceful Mr Dace and his wife were on the road south for ten days.

We had reached the river Loire when the Germans caught up with us. We took refuge in the village of Montsoreau near Saumur. Here I was able to get false French identity papers.

As the Germans had ordered all refugees from the north to return to their homes I borrowed a car and drove my wife and two other refugees back to a friend's home in Normandy, in the hamlet of Le Hamet. Here I registered as a refugee farm worker.

And there he stayed for the duration as a farm worker and as an agent for the Resistance.

WITH THE EVACUATION from Dunkirk and the fall of France, the home front prepared for battle. This time it was for real. On May 22nd, an extension of the 1939 Emergency Powers Act gave the government almost total control over persons and property. The necessary legislation was passed on the nod by the House of Commons. Attlee set the tone.

> A great battle is now proceeding. Our men at sea, on land and in the air, are fighting with splendid courage, devotion and skill, in company with the freedom-loving people who are our Allies. The result of that battle we cannot know, but it must be clear to all that the next few weeks will be critical. Our ruthless enemy, who is restrained by no considerations of international law, of justice or humanity, is throwing everything into the scale to force a decision. We are resolved that he shall not succeed. The Government are convinced that now is the time when we must mobilise to the full the whole resources of this country. We must throw all our weight into the struggle. Every private interest must give way to the urgent needs of the community. We cannot know what the next few weeks or even days may bring forth, but whatever

may come we shall meet it as the British people in the past have met dangers and overcome them.

As the minister of labour, Ernest Bevin had power 'to direct any person to perform any service required of him'. A blunt, pugnacious former trade union leader, Bevin was loved by the workers and feared by the middle class who, taking their cue from the Archbishop of Canterbury, saw a socialist dictator in the making. They were seriously misinformed. Bevin was a democrat through and through, one who had made his reputation in labour relations by fighting off the attentions of the totalitarian far left. It would have been hard to find anyone better qualified to mobilise the nation's workforce.

Wages and profits came under central control. Excess Profits Tax was set at 100 per cent. And not before time, was the consensus.

To the fear of bombing was now added the fear of invasion, the expectation being that Britain was next on the list for German conquest. To frustrate enemy intruders, barricades went up on country roads, and open spaces such as golf courses were smattered with improvised bulwarks such as felled trees or abandoned vehicles. One bright idea that had a limited take-up was to impede the progress of invading forces by laying soup plates upside down in the streets in the hope that they would be mistaken for anti-tank mines.

The suffocating grip of the regulatory regime grew ever tighter. Careful householders checked their bookcases for publications that might hint at unpatriotic sympathies. Children were warned not to speak out of turn. As a five-year-old, this writer got into trouble when he was unable to disguise his pleasure at a stray bomb falling on the local church hall, an act of benevolence that spared me further attendance at Sunday school.

Advice from the Ramblers' Association was for members not to be too ostentatious in their use of maps and to refrain from night walking. 'There is always the possibility that some over-zealous person will fire first and ask questions afterwards.' Photographers and painters were told to play safe in their choice of subject. One never knew who might misinterpret art for artifice.

If fewer evacuees fell suspect to nefarious activities it was because, quite simply, there were fewer evacuees. By late spring 1940 there were only around 460,000 children and 60,000 adults billeted in safer areas of England and Wales. In Scotland, of the 175,000 in the first exodus from Glasgow and other cities, only 27,000 had stayed away from home. With the increasing likelihood of the experience in France being repeated in Britain, the evacuation was relaunched but with more attention to the sensibilities of the reception areas. At the same time the most vulnerable were resistant to another venture into the countryside. Once was enough. When the blitz started in September 1940, there were 520,000 children of school age marooned in London.[5]

At the outbreak of war, the Home Office had ruled that refugees from enemy territories would no longer be allowed entry under any circumstances. But no decree can be all-embracing. Among the outcasts from Nazi rule who managed to escape over the border into Holland there were those who managed to buy or beg a passage across the water on the *Bodegraven* on May 14th, the last boat to sail from north Holland before the German occupation.

The *Bodegraven* was an elderly steam freighter, serviceable for short hauls but not suited to military action. Fortunately, there was much to divert the passengers from the risks they were taking. As Ya'acov Friedler recalls:

As we walked towards the vessel we noticed the arrival of two small warships – they must have been torpedo boats – from which soldiers wearing dark blue uniforms and British-style steel helmets were disembarking. The dozen or so men, Royal Marines I guess they must have been, were staggering under the weight of their kitbags and the heavy machine-guns they were bringing ashore. We crossed paths as they walked off the pier and we walked on to it. They smiled and gave us the thumbs-up sign, shouting words of encouragement at us. We did not understand their language, but there was no mistaking the tone.

The *Bodegraven* had a hard time clearing Dutch waters. As it pulled away, two German planes attacked the harbour.

We could see them making their run and diving to release their bombs, which dropped slowly to explode below. It was like watching some spectacular fireworks. Then, suddenly the two bombers turned towards the sea and made straight for our ship. They swooped low as they approached and we could see their Luftwaffe markings. The planes started sweeping the ship with machine-gun fire and we instinctively threw ourselves face down. The captain issued rifles to the crew who took ineffective pot shots at the planes.

This continued for a few moments. Then the captain announced that Holland had surrendered and ordered his crew to cease fire. The men lowered their rifles and pressed against the side of the superstructure for cover.

There was one more attack to come, not from German planes but from British gunners. Thrown off course in dense fog, the *Bodegraven* drifted south towards the Kent coast, where it was spotted by a local defence unit. At the sound of gunfire the refugee ship turned away and made off round the southern counties and up towards Liverpool, where it was finally recognised as a friendly vessel. The *Bodegraven* docked to a hero's welcome.

For those who disembarked, bringing with them little except the clothes they had on and a few personal items, it was the start of a new life. But in this, at least, they had something in common with those who took them in. In May 1940, every British citizen had to face up to changes that amounted to a new life. The Phoney War was over. The real war was about to begin.

BIBLIOGRAPHY

Agate, James, *A Shorter Ego*, 1945

Arnold, Ralph, *A Very Quiet War*, 1962

Balfour, Michael, *Propaganda in War, 1939–45*, 1979

Beardmore, George, *Civilians at War: Journals 1938–1946*, 1984

Bekker, C.D., *Swastika at Sea*, 1953

Bentley, Nicolas, *A Version of the Truth*, 1989

Best, Captain S. Payne, *The Venlo Incident*, 1950

Bishop, Patrick, *Air Force Blue*, 2017

Bishop, Patrick, *Bomber Boys*, 2007

Blake, Leonardo, *Hitler's Last Year in Power*, 1939

Bloom, Ursula, *War Isn't Wonderful*, 1961

Bowyer, Michael J.F., *2 Group RAF: A Complete History 1936–45*, 1974

Brendon, Piers, *The Dark Valley: A Panorama of the 1930s*, 2001

Briggs, Asa, *The History of Broadcasting in the UK*, Vol. III, *The War of Words*, 1995

Brown, Anthony Cave, *The Secret Servant: The Life of Sir Stewart Menzies*, 1988

Channon, Chips, *Chips – The Diary of Sir Henry Channon*, 1967

Carey, John, *The Intellectuals and the Masses*, 1992

Caulfield, Max, *A Night of Terror*, 1958

Churchill, W.S., *The Second World War: The Gathering Storm*, 1953

Cockett, Richard, *Twilight of Truth*, 1989

Cooper, Duff, *Old Men Forget*, 1958

Corrigan, Gordon, *Blood, Sweat and Arrogance*, 2006

Cox, Geoffrey, *Countdown to War*, 1988

Crompton, Richmal, *William and ARP*, 1979

Cudlipp, Hugh, *Publish and be Damned*, 1953

Dallek, Robert, *Franklin D. Roosevelt*, 2017

Danchev, Alex and Todman, Daniel (eds), *Alanbrooke War Diaries 1939–1945*, 2001

Dawson, Sandra Trudgen, *Holiday Camps in Twentieth-Century Britain*, 2011

Douglas, Roy, *The Advent of War, 1939–40*, 1978

Egerton, David, *Britain's War Machine*, 2011

Faber, David, *Munich: The Appearance of Crisis*, 2008

Fawkes, Richard, *Fighting for a Laugh*, 1978

Garfield, Simon, *We Are At War*, 2009

Gielgud, Val, *Years of the Locust*, 1947

Gillman, Peter and Leni, *'Collar the Lot!' – How Britain Interned and Expelled its Wartime Refugees*, 1980

Griffiths, Richard, *Fellow Travellers of the Right*, 1980

Hammerton, Sir John, *As Days Go By*, 1945

Hanson, Neil and Priestley, Tom (eds), *Priestley's Wars*, 2008

Harrisson, Tom and Madge, Charles (eds), *War Begins at Home (Mass-Observation)*, 1940

Hart, Bradley W., *George Pitt-Rivers and the Nazis*, 2015

Henderson, Donald, *Mr Bowling Buys a Newspaper*, 1943

Hinsley, F.H., *British Intelligence in the Second World War*, 1990

Hodson, James Lansdale, *Through the Dark Night*, 1941

Hucker, Daniel, *Public Opinion and the End of Appeasement in Britain*, 2011

Hughes, Randolph, *The New Germany*, 1936

Ifould, Lloyd C., *Immortal Era: The Birth of British Aviation*, 1948

Ingram, Norman, *The Politics of Dissent: Pacifism in France 1919–1939*, 1991

Ismay, Lord, *The Memoirs of General Lord Ismay*, 1960

Kavanagh, Ted, *Tommy Handley*, 1949

Kee, Robert, *The World We Left Behind*, 1984

Kershaw, Ian, *Hitler*, 2000

Kershaw, Ian, *Making Friends with Hitler*, 2004

Khrushchev, Nikita, *Khrushchev Remembers*, 1974

Kiszely, John, *Anatomy of a Campaign*, 2017

Knightley, Phillip, *The First Casualty*, 1975

Lukacs, John, *Five Days in London: May 1940*, 2001

Mackay, Robert, *Half the Battle: Civilian Morale in Britain during the Second World War*, 2002

Mackintosh, Sir Alexander, *Echoes of Big Ben*, 1946

Macleod, Iain, *Neville Chamberlain*, 1961

Macnab, Geoffrey, *J. Arthur Rank and the British Film Industry*, 1993

Malcolmson, Patricia and Robert, *Women at the Ready*, 2013

Marwick, Arthur, *The Home Front: The British and the Second World War*, 1976

McLaine, Ian, *Ministry of Morale*, 1979

Millgate, Helen D. (ed.), *Mr Brown's War: A Diary of the Second World War*, 1998

Minney, R.J., *The Private Papers of Hore-Belisha*, 1960

Montgomery, Field Marshal Viscount, *The Memoirs of Field Marshal Viscount Montgomery of Alamein*, 1958

Morton, H.V., *I Saw Two Englands*, 1940

Mosley, Leonard O., *Report From Germany*, 1945

Muggeridge, Malcolm, *The Thirties: 1930–1940 in Great Britain*, 1940

Murray, William, *Luftwaffe*, 1985

Murrow, Edward R., *This is London*, 1941

O'Brien, Terence H., *Civil Defence*, 1955

Overy, Richard, *The Morbid Age: Britain Between the Wars*, 2009

Padley, Richard and Cole, Margaret, *Evacuation Survey*, 1940

Perry, George, *The Great British Picture Show*, 1974

Possony, Stephen, *Tomorrow's War: Its Planning, Management and Cost*, 1938

Price, George Ward, *Year of Reckoning*, 1939

Rice, Joan, *Sand in My Shoes*, 2006

Ritchie, Charles, *The Siren Years: Undiplomatic Diaries, 1937–45*, 1974

Roberts, Andrew, *The Holy Fox: A Biography of Lord Halifax*, 1991

Schellenberg, Walter, *The Schellenberg Memoirs*, 1956

Schmidt, Paul, *Hitler's Interpreter*, 2016

Scott, Sir Harold, *Your Obedient Servant*, 1959

Seth, Ronald, *The Day War Broke Out*, 1963

Smith, Daniel, *The Spade as Mighty as the Sword*, 2011

Smith, Harold L. (ed.), *War and Social Change*, 1986

Strang, Lord, *Home and Abroad*, 1956

Summers, Julie, *Our Uninvited Guests*, 2018

Teeling, William, *Why Britain Prospers*, 1938

Templewood, Viscount (The Rt. Hon. Sir Samuel Hoare), *Nine Troubled Years*, 1954

Titmuss, Richard, *Problems of Social Policy*, 1950

Todman, Daniel, *Britain's War 1937–1941*, 2016

Turner, E.S., *The Phoney War on the Home Front*, 1961

Vansittart, Peter, *Paths from the White Horse*, 1985

Von Ribbentrop, Joachim, *Germany Speaks*, 1937

Wallington, Neil, *Firemen at War*, 1981

Warner, Jack, *Jack of All Trades*, 1995

Watt, Donald Cameron, *How War Came*, 1989

Weber, Eugen, *The Hollow Years*, 1995

Welshman, John, *Churchill's Children: The Evacuee Experience in Wartime Britain*, 2010

West, W.J., *Truth Betrayed*, 1987

Winton, John (ed.), *The War at Sea 1939–1945*, 1967

Woodman, Richard, *The Battle of the River Plate*, 2008

Wrench, John Evelyn, *Geoffrey Dawson and our Times*, 1955

Wyatt, Woodrow, *Confessions of an Optimist*, 1985

Yeats-Brown, Francis, *European Jungle*, 1939

NOTES

_____

(Unless otherwise stated, the letters quoted are from the author's collection.)

Chapter 1

1. Paul Schmidt, *Hitler's Interpreter*, 2016 edition; p. 158.
2. Ibid; p. 159.
3. Donald Cameron Watt, *How War Came*, 1989; p. 602.
4. R.J. Minney, *The Private Papers of Hore-Belisha*, 1960; p. 394.
5. *Hansard*, September 3rd, 1939.
6. Professor H.N. Fieldhouse, Toronto University, speaking in London, June 1938.
7. Ursula Bloom, *War Isn't Wonderful*, 1961.
8. Charles Ritchie, *The Siren Years: Undiplomatic Diaries, 1937–45*, 1974, p. 42.

Chapter 2

1. *The Times*, January 24th, 1933.
2. Chips Channon, *Diary*, August 6th, 1936; p. 106.
3. Randolph Hughes, *The New Germany*, 1936; p. 11.
4. Ian Kershaw, *Making Friends with Hitler*, 2004; p. 15.
5. Joachim von Ribbentrop, *Germany Speaks*, 1937; p. 79.
6. Peter Vansittart, *Paths from the White Horse*, 1985; pp. 117, 118.
7. Lord Lothian quoted by W.S. Churchill in *The Second World War: The Gathering Storm*, 1953; p. 176.

8. Donald Cameron Watt, *How War Came*, 1989; p. 79.
9. William Teeling, *Why Britain Prospers*, 1938; p. 201.
10. Andrew Roberts, *The Holy Fox: A Biography of Lord Halifax*, 1991; p. 115.
11. Neil Hanson and Tom Priestley (eds), *Priestley's Wars*, 2008; p. 174.
12. Ironside to Colonel R. Macleod, undated.
13. Defence White Paper, March 3rd, 1936.
14. *Hansard*, November 10th, 1932.
15. *Hansard*, November 28th, 1934.
16. Michael J.F. Bowyer, *2 Group RAF: A Complete History 1936–45*, 1974; pp. 34, 35.
17. Lloyd C. Ifould, *Immortal Era: The Birth of British Aviation*, 1948; p. 145.
18. Ibid; p. 129.
19. William Murray, *Luftwaffe*, 1985; p. 8.
20. Stephen Possony, *Tomorrow's War: Its Planning, Management and Cost*, 1938.
21. Terence H. O'Brien, *Civil Defence*, 1955; p. 39.

Chapter 3
1. Malcolm Muggeridge, *The Thirties: 1930–1940 in Great Britain*, 1940; p. 295.
2. Lord Strang, *Home and Abroad*, 1956; p. 137.
3. Leonardo Blake, *Hitler's Last Year in Power*, 1939; p. 6.
4. *The Times*, March 16th, 1939.
5. Lord Strang, *Home and Abroad*, 1956; p. 161.
6. Francis Yeats-Brown, *European Jungle*, 1939; p. 11.
7. George Ward Price, *Year of Reckoning*, 1939; p. 10.
8. Sir Harold Scott, *Your Obedient Servant*, 1959; p. 63.
9. Ibid; p. 106.
10. Ibid; pp. 109–10.
11. Ibid; pp. 113, 114.
12. Ibid; pp. 117, 118.
13. Ibid; p. 118.
14. Terence O'Brien, *Civil Defence*, 1955; pp. 150, 151.
15. Ibid; p. 151.

16. James Agate, *A Shorter Ego*, 1945; p. 14.
17. Tom Harrisson and Charles Madge (eds), *War Begins at Home*, Mass-Observation, 1940; p. 114.
18. Julie V. Gottlieb, *War of Nerves*, *History Today*, September 2018.
19. Marion Rees, Diary, September 11, 1939.
20. Leonard O. Mosley, *Report From Germany*, 1945.

Chapter 4

1. *International Affairs*, Vol. XVII, No. 3, May–June 1938.
2. Richard Titmuss, *Problems of Social Policy*, 1950; p. 88.
3. Charles Ritchie, *The Siren Years 1937–45*, 1974; p. 47.
4. Sir Harold Scott, *Your Obedient Servant*, 1959; pp. 115, 116.
5. Lord Ismay, *The Memoirs of General Lord Ismay*, 1960; p. 86.
6. Ibid; p. 86.
7. Sir Kenneth Clark on the BBC Empire Service, August 29th, 1939.
8. Julie Summers, *Our Uninvited Guests*, 2018; pp. 18, 22.

Chapter 5

1. Neil Hanson and Tom Priestley (eds), *Priestley's Wars*, 2008; p. 191.
2. Charles Ritchie, *The Siren Years 1937–45*, 1974; p. 45.

Chapter 6

1. George Beardmore, *Civilians at War: Journals 1938–1946*, 1984; p. 45.
2. *North London Collegiate Magazine*, December 1939.

Chapter 7

1. Imperial War Museum; 96/13/2.
2. Patricia and Robert Malcolmson, *Women at the Ready*, 2013; pp. 13, 14.
3. Richard Padley and Margaret Cole, *Evacuation Survey*, 1940.
4. Richard Titmuss, *Problems of Social Policy*, 1950; p. 138.
5. Sir John Hammerton, *As the Days Go By*, 1945.
6. Richard Titmuss, *Problems of Social Policy*, 1950; p. 109.
7. Simon Garfield, *We Are At War*, 2009; p. 60.

8. Richard Titmuss, *Problems of Social Policy*, 1950; pp. 168, 169.
9. Sandra Trudgen Dawson, *Holiday Camps in Twentieth-Century Britain*, 2011.

Chapter 8
1. Tom Harrisson and Charles Madge (eds), *War Begins at Home*, Mass-Observation, 1940; p. 157.
2. Letter to Colonel R. Macleod, December 4th, 1942.
3. Ralph Arnold, *A Very Quiet War*, 1962; p. 27.
4. Final Report on the circumstances leading to the termination of Henderson's mission to Berlin, September 20th, 1939.

Chapter 9
1. Anthony Cave Brown, *The Secret Servant: The Life of Sir Stewart Menzies*, 1988; p. 195.
2. Geoffrey Cox, *Countdown to War*, 1988; p. 130.
3. James Lansdale Hodson, *Through the Dark Night*, 1941; p. 12.
4. Alex Danchev and Daniel Todman (eds), *Alanbrooke War Diaries 1939–1945*, 2001; p. 20 (diary entry for November 28th, 1939).
5. H.V. Morton, *I Saw Two Englands*, 1940; p. 67.
6. James Lansdale Hodson, *Through the Dark Night*, 1941; p. 17.
7. Edward R. Murrow, *This is London*, December 14th, 1939; pp. 86, 87.
8. Woodrow Wyatt, *Confessions of an Optimist*, 1985; pp. 80, 81.
9. Ibid; p. 81.
10. Ralph Arnold, *A Very Quiet War*, 1962; p. 21.
11. *The Day War Broke Out*, BBC Radio 4, April 14th, 1969.
12. Joan Rice, *Sand in My Shoes*, 2006.
13. Captain S. Payne Best, *The Venlo Incident*, 1950; p. 8.
14. Walter Schellenberg, *The Schellenberg Memoirs*, 1956; p. 831.
15. Captain S. Payne Best, *The Venlo Incident*, 1950; p. 17.

Chapter 10
1. Patrick Bishop, *Air Force Blue*, 2017; p. 119.
2. Ibid; p. 120.

3. Patrick Bishop, *The Bombers*, 2007; p. 66.

4. Patrick Bishop, *Air Force Blue*, 2017; p. 133.

5. *The War at Sea 1939–1945*; an anthology edited by John Winton, 1967; p. 11.

6. Edward R. Murrow, *This is London*, 1941; p. 48.

7. Max Caulfield, *A Night of Terror*, 1958; p. 72.

8. Francis M. Carroll, *History Ireland*, Vol. 19, No. 1, January–February 2011; pp. 42, 43, 44, 45.

9. Tom Harrisson and Charles Madge (eds), *War Begins at Home*, Mass-Observation, 1940; pp. 160, 161.

10. *The Memoirs of Field-Marshal Viscount Montgomery of Alamein*, 1958.

11. Nikita Khrushchev, *Khrushchev Remembers*, 1974; p. 71.

12. Geoffrey Cox, *Countdown to War*, 1988; p. 141.

13. Neil Wallington, *Firemen at War*, 1981; p. 40.

14. *The War at Sea 1939–1945*; an anthology edited by John Winton, 1967; pp. 13, 14.

15. Richard Woodman, *The Battle of the River Plate*, 2008; pp. 355, 356.

16. C.D. Bekker, *Swastika at Sea*, 1953.

Chapter 11

1. Helen D. Millgate (ed), *Mr Brown's War: A Diary of the Second World War*, 1998; p. 21.

2. Richard Titmuss, *Problems of Social Policy*, 1950; p. 322.

3. Tom Harrisson and Charles Madge (eds), *War Begins at Home*, Mass-Observation, 1940; p. 210.

4. Ibid; p. 107.

5. Nicolas Bentley, *A Version of the Truth*, 1960; pp. 178, 179.

6. Nicolas Bentley, *A Version of the Truth*, 1960; p. 180.

7. Neil Wallington, *Fireman at War*, 1981; p. 38.

8. *BBC History* magazine, September 4th, 2015.

9. Imperial War Museum; 90/16/1.

10. Tom Harrisson and Charles Madge (eds), *War Begins at Home*, Mass-Observation, 1940; p. 120.

Chapter 12

1. George Perry, *The Great British Picture Show*, 1974; p. 85.
2. Richard Cockett, *Twilight of Truth*, 1989; p. 27.
3. Ibid; p. 101.
4. Ibid; p. 104.
5. Hugh Cudlipp, *Publish and be Damned*, 1953; p. 138.
6. Viscount Templewood (Sir Samuel Hoare), *Nine Troubled Years*, 1954; p. 421.
7. Ian McLaine, *Ministry of Morale*, 1979; p. 27.
8. Ibid; p. 28.
9. Ibid; p. 29.
10. Duff Cooper, *Old Men Forget*, 1958; p. 285.
11. H.V. Morton, *I Saw Two Englands*, 1940; p. 280, 281.
12. Sir Harold Scott, *Your Obedient Servant*, 1959; p. 120.
13. Phillip Knightley, *The First Casualty*, 1975; p. 206.
14. Viscount Templewood (Sir Samuel Hoare), *Nine Troubled Years*, 1954; p. 422.
15. Tom Harrisson and Charles Madge (eds), *War Begins at Home*, Mass-Observation, 1940; p. 56.
16. Malcolm Muggeridge, *The Thirties: 1930–1940 in Great Britain*, 1940; p. 317.
17. Donald Henderson, *Mr Bowling Buys a Newspaper*, 1943; p. 49.
18. W.J. West, *Truth Betrayed*, 1987; p. 86.
19. Stuart Hood, 'Battle of the Airwaves', *The Listener*, November 12th, 1987.
20. Asa Briggs, *The History of Broadcasting in the UK*, Vol. III, *The War of Words*, 1995; p. 71.
21. H.V. Morton, *I Saw Two Englands*, 1940; p. 249.

Chapter 13

1. Tom Harrisson and Charles Madge (eds), *War Begins at Home*, Mass-Observation, 1940; p. 230.
2. Edward R. Murrow, *This is London*, September 19th, 1939.

3. Tom Harrisson and Charles Madge (eds), *War Begins at Home*, Mass-Observation, 1940; p. 187.

4. Edward R. Murrow, *This is London*, 1941; pp. 34, 35.

5. Tom Harrisson and Charles Madge (eds), *War Begins at Home*, Mass-Observation, 1940; p. 155.

6. Richard Fawkes, *Fighting for a Laugh*, 1978; p. 17.

7. Ibid; p. 16.

8. Richmal Crompton, *William and ARP*, 1939; p. 13.

9. Geoffrey Macnab, *J. Arthur Rank and the British Film Industry*, 1993; p. 36.

10. Val Gielgud, *Years of the Locust*, 1947; p. 167.

11. Ibid; p. 168.

12. Ibid; p. 169.

13. Ibid; p. 171.

14. Ted Kavanagh, *Tommy Handley*, 1949; pp. 101–02.

15. Jack Warner, *Jack of All Trades*, 1995; pp. 61–2.

16. George Beardmore, *Civilians at War: War Journals 1938–1946*, 1984; p. 43.

Chapter 14

1. H.V. Morton, *I Saw Two Englands*, 1940; p. 201.

2. Charles Ritchie, *The Siren Years 1937–45*, 1974; p. 44, 45.

3. Tom Harrisson and Charles Madge (eds), *War Begins at Home*, Mass-Observation, 1940; p. 376.

4. Daniel Smith, *The Spade as Mighty as the Sword*, 2011; p. 20.

5. Ibid; p. 56.

6. H.V. Morton, *I Saw Two Englands*, 1940; p. 274.

Chapter 15

1. Peter and Leni Gillman, *'Collar the Lot!' – How Britain Interned and Expelled its Wartime Refugees*, 1980; p. 45.

2. Bradley W. Hart, *George Pitt-Rivers and the Nazis*, 2015.

3. John Carey, *The Intellectuals and the Masses*, 1992; p. 13.

4. Malcolm Muggeridge, *The Thirties: 1930–1940 in Great Britain*; p. 263.
5. William Hickey, *Daily Express*, October 2nd, 1939.
6. Barry Turner, *And the Policeman Smiled*, 1990.

Chapter 16
1. Lord Ismay, *The Memoirs of General Lord Ismay*, 1960; pp. 118, 119.
2. Sir Alexander Mackintosh, *Echoes of Big Ben*, 1946; p. 153.
3. John Kiszely, *Anatomy of a Campaign*, 2017; pp. 129, 179.
4. Alex Danchev and Daniel Todman (eds), *Alanbrooke War Diaries 1939–1945*, 2001; p. 36.
5. Richard Titmuss, *Problems of Social Policy*, 1950; p. 357.

ACKNOWLEDGEMENTS

In researching this book I am indebted to the London Library, the depository of so many memoirs and records of the period. All praise goes to the staff of this noble institution who have given unfailing support.

Fulsome thanks also go to my agent, Michael Alcock, the font of sound advice, to Jill Fenner who made sense of my scrawl and, most particularly, to Duncan Heath, the prince of editors.

I dedicate this book to our five grandchildren – Eve, Max, Leo, Frøya and Aksel – in the confident expectation that they and their generation will overcome the political inanities that even now threaten our survival.

INDEX